Betty Crocker
easy everyday
VEGETARIAN

Meatless Main Dishes You'll Love!

WILEY

Wiley Publishing, Inc.

Library of Congress Cataloging-in-Publication Data:

Betty Crocker easy everyday vegetarian : meatless main dishes
you'll love / Betty Crocker editors.—2nd ed.
   p. cm.
  Includes index.
  ISBN-13: 978-0-471-75304-9 (cloth)
  ISBN-10: 0-471-75304-1 (cloth)
  1. Vegetarian cookery. I. Crocker, Betty.
  TX837.C782 2006
  641.5'636--dc22   2005032312

Manufactured in the United States of America
10 9 8 7 6 5 4 3 2 1

Second Edition

Cover photo: Home-Style Vegetable Chili (page 228)

General Mills, Inc.

Director, Book and Online Publishing: Kim Walter

Manager, Cookbook Publishing: Lois Tlusty

Editor: Lori Fox

Recipe Development and Testing: Betty Crocker Kitchens

Photography and Food Styling: General Mills Photography Studios

Wiley Publishing, Inc.

Publisher: Natalie Chapman

Executive Editor: Anne Ficklen

Editor: Kristi Hart

Production Editor: Michael Olivo

Cover Design: Suzanne Sunwoo

Interior Design and Layout: Holly Wittenberg

Photography Art Direction: General Mills Photography Studios

Manufacturing Manager: Kevin Watt

Spot Art: © Digital Vision

The Betty Crocker Kitchens seal guarantees
success in your kitchen. Every recipe has been
tested in America's Most Trusted Kitchens™
to meet our high standards of reliability, easy
preparation and great taste.

FIND MORE GREAT IDEAS AND SHOP
FOR NAME-BRAND HOUSEWARES AT

BettyCrocker.com

Dear Friends,

Eating vegetarian isn't just for vegetarians any more! More and more people enjoy eating vegetarian meals, without committing to a complete vegetarian lifestyle. And why not? Veggie meals are inventive, yummy—and, oh yes—good for you.

Whip up Moroccan Garbanzo Beans with Raisins or Three-Mushroom Risotto—both are great new taste treats that everyone will love. Want to use those great new soy-based convenience products? Try the Italian "Veggie Burger" Bake or bring out the slow cooker and stir up a big batch of Veggie Joes—perfect for potlucks.

Eating vegetarian today is so easy—not to worry if one of the kids has turned full-time vegetarian, or if you need to serve vegetarian friends. With recipes this good, you'll be making them often and no one will care if they are vegetarian or not. They'll just know they taste great!

Warmly,

Betty Crocker

contents

the everyday VEGETARIAN

Dig in and enjoy the wonderful, flavor-filled and versatile repertoire of vegetarian cuisine. Think of a bowl of steaming spaghetti topped with marinara sauce, margherita pizza with fresh tomatoes and basil or cheese enchiladas smothered in red sauce. These enticing foods are your gateway to the pleasures of meatless eating and the vegetarian table! Pull up a chair and get ready to savor the wonderful diversity of vegetarian meals. This book isn't about one definition of vegetarian eating—there are many ways to be "vegetarian" these days. Vegetarians may choose not to eat meat, poultry, fish, seafood or any animal by-products for health, ethical, environmental or economical reasons. Others choose various styles of vegetarian diets simply for the food itself—it offers great taste and so many options. There are other reasons for embracing a vegetarian diet, too. Many of us are eating a healthier diet by increasing the amounts of grains, legumes, vegetables and fruits we eat and, along the way, including more meatless meals, so we fit right in!

Enjoy recipes in this book from the familiar and comforting to the imaginative and sophisticated. Look for recipes offering variations to include meat, poultry, fish or seafood for those times when you want a little flexibility. All are easy enough for everyday cooking!

Vegetarians Defined

Many people call themselves vegetarians, yet each can sit down to a meal that is very different. How vegetarians choose to eat is a matter of choice, and there is so much delicious variety to choose from! Some popular styles of vegetarianism are described below.

OVO-LACTO VEGETARIAN

Health is cited as the main reason for following this style. The diet includes eggs (ovo) and dairy products (lacto), but eliminates meat, poultry, fish and seafood. This diet provides a wide variety of food options, so eating away from home rarely is a problem.

DIET INCLUDES: Vegetables, fruits, grains, legumes, nuts, seeds, eggs and dairy products like milk and milk-based foods.

DIET DOESN'T INCLUDE: Meat, poultry, fish or seafood. May not eat animal-based broths like beef, chicken, fish or seafood.

LACTO-VEGETARIAN

This style is popular for those trying to lower cholesterol or avoid egg allergies. Some people following a subcategory of this diet may also eliminate milk and milk products in addition to eggs due to an allergy or for ethical reasons.

DIET INCLUDES: Vegetables, fruits, grains, legumes, nuts, seeds and dairy products like milk and milk-based foods.

DIET DOESN'T INCLUDE: Eggs, meat, poultry, fish or seafood. May not eat animal-based broths like beef, chicken, fish or seafood.

VEGANS

This is the strictest style of vegetarianism because the diet includes no animal products or by-products. A main reason why someone might choose this style is for ethical reasons. It can be very difficult to eat away from home when following a vegan diet.

DIET INCLUDES: Vegetables, fruits, grains, legumes, nuts and seeds.

DIET DOESN'T INCLUDE: Meat, poultry, fish, seafood, eggs, dairy products like milk and milk-based foods or foods containing animal products like beef, chicken, fish or seafood broth, lard or gelatin. Vegans may not use animal products or animal by-products like honey, leather, fur, silk, wool, and cosmetics and soaps that contain animal by-products.

SEMI-VEGETARIAN
(ALSO KNOWN AS "FLEXITARIAN")

This style of eating continues to grow, but it's often not considered a legitimate style of vegetarianism. It can refer to people who eat meatless meals the majority of the time but occasionally eat fish, seafood, poultry and meat. Or it may define those who eat fish, seafood and poultry but no red meat. People who eat this way include more grains, legumes, vegetables and fruits in their diet, which contributes to a healthy lifestyle. This rarely creates problems when eating away from home.

DIET INCLUDES: Vegetables, fruits, grains, legumes, nuts, seeds, eggs and dairy products like milk and milk-based foods. May include poultry, fish and seafood but usually limit these foods to occasional use.

DIET DOESN'T INCLUDE: Usually avoid red meat.

Vegetarian Is Healthy!

Our specific food choices can lead to a healthy lifestyle or contribute to health problems down the road. Embracing a vegetarian way of eating—largely diets that are low in fat and saturated fat and high in fiber—has been shown to provide health and nutrition benefits.

Many people follow healthy lifestyle habits in addition to dietary changes that may help to decrease the risk of disease. These habits often include choosing not to smoke, refraining from or moderating use of alcoholic beverages, getting regular exercise, getting adequate rest and sleep, monitoring health and well-being, and actively seeking help or treatment for health problems. Research data support that vegetarians are at less risk for the following disorders: high blood pressure, heart disease, Type II (adult-onset) diabetes and gallstones. Studies also show that vegetarians have a lower body mass index, which is a measure of obesity. Some data support a reduced risk of diverticular disease, colon cancer and prostate cancer.

A reduced risk of certain diseases indeed may be due to a combination of both lifestyle and the foods we choose to eat. More studies are necessary to determine the true benefits for vegetarians and whether they can translate to a larger population. In any event, all signs point to a vegetarian diet—even a semi-vegetarian diet—as being a healthy choice.

"VEGGIE"-WISE NUTRITION

There are a number of popular misconceptions about vegetarians getting inadequate nutrients. To help you sort fact from fiction, follow these nutrition guidelines to ensure a healthy vegetarian diet:

Protein—Don't Worry About It

Yes, you can get enough protein on a vegetarian diet. Eliminating or cutting back significantly on animal protein will decrease protein intake, but vegetarian diets usually meet or even exceed the Recommended Dietary Allowance (RDA).

The recommended daily amounts of protein by age are:

Girls 15–18: 46 grams	Boys 15–18: 52 grams
Adult Women: 46 grams	Adult Men: 56 grams

Recent studies confirm that as long as you eat a variety of foods each day, you'll most likely get enough protein to meet your needs. Vegetarians, not eating protein from animal sources, rely on protein found in combinations of legumes, grains, pastas, cereals, breads, nuts, seeds and dairy foods. Read more about protein in Vegetarian Myth Busters on page 9.

Vitamin B$_{12}$

Vitamin B$_{12}$ is necessary for all body cells to function properly. It occurs naturally only in animal foods but can be found in supplements and foods fortified with vitamin B$_{12}$. Vegans are the only vegetarians who need to supplement their diets with B$_{12}$. A B$_{12}$ deficiency can lead to anemia and nerve damage.

Iron

Teenage girls, and women in general, even non-vegetarians, have some difficulty getting enough iron in their diets. The RDA for iron for women ages 19 to 50 is 18 milligrams. Taking an iron supplement is the best way to get the iron you need if you're not eating animal-based foods. Iron supplements, either alone or in a multivitamin, are absorbed more easily when taken with vitamin C, so take them with an orange or orange juice, for example.

13 Best Non-Animal Iron Sources

Food	Amount	Iron (milligrams)
Ready-to-eat cereals (fortified)	1 cup	4.5 to 8.1
Quinoa	1 cup cooked	5.3
Spinach	1 cup cooked	4.0
Black-eyed peas	1/2 cup cooked	3.8
Lentils	1/2 cup cooked	3.4
Swiss chard	1 cup cooked	3.2
Lima beans	1/2 cup cooked	2.9
Prunes	10 dried	2.4
Blackstrap molasses	1 tablespoon	2.3
Millet	1 cup cooked	2.2
Raisins	1/2 cup	1.7
Winter squash (acorn, buttercup, butternut, Hubbard)	1 cup cooked	1.4
Brewer's yeast	1 tablespoon	1.4

Calcium

Teenage girls, and women in general, whether or not they are vegetarians, have difficulty getting enough calcium in their diets.

The recommended daily amounts of calcium by age are:

Before age 19: 1,300mg   19–50: 1,000mg   51+: 1,200mg

If you take a calcium supplement, follow these guidelines to get the most out of it:

Take it with meals to help with absorption.

If not taking multivitamins, look for calcium tablets containing vitamin D, which helps with absorption.

15 Best Calcium Sources

Food	Amount	Calcium (milligrams)
Milk (skim and low-fat)	1 cup	300
Tofu (calcium-fortified)	1/2 cup	258
Yogurt	1 cup	250
Orange juice (calcium-fortified)	1 cup	240
Ready-to-eat cereals (calcium-fortified)	1 cup	200
Mozzarella cheese (part-skim)	1 ounce	183
Canned salmon with bones	3 ounces	181
Collards	1/2 cup cooked	179
Ricotta cheese (part-skim)	1/4 cup	169
Bread (calcium-fortified)	2 slices	160
Cottage cheese (1 percent fat)	1 cup	138
Parmesan cheese	2 tablespoons grated	138
Navy beans	1 cup cooked	128
Turnips	1/2 cup cooked	125
Broccoli	1 cup cooked	94

Zinc

Some vegetarians don't get enough zinc, which helps repair body cells and is important in energy production. The zinc found in plant foods isn't absorbed by the body as well as zinc from animal foods, but it will still do the trick. Whole grains, legumes, tofu, seeds and nuts all provide vegetarian sources of zinc. Vitamin supplements also are an option.

Vegetarian Kids

Teens and young adults make up the fastest-growing segment of the U.S. population that is interested in becoming or choosing to become vegetarians. It's appealing for ethical or environmental reasons or because their peers are also trying out a vegetarian diet.

Panic is often the first reaction nonvegetarian parents have when their kids say, "I want to be a vegetarian." Nutrition and meal planning are the biggest concerns, after all, and this is brand-new territory!

Fear not, the majority of vegetarian diets are healthy and incorporate the principles of the U.S. Department of Agriculture (USDA) and U.S. Department of Health & Human Services food guidelines that emphasize eating plenty of grains, legumes, vegetables and fruit. And with some minor alterations, only one family meal needs to be made instead of cooking separate, highly specialized meals for vegetarian kids. For example, if you're making spaghetti and all but one person wants meat in their sauce, take out a portion of the sauce for that person before adding meat or sausage. And, trying a vegetarian meal with your kid isn't a bad idea—you may enjoy a sauce without meat—not every time, but sometimes. The key to a healthy, successful vegetarian diet is variety—entire cultures have lived as vegetarians for centuries—there are endless ways to enjoy a vegetarian lifestyle and still be well fed. You may be surprised at how satifying a vegetarian meal can be!

Encourage your kids to generate ideas for their own recipe creations, and let them shop for the ingredients and make meals for the family. If your kids are very strict about what they eat, they may want to help make their own part of the family meal. Letting that type of initiative and creativity shine through makes the transition to vegetarianism easier for everyone.

Vegetarian Myth Busters

MYTH: I HAVE TO EAT WEIRD FOODS!

FACT: You've probably been eating meatless or vegetarian for a long time but just didn't think of it that way. Take a look at the vegetarian foods most of us eat regularly! Cheese or vegetable pizza, grilled cheese sandwiches, spaghetti with pasta sauce, vegetable omelets, macaroni and cheese, peanut butter and jelly sandwiches, cheese quesadillas, cheese enchiladas and pasta primavera. They all qualify as a style of vegetarian eating.

MYTH: I WON'T GET ENOUGH PROTEIN.

FACT: Meatless foods can provide enough protein for the growth and maintenance of body tissues.

Proteins are made of building blocks called *amino acids*. Some of these amino acids we can make in our bodies. Those we can't produce, called *essential amino acids*, must come from the foods we eat.

Proteins that contain all our essential amino acids, called *complete* or *high-quality proteins*, come from animal sources like meat, eggs, chicken, fish and dairy products. Nonanimal protein sources, like legumes, grains, pastas, cereals, breads, nuts and seeds, are *incomplete* or *lower-quality proteins* because the protein they provide is missing at least one of the essential amino-acid building blocks. But they can be combined to make complete proteins.

MYTH: I HAVE TO COMBINE PROTEINS AT EVERY MEAL TO GET THE ESSENTIAL AMINO ACIDS I NEED.

FACT: You don't have to combine protein foods at the same meal to reap the benefits of complete protein. Recent studies show that as long as you eat a variety of foods every day, you'll get enough complete protein to meet your needs. If you want to combine proteins, however, you certainly can. Combining lower-quality protein foods can complement or complete the amino acids missing from one another to create complete proteins equaling the quality of animal proteins.

Here's a snapshot of how combining works. Grain foods complement legumes; legumes complement nuts and seeds. The pairings are almost endless. Familiar examples of combinations that create high-quality protein include peanut butter on whole wheat bread, macaroni and cheese, and a bean and cheese enchilada.

MYTH: I WILL HAVE TO EAT MUSHY, BLAND MEALS.

FACT: Variety is what makes any diet exciting, offering different tastes, textures and colors to your meals. Sprinkle toasted nuts or seeds on a salad or casserole for added pizzazz. Go on an adventure using herbs and spices, flavored vinegars, condiments and fresh citrus juice or peel. A dash of vinegar or lemon juice added just before serving a legume soup provides a kick of flavor. Cook vegetables just until they are tender or crisp-tender for texture, and sprinkle with chopped fresh herbs.

MYTH: IT WILL COST ME MORE TIME AND MONEY IF I BECOME A VEGETARIAN.

FACT: Anything new takes a little extra attention, but once you're used to this new way of eating, it will be easier. Years ago, eating vegetarian might have been more difficult, but now it's mainstream. Supermarkets carry a wide variety of vegetarian foods plus convenience foods like pre-cut vegetables and fruits. The number of whole-food and co-op stores has increased, offering even more options. Many grains, legumes, vegetables, soy-protein and nut products are less expensive per pound than meat, poultry, fish and seafood, so a vegetarian diet can be very easy on your budget!

MYTH: I CAN EAT ONLY SALADS AT RESTAURANTS.

FACT: More and more restaurants offer vegetarian entrées on their menus or are very willing to make something to order. Asian, Indian, Mexican, Middle Eastern and other ethnic restaurants have vegetarian options because these dishes are part of their traditional diet. Be creative as you check the menu. The appetizer section often offers meatless choices that you can make into a meal by ordering several— think dim sum, meze and tapas! Or combine an appetizer with a few vegetable side dishes. Also, if you don't see anything that you can eat, ask your server if he or she can make a suggestion for you.

MYTH: I HAVE TO BE YOUNG TO BECOME A VEGETARIAN.

FACT: People of all ages are turning to a vegetarian diet, or reducing meat and animal by-products, because of health concerns. Many are combating weight gain, higher cholesterol and blood pressure, increased cancer risk and digestion problems. So just go for it!

STRING CHEESE STICKS with dipping sauce *(page 18)*

CHAPTER 1 snacks, bites & nibbles

Try substituting hummus for the pizza sauce and leftover grilled vegetables for the fresh uncooked vegetables, then garnish each pizzette with whatever fresh herbs you have available.

easy PIZZETTES

prep time: 5 minutes   **start to finish:** 15 minutes   16 pizzettes

1 cup pizza sauce
8 English muffins, split, toasted
2 cups shredded provolone cheese (8 oz)
Assorted toppings (2/3 cup each sliced mushrooms, sliced ripe olives, chopped bell pepper and chopped red onion)

1. Heat oven to 425°F. Spread 1 tablespoon pizza sauce over each English muffin half. Sprinkle each with 1 tablespoon of the cheese.

2. Arrange toppings on pizzas. Sprinkle with remaining cheese. Place on ungreased cookie sheet.

3. Bake 5 to 10 minutes or until cheese is melted.

1 pizzette: Calories 130 (Calories from Fat 45); Total Fat 5g (Saturated Fat 2.5g; Trans Fat 0g); Cholesterol 10mg; Sodium 370mg; Total Carbohydrate 16g (Dietary Fiber 1g; Sugars 5g); Protein 6g
% daily value: Vitamin A 4%; Vitamin C 6%; Calcium 15%; Iron 8%   **exchanges:** 1 Starch, 1/2 High-Fat Meat   **carbohydrate choices:** 1

Make sure to use marinated artichoke hearts instead of just canned artichokes because the marinade adds lots of flavor!

artichoke–rosemary BRUSCHETTA

prep time: 10 minutes   **start to finish:** 35 minutes   12 slices

1 loaf (1 lb) French bread, cut in half horizontally
1 cup shredded mozzarella cheese (4 oz)
1/2 cup grated Parmesan cheese
1 tablespoon chopped fresh or 1 teaspoon dried rosemary leaves, crushed
2/3 cup mayonnaise or salad dressing
1 jar (6 to 7 oz) marinated artichoke hearts, drained, chopped

1. Heat oven to 375°F. On ungreased cookie sheet, place bread, cut sides up. Bake 10 minutes.

2. Meanwhile, in medium bowl, mix 1/2 cup of the mozzarella cheese, the Parmesan cheese, rosemary, mayonnaise and artichokes.

3. Spread cheese mixture on baked bread. Sprinkle with remaining 1/2 cup mozzarella cheese.

4. Bake 15 to 20 minutes or until cheese is melted.

1 slice: Calories 250 (Calories from Fat 130); Total Fat 14g (Saturated Fat 4g; Trans Fat 0g); Cholesterol 15mg; Sodium 460mg; Total Carbohydrate 21g (Dietary Fiber 2g; Sugars 0g); Protein 8g
% daily value: Vitamin A 2%; Vitamin C 0%; Calcium 15%; Iron 8%   **exchanges:** 1 1/2 Starch, 1/2 Medium-Fat Meat, 2 Fat
carbohydrate choices: 1 1/2

Dress up these simple toasts with a slice of cherry tomato and a snip of fresh cilantro.

southwest CHEESE BREAD (LOW fat)

prep time: 10 minutes   **start to finish:** 15 minutes   8 slices

1/4 cup mayonnaise or salad dressing
2 tablespoons finely chopped bell pepper
2 tablespoons finely chopped green onion
1 teaspoon chopped fresh cilantro or parsley, if desired
8 slices French bread (1/2 inch thick)
1/2 cup shredded Colby-Monterey Jack cheese blend (2 oz)

1. Heat oven to 400°F. In small bowl, mix all ingredients except bread and cheese.

2. Spread mixture on 1 side of each bread slice. Sprinkle with cheese. Place on ungreased cookie sheet.

3. Bake 5 to 6 minutes or until cheese is melted and bread is slightly toasted on bottom.

1 slice: Calories 130 (Calories from Fat 80); Total Fat 8g (Saturated Fat 2.5g; Trans Fat 0g); Cholesterol 10mg; Sodium 190mg; Total Carbohydrate 10g (Dietary Fiber 0g; Sugars 0g); Protein 3g
% daily value: Vitamin A 2%; Vitamin C 0%; Calcium 6%; Iron 4%   **exchanges:** 1 Starch, 1 1/2 Fat   **carbohydrate choices:** 1/2

southwest CHEESE BREAD

Hard or soft pretzels, breadsticks, pita wedges, slices of cocktail rye or raw vegetables all make interesting and tasty dippers.

appetizer beer–cheese FONDUE

prep time: 35 minutes   **start to finish:** 35 minutes   16 servings (2 tablespoons fondue and 1/2 cup bread cubes each)

1 loaf (1 lb) French bread, cut into 1-inch cubes
1 loaf (16 oz) prepared cheese product, cubed
1 1/2 cups frozen chopped broccoli (from 1-lb bag), cooked, drained
1/4 cup regular or nonalcoholic beer
1 jar (2 oz) diced pimientos, drained
1 teaspoon ground mustard

1. Heat oven to 350°F. In ungreased 15 × 10 × 1-inch pan, place bread cubes. Bake about 10 minutes, stirring twice, until lightly toasted. Transfer to serving bowl or basket.

2. Meanwhile, in 2-quart saucepan, melt cheese over medium heat, stirring occasionally. Stir in broccoli, beer, pimientos and mustard. Cook, stirring occasionally, until hot. Pour cheese mixture into ceramic fondue pot over Low heat or into 1 1/2-quart slow cooker on Low heat setting.

3. To serve, skewer toasted bread pieces with fondue forks or wooden skewers and dip into cheese mixture. Cheese mixture will hold in slow cooker on Low heat setting up to 2 hours.

1 serving: Calories 170 (Calories from Fat 70); Total Fat 7g (Saturated Fat 4g; Trans Fat 0g); Cholesterol 25mg; Sodium 590mg; Total Carbohydrate 18g (Dietary Fiber 1g; Sugars 3g); Protein 8g
% daily value: Vitamin A 10%; Vitamin C 6%; Calcium 15%; Iron 6%   **exchanges:** 1 Starch, 1/2 High-Fat Meat, 1/2 Fat   **carbohydrate choices:** 1

Fresh mozzarella can be shaped into rounds, braids or small balls called bocconcini; it's usually stored in water or whey. The small balls of mozzarella can be used whole in this recipe.

MOZZARELLA AND BASIL
with marinara sauce

prep time: 5 minutes **start to finish:** 15 minutes **10 servings** (1/4 cup sauce and 3 slices bread each)

8 oz fresh mozzarella cheese, cubed
2 tablespoons chopped fresh basil leaves
2 cups chunky marinara sauce
1 loaf (10 oz) French baguette bread, cut into 30 slices

1. Heat oven to 350°F. In shallow 2-quart casserole, place cheese cubes. Sprinkle with basil. Spoon marinara sauce around cheese.

2. Bake uncovered 8 to 10 minutes or until cheese is hot and bubbly. Serve with baguette slices.

1 serving: Calories 200 (Calories from Fat 70); Total Fat 7g (Saturated Fat 3.5g; Trans Fat 0g); Cholesterol 10mg; Sodium 530mg; Total Carbohydrate 24g (Dietary Fiber 1g; Sugars 4g); Protein 9g
% daily value: Vitamin A 10%; Vitamin C 6%; Calcium 20%; Iron 6%   **exchanges:** 1 1/2 Starch, 1/2 Medium-Fat Meat, 1 Fat
carbohydrate choices: 1 1/2

Say no to deep-fat frying! These melt-in-your-mouth dough-covered cheese sticks are baked in the oven. If you don't have pizza sauce on hand, warm up spaghetti sauce or salsa for dipping.

STRING CHEESE STICKS
with dipping sauce

prep time: 10 minutes   **start to finish:** 20 minutes   4 servings (2 cheese sticks and 3 tablespoons sauce each)

2 1/4 cups Original Bisquick® mix
2/3 cup milk
1 package (8 oz) plain or smoked string cheese
1 tablespoon butter or margarine, melted
1/4 teaspoon garlic powder
1 can (8 oz) pizza sauce, heated

1. Heat oven to 450°F. In medium bowl, stir Bisquick mix and milk until soft dough forms; beat 30 seconds with spoon. Place dough on surface sprinkled with Bisquick mix; gently roll in Bisquick mix to coat. Shape into a ball; knead 10 times.

2. With rolling pin, roll dough until 1/4 inch thick. Cut into eight 6 × 2-inch rectangles. Roll each rectangle around 1 piece of cheese. Pinch edge into roll to seal; seal ends. Roll on surface to completely enclose cheese sticks. On ungreased cookie sheet, place sticks, seam sides down.

3. Bake 8 to 10 minutes or until golden brown. In small bowl, mix butter and garlic powder; brush over warm cheese sticks before removing from cookie sheet. Serve warm with pizza sauce for dipping.

1 serving: Calories 500 (Calories from Fat 220); Total Fat 24g (Saturated Fat 11g; Trans Fat 2g); Cholesterol 40mg; Sodium 1550mg; Total Carbohydrate 50g (Dietary Fiber 2g; Sugars 10g); Protein 22g
% daily value: Vitamin A 10%; Vitamin C 2%; Calcium 60%; Iron 20%   **exchanges:** 2 1/2 Starch, 1/2 Other Carbohydrate, 2 Medium-Fat Meat, 2 1/2 Fat   **carbohydrate choices:** 3

Italian Gorgonzola is rich and creamy with a mild, yet slightly pungent flavor and aroma. If you can't find it, use blue cheese instead. Slivered almonds, pistachios or walnuts would do just fine in place of hazelnuts.

gorgonzola- and hazelnut-stuffed
MUSHROOMS (LOW fat)

prep time: 30 minutes   **start to finish:** 50 minutes   about 35 mushrooms

1 lb fresh whole mushrooms
1/3 cup crumbled Gorgonzola cheese
1/4 cup Italian-style dry bread crumbs
1/4 cup chopped hazelnuts (filberts)
1/4 cup finely chopped red bell pepper
4 medium green onions, chopped (1/4 cup)
1/2 teaspoon salt

1. Heat oven to 350°F. Remove stems from mushroom caps; reserve caps. Finely chop enough stems to measure about 1/2 cup. Discard remaining stems.

2. In small bowl, mix chopped mushroom stems and remaining ingredients until well blended. Spoon into mushroom caps, mounding slightly. In ungreased 15 × 10 × 1-inch pan, place mushrooms, filled sides up.

3. Bake 15 to 20 minutes or until heated through. Serve warm.

1 mushroom: Calories 20 (Calories from Fat 10); Total Fat 1g (Saturated Fat 0g; Trans Fat 0g); Cholesterol 0mg; Sodium 65mg; Total Carbohydrate 1g (Dietary Fiber 0g; Sugars 0g); Protein 0g
% daily value: Vitamin A 0%; Vitamin C 2%; Calcium 0%; Iron 0%   **exchanges:** Free   **carbohydrate choices:** 0

Extra-firm tofu holds up to frying and gives these golden brown nuggets a slightly chewy texture.

tofu NUGGETS

prep time: 20 minutes   **start to finish:** 20 minutes   **10 servings** (4 nuggets and 1 tablespoon sauce each)

3 tablespoons all-purpose flour
6 tablespoons cold water
2/3 cup unseasoned dry bread crumbs
1 teaspoon salt
Dash of ground red pepper (cayenne)
1 package (12 oz) extra-firm tofu packed in water, drained,
   cut into 1-inch cubes
Vegetable oil
2/3 cup barbecue sauce, sweet-and-sour sauce, salsa or ketchup

1. In small bowl, beat flour and water with wire whisk or hand beater until smooth. In shallow dish or pie plate, toss bread crumbs, salt and red pepper.

2. Dip tofu cubes into batter, then roll in bread crumb mixture to coat.

3. In 10-inch skillet, heat oil (1/2 inch) over medium–high heat. Cook 15 nuggets at a time in oil about 1 minute, turning once, until golden brown. Drain nuggets on paper towels. Serve hot with barbecue sauce.

1 serving: Calories 160 (Calories from Fat 80); Total Fat 9g (Saturated Fat 1.5g; Trans Fat 0g); Cholesterol 0mg; Sodium 470mg; Total Carbohydrate 14g (Dietary Fiber 0g; Sugars 5g); Protein 5g
% daily value: Vitamin A 0%; Vitamin C 0%; Calcium 6%; Iron 8%   **exchanges:** 1 Starch, 1 1/2 Fat   **carbohydrate choices:** 1

Make the crisps up to 4 hours ahead, then store them tightly covered at room temperature. Top them just before serving.

guacamole–cheese CRISPS

prep time: 25 minutes **start to finish:** 25 minutes 16 servings

1 cup finely shredded Mexican-style Cheddar-Jack cheese blend
   with jalapeño peppers (from 8-oz package)
1 ripe avocado, pitted, peeled and chopped
1 tablespoon lime juice
1 clove garlic, finely chopped
3 tablespoons sour cream
3 tablespoons chunky-style salsa

1. Heat oven to 400°F. Line cookie sheet with cooking parchment paper. For each cheese crisp, spoon 1 tablespoon cheese (loosely packed) onto paper-lined cookie sheet; pat into 2-inch round.

2. Bake 6 to 8 minutes or until edges are light golden brown. Immediately remove from cookie sheet to wire rack. Cool 5 minutes or until crisp.

3. In small bowl, mix avocado, lime juice and garlic; mash avocado with fork and mix with ingredients. Spoon 1 1/2 teaspoons avocado mixture onto each cheese crisp; top with about 1/2 teaspoon each sour cream and salsa.

1 serving: Calories 50 (Calories from Fat 40); Total Fat 4.5g (Saturated Fat 2g; Trans Fat 0g); Cholesterol 10mg; Sodium 70mg; Total Carbohydrate 2g (Dietary Fiber 0g; Sugars 0g); Protein 2g
% daily value: Vitamin A 4%; Vitamin C 0%; Calcium 6%; Iron 0% **exchanges:** 1 Fat **carbohydrate choices:** 0

To make this nifty dip with a kick ahead of time, follow directions through step 2, then cover and refrigerate up to 24 hours. Bake as directed.

chipotle–black bean DIP

prep time: 20 minutes   **start to finish:** 45 minutes   15 servings (2 tablespoons dip and 3 chips each)

2 large dried chipotle chilies
1 cup chunky-style salsa
1/2 cup jalapeño black bean dip
2 tablespoons chopped fresh cilantro
1 cup shredded Colby-Monterey Jack cheese blend (4 oz)
2 medium green onions, chopped (2 tablespoons)
Sweet red cherry chili half, if desired
Tortilla chips

1. Heat oven to 350°F. In small bowl, cover dried chilies with boiling water; let stand 10 minutes. Drain chilies; remove seeds. Chop chilies.

2. In small bowl, mix chilies, salsa and bean dip; stir in cilantro. Spoon into shallow 1-quart ovenproof serving dish. Sprinkle with cheese.

3. Bake about 15 minutes or until mixture is hot and cheese is melted. Sprinkle with onions. Garnish with cherry chili half if desired. Serve with tortilla chips.

1 serving: Calories 80 (Calories from Fat 45); Total Fat 5g (Saturated Fat 2g; Trans Fat 0g); Cholesterol 10mg; Sodium 210mg; Total Carbohydrate 6g (Dietary Fiber 0g; Sugars 1g); Protein 3g

% daily value: Vitamin A 10%; Vitamin C 2%; Calcium 6%; Iron 4%   **exchanges:** 1/2 Starch, 1 Fat   **carbohydrate choices:** 1/2

Slash the fat to 2 grams and the calories to 40 per serving by using 1/2 cup fat-free mayonnaise or salad dressing and 1/2 cup plain fat-free yogurt instead of the regular mayonnaise.

spinach–artichoke DIP

prep time: 10 minutes   **start to finish:** 1 hour 25 minutes   24 servings (2 tablespoons dip and 3 slices bread each)

1 cup mayonnaise or salad dressing
1 cup freshly grated Parmesan cheese
1 can (14 oz) artichoke hearts, drained, coarsely chopped
1 box (9 oz) frozen spinach, thawed, squeezed to drain
1/2 cup chopped red bell pepper
1/4 cup shredded Monterey Jack or mozzarella cheese (1 oz)
2 loaves (10 oz each) French baguette bread, cut into 1/2-inch slices (toasted if desired)

1. Spray inside of 1- to 2 1/2-quart slow cooker with cooking spray. In medium bowl, mix mayonnaise and Parmesan cheese. Stir in artichoke hearts, spinach and bell pepper. Spoon into slow cooker. Sprinkle with Monterey Jack cheese.

2. Cover; cook on Low heat setting 1 hour to 1 hour 15 minutes or until cheese is melted. Serve warm with baguette slices. Dip will hold up to 3 hours.

1 serving: Calories 160 (Calories from Fat 90); Total Fat 10g (Saturated Fat 2.5g; Trans Fat 0g); Cholesterol 10mg; Sodium 310mg; Total Carbohydrate 14g (Dietary Fiber 2g; Sugars 0g); Protein 5g
% daily value: Vitamin A 15%; Vitamin C 6%; Calcium 10%; Iron 6%   **exchanges:** 1 Starch, 2 Fat   **carbohydrate choices:** 1

Sweet potatoes and carrots are loaded with vitamin A and sweet flavor. If you can, choose the intensely colored and flavored red garnet sweet potatoes, but any of the deep-orange variety will work fine.

roasted carrot and herb SPREAD

prep time: 10 minutes   **start to finish:** 55 minutes   **20 servings** (2 tablespoons spread and 3 slices bread each)

2 lb ready-to-eat baby-cut carrots
1 large sweet potato, peeled, cut into 1-inch pieces
1 medium onion, cut into 8 wedges, separated
1/4 cup olive or vegetable oil
2 tablespoons chopped fresh or 1 teaspoon dried thyme leaves
2 cloves garlic, finely chopped
3/4 teaspoon salt
1/4 teaspoon freshly ground pepper
2 loaves (10 oz each) French baguette bread, each cut into 30 slices

1. Heat oven to 350°F. Spray 15 × 10 × 1-inch pan with cooking spray. Place carrots, sweet potato and onion in pan. Drizzle with oil. Sprinkle with thyme, garlic, salt and pepper. Stir to coat.

2. Roast uncovered 35 to 45 minutes, stirring occasionally, until vegetables are tender.

3. In food processor, place vegetable mixture. Cover; process until blended. Spoon into serving bowl. Serve warm, or cover and refrigerate until serving. Serve with baguette slices.

1 serving: Calories 130 (Calories from Fat 35); Total Fat 4g (Saturated Fat 0.5g; Trans Fat 0g); Cholesterol 0mg; Sodium 270mg; Total Carbohydrate 22g (Dietary Fiber 2g; Sugars 4g); Protein 3g
% daily value: Vitamin A 190%; Vitamin C 6%; Calcium 4%; Iron 6%   **exchanges:** 1 1/2 Starch, 1/2 Fat   **carbohydrate choices:** 1 1/2

roasted carrot and herb SPREAD

This recipe can be made up to one day ahead of time; just cover and refrigerate until serving.

roasted-garlic HUMMUS (LOW fat)

prep time: 10 minutes **start to finish:** 1 hour 20 minutes   **16 servings (2 tablespoons hummus and 2 pita wedges each)**

1 bulb garlic, unpeeled
2 teaspoons olive or vegetable oil
1 can (15 to 16 oz) great northern beans, drained, 2 tablespoons liquid reserved
3 tablespoons lemon juice
1/2 teaspoon salt
Chopped fresh parsley
4 pita breads, each cut into 8 wedges

1. Heat oven to 350°F. Cut 1/2-inch slice off top of garlic bulb. Drizzle oil over garlic bulb. Wrap garlic in foil.

2. Bake 50 to 60 minutes or until garlic is soft when pierced with a knife. Cool slightly, about 10 minutes.

3. Squeeze garlic into food processor. Add beans, reserved bean liquid, lemon juice and salt. Cover; process until uniform consistency.

4. Spoon dip into serving dish. Sprinkle with parsley. Serve with pita bread wedges.

1 serving: Calories 80 (Calories from Fat 5); Total Fat 1g (Saturated Fat 0g; Trans Fat 0g); Cholesterol 0mg; Sodium 135mg; Total Carbohydrate 14g (Dietary Fiber 2g; Sugars 0g); Protein 4g
% daily value: Vitamin A 0%; Vitamin C 0%; Calcium 4%; Iron 8%   **exchanges:** 1 Starch   **carbohydrate choices:** 1

For the very best flavor, stick with Kalamata or Gaeta olives; if you can't find them, try large pitted ripe olives instead. To make ahead, cover tightly and store in the fridge up to one week.

greek marinated ROASTED PEPPERS, OLIVES AND FETA

prep time: 55 minutes **start to finish:** 1 hour 10 minutes 32 servings (1/4 cup pepper mixture and 3 slices bread each)

5 large red bell peppers
1/4 cup olive or vegetable oil
3 tablespoons lemon juice
1/2 cup chopped fresh parsley
1/4 cup finely chopped red onion
2 tablespoons chopped fresh or 2 teaspoons dried oregano leaves
2 cloves garlic, finely chopped
2 cups pitted Kalamata olives
1 piece (8 oz) feta cheese, cut into 1/2-inch cubes (1 cup)
2 1/2 loaves (10 oz each) French baguette bread, cut into 1/2-inch slices

1. Set oven control to broil. On cookie sheet, place bell peppers. Broil with tops about 5 inches from heat, turning occasionally, until skin is blistered and evenly browned. Place in plastic bag; close tightly. Let stand 20 minutes.

2. Meanwhile, in tightly covered container, shake oil, lemon juice, parsley, onion, oregano and garlic.

3. Remove skins, stems, seeds and membranes from peppers. Cut peppers into 1-inch pieces.

4. In glass bowl or jar, place peppers, olives and cheese. Pour oil mixture over pepper mixture. Serve with slotted spoon. Serve with baguette slices.

1 serving: Calories 110 (Calories from Fat 45); Total Fat 5g (Saturated Fat 1.5g; Trans Fat 0g); Cholesterol 5mg; Sodium 290mg; Total Carbohydrate 14g (Dietary Fiber 2g; Sugars 2g); Protein 3g
% daily value: Vitamin A 35%; Vitamin C 40%; Calcium 6%; Iron 6%   **exchanges:** 1 Starch, 1 Fat   **carbohydrate choices:** 1

kid-pleasing MEAL OPTIONS

Vegetarian kids are often more adventurous when it comes to eating and are willing to try new and different foods. Go ahead and ask them for some of their own meal ideas, and keep this list handy for more great opportunities!

- Baked regular potatoes or sweet potatoes topped with cheese sauce, cheese, meatless chili, canned dried beans, salsa, pesto or vegetables

- Cheese or vegetable pizza

- Cottage cheese, plain or with fruit, beans or vegetables

- Eggs, any style, served plain or with vegetables or cheese

- Grilled cheese sandwiches with soup

- Macaroni and cheese

- Meatless chili

- Pancakes, waffles and French toast

- Pasta, cheese-filled ravioli or cheese-filled tortellini topped with pasta sauce, or pasta tossed with olive oil or melted butter and grated or shredded cheese; serve plain or add vegetables or beans

- Quesadillas filled with foods like cheese, beans, vegetables or bits of leftovers

- Rice tossed with olive oil or melted butter and grated or shredded cheese; serve plain or add vegetables or beans

- Soy-protein burgers, hot dogs and "chicken" nuggets

- Tacos filled with foods like shredded lettuce, tomatoes, beans, cheese, guacamole and salsa

- Vegetable stir-fry with rice or pasta

- Vegetarian baked beans

- Whole-grain cereal with fresh fruit and vanilla-flavored reduced-fat soy milk

- Wraps or burritos—fill flour tortillas with foods like shredded lettuce, cabbage or carrots, chopped vegetables, rice, beans, cheese, peanut sauce, peanut butter and jelly, salsa or bits of leftovers

- Yogurt parfaits—layer yogurt, granola or slightly crushed cereal, and fresh fruit

Turn this simple appetizer "fashion forward" by lining the serving plate with shredded lettuce before creating the layered dip. Top it all off with sliced ripe olives or chopped fresh cilantro, then add a few cilantro sprigs.

tex-mex layered DIP

prep time: 20 minutes   **start to finish:** 20 minutes   32 servings (2 tablespoons dip and 3 chips each)

1 can (15 oz) black beans, drained, rinsed
2 tablespoons chunky-style salsa
1 1/2 cups sour cream
1 cup guacamole
1 cup shredded Cheddar cheese (4 oz)
1 small tomato, seeded, chopped (1/2 cup)
2 medium green onions, chopped (2 tablespoons)
Tortilla chips

1. In small bowl, mix beans and salsa. On 12- or 13-inch serving plate, spoon bean mixture into 10-inch circle.

2. Spoon sour cream over beans, leaving about 1-inch border of beans around edge. Spread guacamole over sour cream, leaving border of sour cream showing.

3. Sprinkle cheese, tomato and onions over guacamole. Serve immediately, or cover with plastic wrap and refrigerate up to 6 hours. Serve with tortilla chips.

1 serving: Calories 100 (Calories from Fat 50); Total Fat 6g (Saturated Fat 2.5g; Trans Fat 0g); Cholesterol 10mg; Sodium 100mg; Total Carbohydrate 8g (Dietary Fiber 2g; Sugars 1g); Protein 3g
% daily value: Vitamin A 4%; Vitamin C 6%; Calcium 4%; Iron 4%   **exchanges:** 1/2 Starch, 1 Fat   **carbohydrate choices:** 1/2

This awesome dip is based on romesco, a classic Spanish sauce served with fish and poultry. Almonds, red bell pepper, tomato, onion and garlic are what make it special.

ASPARAGUS with creamy spanish dip

prep time: 40 minutes **start to finish:** 40 minutes 15 servings (3 asparagus spears and 1 tablespoon dip each)

1/2 cup slivered almonds, toasted*
1/2 cup roasted red bell peppers (from 7-oz jar), drained, chopped
1/4 teaspoon crushed red pepper
1/2 cup garlic-and-herb spreadable cheese (from 4- or 6.5-oz container)
1/4 cup chili sauce
1 to 2 tablespoons milk
1 lb fresh asparagus spears

1. In food processor, place almonds. Cover; process 10 to 15 seconds or until finely ground. Add roasted peppers and crushed red pepper. Cover; process about 10 seconds or until finely ground. Add cheese, chili sauce and 1 tablespoon of the milk. Cover; process about 10 seconds or until well mixed. Add remaining 1 tablespoon milk if needed for dipping consistency.

2. In 12-inch skillet, heat 3/4 inch water to boiling. Add asparagus. Cover and cook 2 minutes; drain. Plunge asparagus into ice water until cold; drain.

3. On serving platter, arrange asparagus spears. Serve with dip.

To toast nuts, cook in an ungreased heavy skillet over medium-low heat 5 to 7 minutes, stirring frequently until browning begins, then stirring constantly until golden brown.

1 serving: Calories 60 (Calories from Fat 40); Total Fat 4.5g (Saturated Fat 2g; Trans Fat 0g); Cholesterol 5mg; Sodium 85mg; Total Carbohydrate 3g (Dietary Fiber 1g; Sugars 1g); Protein 2g
% daily value: Vitamin A 10%; Vitamin C 10%; Calcium 2%; Iron 2% **exchanges:** 1 Fat **carbohydrate choices:** 0

SHRIMP AND ASPARAGUS with creamy spanish dip: Arrange 1 pound cooked peeled deveined large shrimp with tails (26 to 30 count) with the asparagus on the serving platter.

Instead of an olive slice, top each egg half with a cherry tomato wedge. To make ahead, store stuffed eggs tightly covered in the fridge up to 24 hours before serving.

olive and herb DEVILED EGGS

prep time: 1 hour   **start to finish:** 1 hour   16 deviled eggs

8 eggs
1/3 cup mayonnaise or salad dressing
2 tablespoons finely chopped parsley
2 tablespoons finely chopped fresh marjoram leaves
2 tablespoons finely chopped fresh chives
1/2 teaspoon garlic-pepper blend
1/2 cup chopped ripe olives
8 pitted ripe olives
Fresh parsley or marjoram sprigs or leaves, if desired

1. In 3-quart saucepan, place eggs in single layer; add enough cold water to cover eggs by 1 inch. Cover; heat to boiling. Remove from heat; let stand covered 15 minutes. Drain. Immediately place eggs in cold water with ice cubes or run cold water over eggs until completely cooled.

2. To remove shell from each egg, crackle it by tapping gently all over; roll between hands to loosen. Peel, starting at large end. With rippled vegetable cutter or sharp knife, cut each egg in half lengthwise.

3. Stir mayonnaise, chopped herbs, garlic-pepper blend and chopped olives into mashed yolks. Carefully spoon mixture into egg white halves, mounding lightly.

4. Cut whole pitted olives into slices; top each egg half with olive slices. Garnish with small herb sprigs or leaves if desired.

1 deviled egg: Calories 80 (Calories from Fat 60); Total Fat 7g (Saturated Fat 1.5g; Trans Fat 0g); Cholesterol 110mg; Sodium 110mg; Total Carbohydrate 0g (Dietary Fiber 0g; Sugars 0g); Protein 3g
% daily value: Vitamin A 4%; Vitamin C 0%; Calcium 2%; Iron 4%   **exchanges:** 1/2 Medium-Fat Meat, 1 Fat   **carbohydrate choices:** 0

Crystallized ginger is fresh gingerroot that has been cooked in a sugar syrup, then coated with sugar. It has that great ginger bite along with the sweet flavor.

FRESH FRUIT with ginger dip (LOW fat)

prep time: 25 minutes   **start to finish:** 25 minutes   24 servings (3 fruit pieces and 1 1/2 tablespoons dip each)

1 cup sour cream
1/4 cup apricot preserves
2 tablespoons finely chopped crystallized ginger
1 tablespoon chopped fresh cilantro
24 fresh strawberries
24 cantaloupe balls (1 inch)
24 honeydew melon balls (1 inch)

1. In small bowl, mix sour cream, preserves and ginger until well blended. Stir in cilantro. Place in small serving bowl.

2. On serving platter, arrange strawberries and melon balls. Serve with dip.

1 serving: Calories 45 (Calories from Fat 20); Total Fat 2g (Saturated Fat 1g; Trans Fat 0g); Cholesterol 5mg; Sodium 10mg; Total Carbohydrate 7g (Dietary Fiber 0g; Sugars 5g); Protein 0g   **% daily value:** Vitamin A 8%; Vitamin C 25%; Calcium 0%; Iron 0%   **exchanges:** 1/2 Other Carbohydrate, 1/2 Fat   **carbohydrate choices:** 1/2

Great Vegetarian Snacks

Vegetarian snack choices are nearly endless, but here are some suggestions to jump-start your "to-have-on-hand" list:

- Cheese and whole-grain crackers
- Chips and bean dip, guacamole or salsa
- Dried fruit and dried fruit leathers and snacks
- Edamame (fresh green soybeans)
- Fresh fruit
- Fruit-filled breakfast bars

- Granola and granola bars
- Hummus (garbanzo bean–based dip/spread) or baba ghanoush (eggplant-based dip/spread) and pita wedges
- Nut butter and whole-grain bread
- Nuts (look for toasted soy nuts for a new crunchy treat)
- Olive tapenade and baguette slices

- Popcorn
- Pretzels
- Raw vegetables
- Rice cakes
- Smoothies (look for ready-to-drink smoothies in the dairy case!)
- String cheese
- Yogurt

Keep these delicious snacking nuts on hand as extra nibbles for parties. Walnut halves or peanuts can be used instead of the pecans.

savory PECANS

prep time: 5 minutes   **start to finish:** 15 minutes   8 servings (1/4 cup each)

2 cups pecan halves
2 medium green onions, chopped (2 tablespoons)
2 tablespoons butter or margarine, melted
1 tablespoon soy sauce
1/4 teaspoon ground red pepper (cayenne)

1. Heat oven to 300°F. In small bowl, mix all ingredients. In ungreased 15 × 10 × 1-inch pan, spread pecans in single layer.

2. Bake uncovered about 10 minutes or until pecans are toasted. Serve warm, or cool completely. Store in airtight container at room temperature up to 3 weeks.

1 serving: Calories 210 (Calories from Fat 190); Total Fat 21g (Saturated Fat 3g; Trans Fat 0g); Cholesterol 10mg; Sodium 135mg; Total Carbohydrate 4g (Dietary Fiber 2g; Sugars 1g); Protein 2g**%   daily value:** Vitamin A 4%; Vitamin C 0%; Calcium 0%; Iron 4%   **exchanges:** 4 1/2 Fat   **carbohydrate choices:** 0

chinese-spiced PECANS: Omit ground red pepper. Stir in 2 teaspoons five-spice powder and 1/2 teaspoon ground ginger.

tex-mex PECANS: Omit soy sauce and ground red pepper. Stir in 1 tablespoon Worcestershire sauce, 2 teaspoons chili powder, 1/4 teaspoon garlic salt and 1/4 teaspoon onion powder.

The sesame sticks may be found in bulk-food bins, in the snacks or chips aisle or near the produce, depending on the store. Make this snack mix up to one week ahead and store in an airtight container.

roasted sesame and honey SNACK MIX

prep time: 10 minutes   **start to finish:** 1 hour 25 minutes   **20 servings** (1/2 cup each)

3 cups Chex® cereal (any variety)
3 cups checkerboard-shaped pretzels
3 cups sesame sticks
1 cup mixed nuts
1/4 cup honey
3 tablespoons butter or margarine, melted
2 tablespoons sesame seed, toasted* if desired

1. Heat oven to 275°F. In ungreased 15 × 10 × 1–inch pan, mix cereal, pretzels, sesame sticks and nuts.

2. In small bowl, mix remaining ingredients. Pour over cereal mixture, stirring until evenly coated.

3. Bake 45 minutes, stirring occasionally. Spread on waxed paper; cool about 30 minutes. Store in airtight container up to 1 week.

To toast sesame seed, cook in a small nonstick skillet over medium heat 1 to 3 minutes, stirring frequently, until light golden brown.

1 serving: Calories 150 (Calories from Fat 60); Total Fat 7g (Saturated Fat 2g; Trans Fat 0g); Cholesterol 0mg; Sodium 280mg; Total Carbohydrate 19g (Dietary Fiber 1g; Sugars 6g); Protein 3g
% daily value: Vitamin A 2%; Vitamin C 0%; Calcium 4%; Iron 10%   **exchanges:** 1 Starch, 1 1/2 Fat   **carbohydrate choices:** 1

BettyCrocker.com

roasted sesame and honey SNACK MIX

LEMON-PEPPER PASTA and asparagus *(page 66)*

CHAPTER 2 grains, risotto & pasta

Condensed Cheddar cheese soup is also delicious in this broccoli dish. Want to save time? Use 1 1/2 pounds frozen broccoli cuts, thawed, for the fresh broccoli. Omit cooking the broccoli and just start with step 2.

broccoli–rice BAKE (LOW fat)

prep time: 10 minutes   **start to finish:** 40 minutes   6 servings

1 1/2 lb broccoli, cut into bite-size pieces
2 cups uncooked instant brown rice
1 can (14 oz) vegetable broth
1 can (10 3/4 oz) condensed cream of broccoli soup
1 jar (2 oz) diced pimientos, drained
1/4 teaspoon pepper
2 tablespoons firm butter or margarine
1/2 cup Original Bisquick® mix

1. Heat oven to 425°F. In 2-quart saucepan, heat 1 inch water to boiling. Add broccoli; return to boiling. Reduce heat to medium; cover and cook about 5 minutes or until crisp-tender. Drain.

2. In ungreased 2-quart casserole, mix broccoli, rice, broth, soup, pimientos and pepper.

3. Cover; bake 20 minutes. Meanwhile, in medium bowl using pastry blender or crisscrossing 2 knives, cut butter into Bisquick mix until crumbly.

4. Sprinkle crumbly mixture over broccoli mixture; bake uncovered 8 to 10 minutes longer or until top is light brown.

1 serving: Calories 290 (Calories from Fat 80); Total Fat 9g (Saturated Fat 3g; Trans Fat 0.5g); Cholesterol 10mg; Sodium 810mg; Total Carbohydrate 45g (Dietary Fiber 6g; Sugars 4g); Protein 7g
% daily value: Vitamin A 30%; Vitamin C 60%; Calcium 10%; Iron 10%   **exchanges:** 3 Starch, 1 1/2 Fat   **carbohydrate choices:** 3

chicken-broccoli rice BAKE: Add 1 cup cubed cooked chicken or turkey with the broccoli and other ingredients in step 2.

Refrigerated tubes of polenta can usually be found in the produce or dairy cases of large supermarkets. For this recipe, you can use plain polenta or one of the flavored varieties, like Italian herb or sun-dried tomato.

POLENTA with garden vegetables

prep time: 35 minutes   **start to finish:** 35 minutes   4 servings

1 tube (16 oz) refrigerated polenta, cut into 1/2-inch slices
2 tablespoons olive or vegetable oil
1 small red onion, cut into thin wedges
2 cloves garlic, finely chopped
8 oz fresh green beans, cut into 3/4-inch pieces
1 medium red bell pepper, coarsely chopped (1 cup)
1 1/2 cups sliced fresh mushrooms (4 oz)
1 small yellow summer squash, cut lengthwise in half,
    then cut crosswise into 1/4-inch slices
1/2 teaspoon fennel seed, crushed
1/4 teaspoon salt
1/4 cup finely shredded mozzarella cheese (1 oz)

1. Heat oven to 350°F. Bake polenta as directed on tube for 10 to 15 minutes.

2. Meanwhile, in 10-inch skillet, heat oil over medium-high heat. Add onion and garlic; cook 3 to 5 minutes, stirring occasionally, until crisp-tender.

3. Stir in green beans and bell pepper. Cover; cook over medium-low heat 8 to 10 minutes, stirring occasionally, until beans are crisp-tender. Stir in mushrooms, squash, fennel and salt. Cover; cook 3 to 5 minutes, stirring occasionally, until squash is crisp-tender.

4. Serve polenta over vegetable mixture. Sprinkle individual servings with cheese.

1 serving: Calories 200 (Calories from Fat 80); Total Fat 9g (Saturated Fat 2g; Trans Fat 0g); Cholesterol 0mg; Sodium 460mg; Total Carbohydrate 25g (Dietary Fiber 4g; Sugars 6g); Protein 6g
% daily value: Vitamin A 50%; Vitamin C 70%; Calcium 10%; Iron 10%   **exchanges:** 1 1/2 Starch, 1 Vegetable, 1 1/2 Fat
carbohydrate choices: 1 1/2

No kidding? It's true, sweet peas are a good source of fiber, and they also rank as one of the top three favorite vegetables in the United States!

vegetable PALLA (LOW fat)

prep time: 20 minutes   **start to finish:** 1 hour 20 minutes   6 servings

1 cup uncooked regular long-grain brown or white rice
2 3/4 cup water
1 lb asparagus, cut into 2-inch pieces
3 cups fresh broccoli florets
2 teaspoons olive or vegetable oil
1 medium red bell pepper, chopped (1 cup)
2 small zucchini, chopped (1 1/4 cups)
1 medium onion, chopped (1/2 cup)
3/4 teaspoon salt
1/2 teaspoon saffron threads or 1/4 teaspoon ground turmeric
2 large tomatoes, seeded and chopped (2 cups)
2 cans (15 to 16 oz each) garbanzo beans, drained, rinsed
1 box (10 oz) frozen sweet peas, thawed, drained
Lettuce leaves, if desired

1. Cook rice in water as directed on package; set aside and keep warm.

2. In 2-quart saucepan, heat 1 inch water to boiling. Add asparagus and broccoli; return to boiling. Boil about 4 minutes or until crisp-tender; drain.

3. In 10-inch skillet, heat oil over medium-high heat. Add asparagus, broccoli, bell pepper, zucchini, onion, salt and saffron; cook 5 minutes, stirring occasionally, until onion is crisp-tender.

4. Stir in remaining ingredients except lettuce leaves. Serve on platter or individual serving plates lined with lettuce if desired.

1 serving: Calories 460 (Calories from Fat 60); Total Fat 7g (Saturated Fat 1g; Trans Fat 0g); Cholesterol 0mg; Sodium 720mg; Total Carbohydrate 81g (Dietary Fiber 19g; Sugars 10g); Protein 20g
% daily value: Vitamin A 60%; Vitamin C 90%; Calcium 10%; Iron 30%   **exchanges:** 4 1/2 Starch, 1/2 Other Carbohydrate, 1 Vegetable, 1/2 Very Lean Meat, 1 Fat   **carbohydrate choices:** 5 1/2

vegetable and chicken PAELLA: Omit 1 can of garbanzo beans. Add 1 1/2 cups chopped cooked chicken or turkey with the remaining ingredients in step 4.

vegetable PAELLA

indian LENTILS AND RICE (LOW fat)

prep time: 15 minutes   **start to finish:** 1 hour   6 servings

4 medium green onions, chopped (1/4 cup)
1 tablespoon finely chopped gingerroot
1/8 teaspoon crushed red pepper
2 cloves garlic, finely chopped
3 cans (14 oz each) vegetable broth
1 1/2 cups dried lentils (12 oz), sorted, rinsed
1 teaspoon ground turmeric
1/2 teaspoon salt
1 cup uncooked regular long-grain white rice
2 cups water
1 large tomato, chopped (1 cup)
1/4 cup shredded coconut
2 tablespoons chopped fresh or 2 teaspoons dried mint leaves
1 1/2 cups plain fat-free yogurt

1. Spray 3-quart saucepan with cooking spray. Add onions, gingerroot, red pepper and garlic; cook over medium heat 3 to 5 minutes, stirring occasionally, until onions are tender.

2. Stir in 5 cups of the broth, the lentils, turmeric and salt. Heat to boiling. Reduce heat to low; cover and simmer 25 to 30 minutes, adding remaining broth if needed, until lentils are tender.

3. Meanwhile, cook rice in water as directed on package.

4. Stir in tomato, coconut and mint. Serve over rice with yogurt.

1 serving: Calories 370 (Calories from Fat 20); Total Fat 2.5g (Saturated Fat 1.5g; Trans Fat 0g); Cholesterol 0mg; Sodium 1440mg; Total Carbohydrate 65g (Dietary Fiber 10g; Sugars 8g); Protein 20g
% daily value: Vitamin A 20%; Vitamin C 10%; Calcium 20%; Iron 40%   **exchanges:** 4 Starch, 1/2 Other Carbohydrate, 1 Very Lean Meat
carbohydrate choices: 4

Garbanzo, chickpea, ceci. This bean with many names shares culinary history with Mediterranean, Middle Eastern, Indian and Mexican cultures. Unlike most cooked legumes, this nutty-flavored bean has a firm texture.

MOROCCAN GARBANZO BEANS
with raisins (LOW fat)

prep time: 20 minutes   **start to finish:** 20 minutes   4 servings

1 1/3 cups uncooked regular long-grain white rice
2 2/3 cups water
1 tablespoon peanut or vegetable oil
1 large onion, sliced
1 medium onion, chopped (1/2 cup)
1 clove garlic, finely chopped
1 cup diced acorn or butternut squash
1/4 cup raisins
1 cup vegetable broth
1 teaspoon ground turmeric
1 teaspoon ground cinnamon
1/2 teaspoon ground ginger
1 can (15 to 16 oz) garbanzo beans, drained, rinsed

1. Cook rice in water as directed on package.

2. Meanwhile, in 3-quart saucepan, heat oil over medium heat. Add sliced onion, chopped onion and garlic; cook about 7 minutes, stirring occasionally, until onions are tender. Stir in remaining ingredients except garbanzo beans.

3. Heat to boiling. Reduce heat; cover and simmer about 8 minutes, stirring occasionally, until squash is tender. Stir in beans; heat thoroughly. Serve over rice.

1 serving: Calories 470 (Calories from Fat 60); Total Fat 6g (Saturated Fat 1g; Trans Fat 0g); Cholesterol 0mg; Sodium 860mg; Total Carbohydrate 88g (Dietary Fiber 11g; Sugars 11g); Protein 14g
% daily value: Vitamin A 10%; Vitamin C 8%; Calcium 10%; Iron 30%   **exchanges:** 5 Starch, 1/2 Fruit, 1/2 Other Carbohydrate, 1/2 Fat
carbohydrate choices: 6

easy italian SKILLET SUPPER (LOW fat)

prep time: 5 minutes   **start to finish:** 30 minutes   4 servings

1 can (14 oz) vegetable broth
1 1/4 cups uncooked rosamarina or orzo pasta (8 oz)
1 can (14.5 oz) diced tomatoes with basil, garlic and oregano, undrained
1 can (15 oz) black beans, drained, rinsed
2 cups frozen broccoli, carrots and cauliflower (from 1-lb bag)
2 tablespoons chopped fresh parsley, if desired
1/2 cup shredded Parmesan cheese

1. In 10-inch skillet, heat broth to boiling. Stir in pasta; return to boiling. Reduce heat to low; cover and simmer 10 to 12 minutes or until liquid is absorbed.

2. Stir in tomatoes, beans and vegetables. Cover; cook over medium heat 5 to 10 minutes, stirring occasionally, until vegetables are tender.

3. Stir in parsley if desired; sprinkle with cheese.

1 serving: Calories 460 (Calories from Fat 50); Total Fat 5g (Saturated Fat 2.5g; Trans Fat 0g); Cholesterol 10mg; Sodium 1070mg; Total Carbohydrate 81g (Dietary Fiber 11g; Sugars 11g); Protein 23g
% daily value: Vitamin A 40%; Vitamin C 25%; Calcium 30%; Iron 30%   **exchanges:** 4 Starch, 1 Other Carbohydrate, 1 Vegetable, 1 Lean Meat   **carbohydrate choices:** 5 1/2

easy italian turkey sausage SKILLET SUPPER: Add 1/2 lb fully cooked smoked turkey sausage ring, cut into 1/4-inch slices, with the vegetables in step 2.

If you just love the taste of crisp, smoky bacon but have dropped it from your diet, why not try bacon flavor bits? These bits are made from soybeans and contain no animal products but still have that salty, smoky flavor you crave.

warm tuscan bean SALAD (LOW fat)

prep time: 30 minutes   **start to finish:** 30 minutes   4 servings

1 tablespoon olive or vegetable oil
2 medium carrots, sliced (1 cup)
1 medium onion, chopped (1/2 cup)
2 cans (15 to 19 oz each) cannellini beans, drained,
    1/2 cup liquid reserved
1 1/2 teaspoons chopped fresh or 1/2 teaspoon
    dried oregano leaves
1/4 teaspoon pepper
4 cups bite-size pieces spinach leaves
1/4 cup red wine vinaigrette or Italian dressing
2 tablespoons bacon flavor bits

1. In 12-inch skillet, heat oil over medium heat. Add carrots and onion; cook 5 to 7 minutes, stirring occasionally, until vegetables are crisp-tender.

2. Stir in beans, 1/2 cup reserved liquid, the oregano and pepper. Cook 5 minutes, stirring occasionally.

3. Line large platter with spinach. Top with bean mixture. Pour vinaigrette over salad; sprinkle with bacon bits.

1 serving: Calories 330 (Calories from Fat 70); Total Fat 7g (Saturated Fat 1g; Trans Fat 0g); Cholesterol 0mg; Sodium 680mg; Total Carbohydrate 49g (Dietary Fiber 13g; Sugars 10g); Protein 17g
% daily value: Vitamin A 170%; Vitamin C 10%; Calcium 15%; Iron 30%   **exchanges:** 2 Starch, 1 Other Carbohydrate, 1 Vegetable, 1 Very Lean Meat, 1 Fat   **carbohydrate choices:** 3

warm tuscan bean and chicken SALAD: **Omit 1 can of cannellini beans. Add 1 1/2 cups cubed cooked chicken or turkey with the beans in step 2.**

Make this super quick by buying already-baked corn muffins or corn bread squares in the bakery or deli section. Then skip the first five ingredients and the first two steps. All you have to do is heat the beans and salsa and pour over the corn bread—so satisfying.

TRIPLE-CORN SQUARES
with bean sauce

prep time: 10 minutes   **start to finish:** 40 minutes   6 servings

1 can (14 to 15 oz) cream-style corn
1 can (8 oz) whole kernel corn, drained
1 pouch (6.5 oz) golden corn muffin and bread mix
1/3 cup butter or margarine, melted
2 eggs
1 can (15 oz) black beans, drained, rinsed
1/3 cup chunky-style salsa
Chopped fresh cilantro, if desired

1. Heat oven to 400°F. Grease 11 × 7-inch (2-quart) glass baking dish. In medium bowl, mix cream-style corn, whole kernel corn, muffin mix (dry), butter and eggs. Pour into baking dish.

2. Bake uncovered about 30 minutes or until casserole springs back when touched lightly in center.

3. During last 5 minutes of baking, in 1-quart saucepan, mix beans and salsa. Cook over medium heat, stirring occasionally, until hot. Cut casserole into squares; top with bean sauce. Sprinkle with cilantro if desired; serve immediately.

1 serving: Calories 420 (Calories from Fat 150); Total Fat 17g (Saturated Fat 7g; Trans Fat 1g); Cholesterol 100mg; Sodium 680mg; Total Carbohydrate 55g (Dietary Fiber 8g; Sugars 11g); Protein 12g
% daily value: Vitamin A 15%; Vitamin C 8%; Calcium 8%; Iron 20%   **exchanges:** 2 1/2 Starch, 1 Other Carbohydrate, 1/2 Very Lean Meat, 3 Fat   **carbohydrate choices:** 3 1/2

TRIPLE-CORN SQUARES with chicken sauce: Omit beans. Increase salsa to 3/4 cup. Heat 1 1/2 cups diced cooked chicken or turkey with the salsa in step 3.

TRIPLE-CORN SQUARES with bean sauce

dilled gouda and barley SALAD

prep time: 15 minutes   **start to finish:** 1 hour   4 servings

1/2 cup uncooked regular barley
2 cups water
1/3 cup sun-dried tomatoes (not oil-packed)
1 cup coarsely chopped zucchini (1 small)
3/4 cup shredded smoked Gouda cheese (3 oz)
1/3 cup reduced-fat mayonnaise or salad dressing
2 teaspoons chopped fresh or 3/4 teaspoon dried dill weed
1 teaspoon lemon juice
1/4 teaspoon salt
Red leaf lettuce

1. Cook barley in water as directed on package.

2. In small bowl, place tomatoes; add enough hot water to cover. Let stand 5 minutes. Drain and chop.

3. In medium bowl, mix barley, tomatoes and remaining ingredients except lettuce. Serve on lettuce-lined plates.

1 serving: Calories 260 (Calories from Fat 120); Total Fat 13g (Saturated Fat 5g; Trans Fat 0g); Cholesterol 30mg; Sodium 600mg; Total Carbohydrate 27g (Dietary Fiber 5g; Sugars 4g); Protein 9g
% daily value: Vitamin A 35%; Vitamin C 4%; Calcium 20%; Iron 8%   **exchanges:** 2 Starch, 1/2 High-Fat Meat, 1 1/2 Fat   **carbohydrate choices:** 2

dilled gouda and chicken SALAD: **Omit barley. Add 2 cups cubed cooked chicken or turkey with the remaining ingredients in step 3.**

Wheat berries are simply whole grains of wheat and can be found in the health food section of the supermarket.

wheat berry SALAD

prep time: 15 minutes   **start to finish:** 2 hours 45 minutes   5 servings

WHEAT BERRIES
3/4 cup uncooked wheat berries
3 cups water

CREAMY VINAIGRETTE DRESSING
1/3 cup vegetable oil
2 tablespoons mayonnaise or salad dressing
2 tablespoons red wine vinegar
1/2 teaspoon salt
1/4 teaspoon garlic powder
1/8 teaspoon pepper

SALAD
1 cup chopped broccoli
1 cup chopped cauliflower
1 cup grape or cherry tomatoes, cut in half
1 small green bell pepper, chopped (1/2 cup)
4 medium green onions, sliced (1/4 cup)
1/2 cup crumbled feta cheese

1. In 3-quart saucepan, soak wheat berries in water 30 minutes.

2. Heat to boiling over high heat. Reduce heat to low; partially cover and simmer 55 to 60 minutes or until wheat berries are tender. Drain; rinse with cold water.

3. In small bowl, mix dressing ingredients until well blended.

4. In large serving bowl, toss wheat berries, salad ingredients and dressing. Cover; refrigerate at least 1 hour before serving.

1 serving: Calories 330 (Calories from Fat 210); Total Fat 23g (Saturated Fat 5g; Trans Fat 0g); Cholesterol 15mg; Sodium 450mg; Total Carbohydrate 25g (Dietary Fiber 5g; Sugars 3g); Protein 7g
% daily value: Vitamin A 15%; Vitamin C 80%; Calcium 10%; Iron 8%   **exchanges:** 1 1/2 Starch, 1/2 Medium-Fat Meat, 4 Fat
carbohydrate choices: 1 1/2

Risottos are very easy to make and will stick to your ribs. To create authentic taste and texture, use Arborio rice, a short-grain rice with a high starch content that lends risotto its creaminess. Add the hot broth a half cup at a time and don't add more until the liquid has been absorbed. This will ensure a wonderful creamy rice dish.

classic RISOTTO

prep time: 55 minutes   **start to finish:** 55 minutes   4 servings

6 cups vegetable broth
2 tablespoons butter or margarine
1/4 cup olive or vegetable oil
1 medium onion, thinly sliced
2 tablespoons chopped fresh parsley
2 cups uncooked Arborio or medium-grain white rice
1 cup dry white wine or vegetable broth
1 cup freshly grated or shredded Parmesan cheese
1/2 teaspoon coarsely ground pepper

1. In 3-quart saucepan, heat broth over medium heat.

2. Meanwhile, in 12-inch nonstick skillet or 4-quart saucepan, heat butter and oil over medium-high heat until butter is melted. Add onion and parsley; cook about 5 minutes, stirring frequently, until onion is tender.

3. Stir in rice. Cook, stirring occasionally, until edges of rice kernels are translucent. Stir in wine. Cook about 3 minutes, stirring constantly, until wine is absorbed.

4. Reduce heat to medium. Pour 1/2 cup of the hot broth over rice mixture. Cook uncovered, stirring frequently, until broth is absorbed. Continue cooking 30 to 35 minutes, adding broth 1/2 cup at a time and stirring frequently, until rice is almost tender and mixture is creamy. Remove from heat.

5. Stir in cheese and pepper.

1 serving: Calories 670 (Calories from Fat 250); Total Fat 27g (Saturated Fat 10g; Trans Fat 0.5g); Cholesterol 35mg; Sodium 2000mg; Total Carbohydrate 88g (Dietary Fiber 2g; Sugars 6g); Protein 18g
% daily value: Vitamin A 35%; Vitamin C 6%; Calcium 40%; Iron 25%   **exchanges:** 4 Starch, 2 Other Carbohydrate, 1 Lean Meat, 4 Fat
carbohydrate choices: 6

CLASSIC RISOTTO with peas: **Just before serving, stir in a 1-lb bag of frozen sweet peas, cooked and drained.**

A classic Northern Italian dish, risotto has a creamy, velvety texture. This version is made con fagioli, *or* "with beans."

RISOTTO florentine (LOW fat)

prep time: 40 minutes   **start to finish:** 45 minutes   3 servings

3 cups vegetable broth
1 tablespoon butter or margarine
1 medium onion, chopped (1/2 cup)
1 clove garlic, finely chopped
1 cup uncooked Arborio or medium-grain white rice
1/2 teaspoon saffron threads or 1/4 teaspoon ground turmeric
1 can (15 to 16 oz) cannellini beans, drained, rinsed
1 box (9 oz) frozen spinach, thawed, squeezed to drain
1/4 cup grated Parmesan cheese

1. In 2-quart saucepan, heat broth over medium heat.

2. Meanwhile, in 10-inch skillet, melt butter over medium-high heat. Add onion and garlic; cook, stirring frequently, until onion is crisp-tender.

3. Stir in rice. Cook, stirring frequently, until rice begins to brown.

4. Reduce heat to medium. Pour 1/2 cup of the hot broth and the saffron over rice mixture. Cook uncovered, stirring frequently, until broth is absorbed. Continue cooking 15 to 20 minutes, adding broth 1/2 cup at a time and stirring frequently, until rice is almost tender and mixture is creamy. Remove from heat.

5. Stir in beans and spinach. Sprinkle with cheese. Cover; let stand 5 minutes.

1 serving: Calories 520 (Calories from Fat 70); Total Fat 8g (Saturated Fat 4g; Trans Fat 0g); Cholesterol 15mg; Sodium 1230mg; Total Carbohydrate 90g (Dietary Fiber 11g; Sugars 5g); Protein 22g
% daily value: Vitamin A 120%; Vitamin C 10%; Calcium 25%; Iron 40%   **exchanges:** 6 Starch, 1/2 Lean Meat, 1/2 Fat
carbohydrate choices: 6

shrimp RISOTTO FLORENTINE: **Add 1 can (4 oz) medium shrimp, drained and rinsed, with the spinach.**

Never rinse rice before making risotto because it washes off some of the grain's starch, which is so important to this creamy dish.

RISOTTO primavera

prep time: 50 minutes   **start to finish:** 50 minutes   3 servings

3 1/2 cups vegetable broth
2 teaspoons olive or vegetable oil
1 medium onion, chopped (1/2 cup)
1 small carrot, cut into julienne strips
1 cup uncooked Arborio or medium-grain white rice
1 cup broccoli flowerets
1 cup frozen sweet peas (from 1-lb bag)
1 small zucchini, cut into julienne strips
2 tablespoons grated Parmesan cheese

1. In 2-quart saucepan, heat broth over medium heat.

2. Meanwhile, in 3-quart nonstick saucepan, heat oil over medium-high heat. Add onion and carrot; cook, stirring frequently, until crisp-tender.

3. Stir in rice. Cook, stirring frequently, until rice begins to brown.

4. Reduce heat to medium. Pour 1/2 cup of the hot broth over rice mixture. Cook uncovered, stirring frequently, until broth is absorbed. Continue cooking 15 to 20 minutes, adding broth 1/2 cup at a time and stirring frequently, until rice is almost tender and mixture is creamy. Add broccoli, peas and zucchini with last addition of broth. Sprinkle with cheese.

1 serving: Calories 370 (Calories from Fat 45); Total Fat 5g (Saturated Fat 1.5g; Trans Fat 0g); Cholesterol 0mg; Sodium 1290mg; Total Carbohydrate 69g (Dietary Fiber 5g; Sugars 8g); Protein 11g
% daily value: Vitamin A 90%; Vitamin C 30%; Calcium 10%; Iron 20%   **exchanges:** 3 Starch, 1 Other Carbohydrate, 1 Vegetable, 1 Fat
carbohydrate choices: 4 1/2

chicken RISOTTO PRIMAVERA: Add 2 cups chopped cooked chicken with the broccoli, peas and zucchini in step 3.

Sweet potatoes are full of vitamins A and C. You can use either mashed fresh cooked or canned sweet potatoes in this dish. For another orange-hued treat, use mashed cooked carrots instead of sweet potatoes.

sweet potato RISOTTO (LOW fat)

prep time: 1 hour   **start to finish:** 1 hour   4 servings

7 1/2 cups vegetable broth
1/4 cup dry white wine or water
2/3 cup chopped onion
2 cloves garlic, finely chopped
2 cups uncooked Arborio or medium-grain white rice
1 cup mashed cooked sweet potato
1/4 cup grated Parmesan cheese
1 teaspoon chopped fresh or 1/2 teaspoon dried rosemary leaves, crumbled
1/4 teaspoon ground nutmeg
Shredded Parmesan cheese, if desired

1. In 3-quart saucepan, heat broth over medium heat.

2. Meanwhile, in 12-inch nonstick skillet or 4-quart saucepan, heat wine to boiling over medium-high heat. Add onion and garlic; cook 3 to 4 minutes, stirring frequently, until onion is tender.

3. Stir in rice. Cook 1 minute, stirring frequently, until rice begins to brown.

4. Reduce heat to medium. Stir in sweet potato and 1/2 cup of the hot broth. Cook uncovered, stirring frequently, until broth is absorbed. Continue cooking 30 to 35 minutes, adding broth 1/2 cup at a time and stirring frequently, until rice is almost tender and mixture is creamy. Remove from heat.

5. Stir in remaining ingredients. Garnish with additional fresh rosemary and shredded Parmesan cheese.

1 serving: Calories 490 (Calories from Fat 25); Total Fat 3g (Saturated Fat 1.5g; Trans Fat 0g); Cholesterol 0mg; Sodium 2000mg; Total Carbohydrate 104g (Dietary Fiber 4g; Sugars 15g); Protein 12g
% daily value: Vitamin A 220%; Vitamin C 15%; Calcium 15%; Iron 25%   **exchanges:** 4 Starch, 3 Other Carbohydrate
carbohydrate choices: 7

four-cheese RISOTTO

prep time: 55 minutes   **start to finish:** 55 minutes   4 servings

7 cups vegetable broth
1/4 cup olive or vegetable oil
1 large onion, chopped (1 cup)
2 cups uncooked Arborio or medium-grain white rice
2 tablespoons dry white wine or vegetable broth
1 cup ricotta cheese
1/2 cup shredded mozzarella cheese (2 oz)
1/2 cup crumbled Gorgonzola or blue cheese
1/2 cup grated or shredded Parmesan cheese
2 tablespoons chopped fresh parsley

1. In 3-quart saucepan, heat broth over medium heat.

2. Meanwhile, in 12-inch nonstick skillet or 4-quart saucepan, heat oil over medium-high heat. Add onion; cook about 5 minutes, stirring frequently, until tender.

3. Stir in rice. Cook about 5 minutes, stirring occasionally, until edges of kernels are translucent. Stir in wine. Cook about 3 minutes, stirring constantly, until wine is absorbed.

4. Reduce heat to medium. Pour 1/2 cup of the hot broth over rice mixture. Cook uncovered, stirring frequently, until broth is absorbed. Continue cooking 30 to 35 minutes, adding broth 1/2 cup at a time and stirring frequently, until rice is almost tender and mixture is creamy. Remove from heat.

5. Stir in cheeses. Sprinkle with parsley.

1 serving: Calories 760 (Calories from Fat 280); Total Fat 31g (Saturated Fat 12g; Trans Fat 0g); Cholesterol 50mg; Sodium 2370mg; Total Carbohydrate 93g (Dietary Fiber 2g; Sugars 8g); Protein 28g

% daily value: Vitamin A 40%; Vitamin C 6%; Calcium 60%; Iron 25%   **exchanges:** 5 1/2 Starch, 1/2 Other Carbohydrate, 1 1/2 Medium-Fat Meat, 4 Fat   **carbohydrate choices**: 6

Chopped fresh garlic, available in jars in the refrigerator or produce section of the supermarket, is a real time-saver. It makes this quick-to-prepare dish even easier.

creamy corn and garlic RISOTTO

prep time: 45 minutes   **start to finish:** 45 minutes   4 servings

3 3/4 cups vegetable broth
4 cloves garlic, finely chopped
1 cup uncooked Arborio or medium-grain white rice
3 cups frozen whole kernel corn
1/2 cup grated Parmesan cheese
1/3 cup shredded mozzarella cheese
1/4 cup chopped fresh parsley

1. In 12-inch skillet or 4–quart saucepan, heat 1/3 cup of the broth to boiling. Add garlic; cook 1 minute, stirring occasionally. Stir in rice and frozen corn. Cook 1 minute, stirring occasionally.

2. Stir in remaining broth; heat to boiling. Reduce heat to medium; cook uncovered 15 to 20 minutes, stirring occasionally, until rice is tender and mixture is creamy. Remove from heat.

3. Stir in cheeses and parsley.

1 serving: Calories 390 (Calories from Fat 60); Total Fat 7g (Saturated Fat 4g; Trans Fat 0g); Cholesterol 15mg; Sodium 1230mg; Total Carbohydrate 68g (Dietary Fiber 4g; Sugars 5g); Protein 15g
% daily value: Vitamin A 25%; Vitamin C 10%; Calcium 30%; Iron 15%   **exchanges:** 3 Starch, 1 1/2 Other Carbohydrate, 1 Lean Meat, 1/2 Fat   **carbohydrate choices:** 4 1/2

creamy corn, chicken and garlic RISOTTO: **Add 2 cups chopped grilled or cooked chicken in step 3; heat through.**

Three varieties of mushrooms are used for this risotto, each bringing its own character to the dish. Rehydrated dried porcini mushrooms have a chewy texture and deep, woodsy flavor that complements the mild flavor of the shiitake, and tender crimini mushrooms add more flavor than regular button or white mushrooms.

three-mushroom RISOTTO

prep time: 1 hour 45 minutes   **start to finish:** 1 hour 45 minutes   3 servings

1 package (about 1.25 oz) dried porcini mushrooms (about 1 cup)
3 1/2 cups vegetable broth
1/4 cup olive or vegetable oil
2 tablespoons chopped fresh parsley
4 cloves garlic, finely chopped
2 medium green onions, sliced (2 tablespoons)
1 cup uncooked Arborio or medium-grain white rice
1 package (about 3.5 oz) fresh shiitake mushrooms, thinly sliced (1 1/2 cups)
1 package (about 5.5 oz) fresh crimini mushrooms, thinly sliced (2 cups)
1/2 cup freshly grated or shredded Parmesan cheese
1 tablespoon balsamic vinegar

1. In small bowl, place porcini mushrooms; add enough warm water to cover. Let stand at room temperature about 1 hour or until tender; drain.

2. In 2-quart saucepan, heat broth over medium heat.

3. Meanwhile, in 10-inch nonstick skillet, heat oil over medium-high heat. Add parsley, garlic and onions; cook about 5 minutes, stirring frequently, until onions are tender.

4. Stir in rice. Cook, stirring, until edges of kernels are translucent. Stir in porcini, shiitake and crimini mushrooms. Cook uncovered about 3 minutes, stirring frequently, until mushrooms are tender.

5. Reduce heat to medium. Pour 1/2 cup of the hot broth over rice mixture. Cook uncovered, stirring frequently, until broth is absorbed. Continue cooking 15 to 20 minutes, adding broth 1/2 cup at a time and stirring frequently, until rice is almost tender and mixture is moist. Remove from heat.

6. Stir in cheese and vinegar.

1 serving: Calories 570 (Calories from Fat 210); Total Fat 24g (Saturated Fat 6g; Trans Fat 0g); Cholesterol 15mg; Sodium 1480mg; Total Carbohydrate 72g (Dietary Fiber 3g; Sugars 7g); Protein 16g
% daily value: Vitamin A 25%; Vitamin C 8%; Calcium 25%; Iron 20%   **exchanges:** 2 1/2 Starch, 2 Other Carbohydrate, 1 Vegetable, 1 Lean Meat, 4 Fat   **carbohydrate choices:** 5

three-mushroom RISOTTO

Chipotle chilies in adobo sauce come in 7- or 11-ounce cans. Recipes usually use only 1 or 2 of these fiery smoked jalapeños. To save the rest, spoon chilies and sauce into a resealable plastic freezer bag, flatten to a thin layer and freeze. To use, just break off the amount you need; freezing makes them a bit milder, so you may need to use more.

chipotle-peanut-noodle BOWLS

prep time: 15 minutes   **start to finish:** 30 minutes   4 servings

1/2 cup creamy peanut butter
1/2 cup apple juice
2 tablespoons soy sauce
2 chipotle chilies in adobo sauce (from 7-oz can), seeded, chopped
1 teaspoon adobo sauce (from can of chilies)
1/4 cup chopped fresh cilantro
4 cups water
2 medium carrots, cut into julienne strips (1 1/2 × 1/4 × 1/4 inch)
1 medium red bell pepper, cut into julienne strips (1 1/2 × 1/4 × 1/4 inch)
1 package (8 to 10 oz) Chinese curly noodles
2 tablespoons chopped peanuts

1. In medium bowl, mix peanut butter, apple juice, soy sauce, chilies and adobo sauce until smooth. Stir in cilantro.

2. In 2-quart saucepan, heat water to boiling. Add carrots and bell pepper; cook 1 minute. With slotted spoon, remove carrots and bell pepper from water. Add noodles to water; cook and drain as directed on package.

3. Toss noodles with peanut butter mixture; divide noodles into 4 individual bowls. Top with carrots and bell pepper. Sprinkle with peanuts.

1 serving: Calories 500 (Calories from Fat 180); Total Fat 20g (Saturated Fat 4g; Trans Fat 0g); Cholesterol 0mg; Sodium 740mg; Total Carbohydrate 62g (Dietary Fiber 7g; Sugars 10g); Protein 18g
% daily value: Vitamin A 150%; Vitamin C 50%; Calcium 4%; Iron 20%   **exchanges:** 3 Starch, 1 Other Carbohydrate, 1 1/2 High-Fat Meat, 1 Fat   **carbohydrate choices:** 4

Beans are a good source of protein and fiber, among other nutrients. Any type of canned bean can be substituted for the black beans—use your favorite.

southwest fettuccine BOWL

prep time: 15 minutes   **start to finish:** 40 minutes   4 servings

8 oz uncooked fettuccine
Olive oil-flavored cooking spray
1 cup chunky-style salsa
1/3 cup frozen whole kernel corn (from 1-lb bag)
1/4 cup water
2 tablespoons chili sauce
1/2 teaspoon ground cumin
1 can (15 oz) black beans, drained, rinsed
1/4 cup chopped fresh cilantro

1. Cook and drain fettuccine as directed on package. In medium bowl, place fettuccine. Spray fettuccine 2 or 3 times with cooking spray, tossing after each spray. Cover to keep warm.

2. In same saucepan, mix remaining ingredients except cilantro. Cook over medium heat 4 to 6 minutes, stirring occasionally, until corn is tender.

3. Divide fettuccine into 4 individual bowls. Top each with about 3/4 cup sauce mixture. Sprinkle with cilantro.

1 serving: Calories 390 (Calories from Fat 45); Total Fat 5g (Saturated Fat 1g; Trans Fat 0g); Cholesterol 50mg; Sodium 640mg; Total Carbohydrate 69g (Dietary Fiber 9g; Sugars 6g); Protein 17g
% daily value: Vitamin A 10%; Vitamin C 10%; Calcium 10%; Iron 30%   **exchanges:** 4 1/2 Starch, 1/2 Very Lean Meat, 1/2 Fat
carbohydrate choices: 4 1/2

Fish sauce gives this noodle dish its distinctive Thai flavor. Look for it in an Asian food store or in the Asian-foods section of your supermarket.

PAD thai

prep time: 40 minutes **start to finish:** 40 minutes **4 servings**

4 cups water
1 package (6 to 8 oz) linguine-style stir-fry
  rice noodles (rice stick noodles)*
1/3 cup fresh lime juice
1/3 cup water
3 tablespoons packed brown sugar
3 tablespoons fish sauce or soy sauce
3 tablespoons soy sauce
1 tablespoon rice vinegar or white vinegar
3/4 teaspoon ground red pepper (cayenne)

3 tablespoons vegetable oil
3 cloves garlic, finely chopped
1 medium shallot, finely chopped, or 1/4 cup
  finely chopped onion
2 eggs, beaten
1/4 cup finely chopped dry-roasted peanuts
3 cups fresh bean sprouts
4 medium green onions, thinly sliced (1/4 cup)
1/4 cup firmly packed fresh cilantro leaves

1. In 3-quart saucepan, heat 4 cups water to boiling. Remove from heat; add noodles (push noodles into water with back of spoon to cover completely with water if necessary). Soak noodles 3 to 5 minutes or until noodles are soft but firm. Drain noodles; rinse with cold water.

2. Meanwhile, in small bowl, mix lime juice, 1/3 cup water, the brown sugar, fish sauce, soy sauce, vinegar, red pepper and 1 tablespoon of the oil; set aside.

3. In nonstick wok or 12-inch nonstick skillet, heat remaining 2 tablespoons oil over medium heat. Add garlic and shallot; cook about 30 seconds, stirring constantly, until they begin to brown. Stir in beaten eggs, cooking and stirring gently about 2 minutes or until scrambled but still moist.

4. Stir in noodles and lime juice mixture. Increase heat to high; cook about 1 minute, tossing constantly with 2 wooden spoons, until sauce begins to thicken. Add remaining ingredients except cilantro; cook 2 to 3 minutes, tossing with wooden spoons, until noodles are tender. Place on serving platter. Sprinkle with cilantro. If desired, garnish with additional chopped dry-roasted peanuts and green onions.

*Thin or thick rice stick noodles can be substituted for the linguine-style stir-fry rice noodles.

1 serving: Calories 490 (Calories from Fat 190); Total Fat 21g (Saturated Fat 3.5g; Trans Fat 0g); Cholesterol 105mg; Sodium 1880mg; Total Carbohydrate 58g (Dietary Fiber 4g; Sugars 14g); Protein 16g
% daily value: Vitamin A 10%; Vitamin C 15%; Calcium 10%; Iron 15% **exchanges:** 2 1/2 Starch, 1 Other Carbohydrate, 1 Vegetable, 1 Medium-Fat Meat, 3 Fat **carbohydrate choices:** 4

PAD THAI with chicken: **Add 2 cups chopped cooked chicken with the remaining ingredients in step 4.**

Look for regular and reduced-fat refrigerated Alfredo sauce next to the fresh pasta. Whole wheat or lupini fettuccine, linguine or spaghetti can be substituted for the plain fettuccine.

FETTUCCINE primavera

prep time: 25 minutes   **start to finish:** 25 minutes   4 servings

8 oz uncooked fettuccine
1 tablespoon olive or vegetable oil
1 cup broccoli flowerets
1 cup cauliflower florets
1 cup frozen sweet peas (from 1-lb bag), rinsed to separate
2 medium carrots, thinly sliced (1 cup)
1 small onion, chopped (1/4 cup)
1 container (10 oz) refrigerated Alfredo sauce
1 tablespoon grated Parmesan cheese

1. Cook and drain fettuccine as directed on package.

2. Meanwhile, in 12-inch skillet, heat oil over medium–high heat. Add broccoli, cauliflower, peas, carrots and onion; cook 6 to 8 minutes, stirring frequently, until vegetables are crisp-tender.

3. Stir in Alfredo sauce; cook until hot. Stir in fettuccine; heat thoroughly. Sprinkle with cheese.

1 serving: Calories 530 (Calories from Fat 260); Total Fat 29g (Saturated Fat 14g; Trans Fat 1g); Cholesterol 120mg; Sodium 620mg; Total Carbohydrate 52g (Dietary Fiber 5g; Sugars 6g); Protein 16g
% daily value: Vitamin A 140%; Vitamin C 30%; Calcium 25%; Iron 20%   **exchanges:** 3 1/2 Starch, 1 High-Fat Meat, 3 1/2 Fat
carbohydrate choices: 3 1/2

Certain foods just have a love affair with one another, and so it is with the combination of Gorgonzola and toasted walnuts. One taste and you're hooked! If you like, sprinkle additional cheese over the pasta and add a sprinkle of fresh parsley.

GORGONZOLA LINGUINE
with toasted walnuts

prep time: 30 minutes   **start to finish:** 30 minutes   4 servings

12 oz uncooked linguine
2 tablespoons butter or margarine
2 cloves garlic, finely chopped
2 tablespoons all-purpose flour
1/2 teaspoon salt
2 cups fat-free half-and-half
1/2 cup dry white wine or vegetable broth
1 cup crumbled Gorgonzola cheese (4 oz)
1/4 cup chopped walnuts, toasted

1. Cook and drain linguine as directed on package.

2. Meanwhile, in 3-quart saucepan, melt butter over medium heat. Add garlic; cook, stirring occasionally, until golden brown. Stir in flour and salt. Cook, stirring constantly, until smooth and bubbly. Remove from heat. Stir in half-and-half and wine. Cook, stirring constantly, until mixture thickens slightly. Reduce heat to medium-low. Stir in cheese. Cook, stirring occasionally, until cheese is melted.

3. Add linguine to sauce; toss. Garnish with walnuts.

1 serving: Calories 630 (Calories from Fat 200); Total Fat 22g (Saturated Fat 11g; Trans Fat 0.5g); Cholesterol 45mg; Sodium 1250mg; Total Carbohydrate 84g (Dietary Fiber 6g; Sugars 9g); Protein 22g
% daily value: Vitamin A 8%; Vitamin C 0%; Calcium 30%; Iron 20%   **exchanges:** 5 Starch, 1/2 Other Carbohydrate, 1 High-Fat Meat, 2 Fat   **carbohydrate choices:** 5 1/2

Store tomatoes at room temperature, not in the refrigerator—cold temperatures destroy the flavor and make the flesh mealy.

ANGEL HAIR PASTA with autumn vegetable ragout

prep time: 30 minutes **start to finish:** 30 minutes 4 servings

3 cups water
1 medium dark-orange sweet potato, peeled, diced
8 oz uncooked angel hair (capellini) pasta
2 tablespoons olive or vegetable oil
3 cloves garlic, finely chopped
4 medium tomatoes, chopped (4 cups)
1 small zucchini, cut lengthwise in half, then cut crosswise into slices
1 small yellow summer squash, cut lengthwise in half,
  then cut crosswise into slices (1 cup)
1/2 teaspoon salt
1/4 teaspoon freshly ground pepper
1/3 cup freshly shredded Parmesan cheese

1. In 4-quart Dutch oven, heat water to boiling over medium-high heat. Add sweet potato; cook 3 to 5 minutes or until crisp-tender. Drain.

2. Cook and drain pasta as directed on package.

3. Meanwhile, in 10-inch skillet, heat oil over medium-high heat. Add garlic; cook 30 seconds, stirring frequently. Stir in tomatoes. Cook about 3 minutes, stirring frequently, until slightly soft. Stir in zucchini, yellow squash, sweet potato, salt and pepper. Cook 2 to 3 minutes, stirring frequently, until vegetables are crisp-tender.

4. Serve vegetables over pasta. Sprinkle with cheese.

1 serving: Calories 420 (Calories from Fat 100); Total Fat 11g (Saturated Fat 2.5g; Trans Fat 0g); Cholesterol 5mg; Sodium 690mg; Total Carbohydrate 66g (Dietary Fiber 8g; Sugars 10g); Protein 14g
% daily value: Vitamin A 150%; Vitamin C 45%; Calcium 15%; Iron 20%   **exchanges:** 3 1/2 Starch, 1/2 Other Carbohydrate, 1 Vegetable, 2 Fat
carbohydrate choices: 4 1/2

The rice and oat "meatballs" are rolled in a small amount of wheat germ, giving them a golden brown color and a bit of crunch. Nutty-flavored wheat germ is oily, so it can turn rancid quickly; store it in the fridge or freezer. If you like using whole grains, substitute cooked brown rice for the white rice and use whole wheat spaghetti.

SPAGHETTI and spicy rice balls

prep time: 30 minutes   **start to finish:** 30 minutes   6 servings

1 package (16 oz) uncooked spaghetti
2 cups cooked white rice
1/2 cup quick-cooking oats
1 medium onion, chopped (1/2 cup)
1/4 cup unseasoned dry bread crumbs
1/4 cup milk
1 tablespoon chopped fresh or 1 teaspoon dried basil leaves
2 teaspoons chopped fresh or 1/2 teaspoon dried oregano leaves
1/4 teaspoon ground red pepper (cayenne)
1 egg, beaten
1/2 cup wheat germ
1 tablespoon vegetable oil
2 cups tomato pasta sauce
Finely shredded Parmesan cheese, if desired

1. Cook and drain spaghetti as directed on package.

2. Meanwhile, in medium bowl, mix rice, oats, onion, bread crumbs, milk, basil, oregano, red pepper and egg. Shape mixture into 10 balls; roll in wheat germ to coat.

3. In 10-inch skillet, heat oil over medium heat. Add rice balls; cook about 10 minutes, turning occasionally, until light golden brown.

4. Heat pasta sauce until hot. Serve sauce and rice balls over spaghetti; sprinkle with Parmesan cheese if desired.

1 serving: Calories 580 (Calories from Fat 90); Total Fat 9g (Saturated Fat 1.5g; Trans Fat 0g); Cholesterol 35mg; Sodium 970mg; Total Carbohydrate 105g (Dietary Fiber 8g; Sugars 10g); Protein 18g
% daily value: Vitamin A 15%; Vitamin C 10%; Calcium 8%; Iron 30%   **exchanges:** 6 Starch, 1 Other Carbohydrate, 1 Fat
carbohydrate choices: 7

SPAGHETTI and spicy rice balls

Fresh asparagus is now available year-round, so this light and refreshing pasta can be enjoyed when you please. For a flavor twist, try fresh lime peel and juice instead of the lemon.

LEMON-PEPPER PASTA and asparagus

prep time: 25 minutes   **start to finish:** 25 minutes   4 servings

2 cups uncooked farfalle (bow-tie) pasta (4 oz)
1/4 cup olive or vegetable oil
1 medium red bell pepper, chopped (1 cup)
1 lb asparagus, cut into 1-inch pieces
1 teaspoon grated lemon peel
1/2 teaspoon salt
1/2 teaspoon freshly ground pepper
3 tablespoons lemon juice
1 can (15 to 16 oz) navy beans, drained, rinsed
Freshly ground black pepper

1. Cook and drain pasta as directed on package.

2. Meanwhile, in 12-inch skillet, heat oil over medium-high heat. Add bell pepper, asparagus, lemon peel, salt and 1/2 teaspoon pepper; cook, stirring occasionally, until vegetables are crisp-tender.

3. Stir in lemon juice and beans. Cook until beans are hot. Add pasta; toss with vegetable mixture. Sprinkle with pepper.

1 serving: Calories 400 (Calories from Fat 130); Total Fat 15g (Saturated Fat 2g; Trans Fat 0g); Cholesterol 0mg; Sodium 410mg; Total Carbohydrate 52g (Dietary Fiber 9g; Sugars 7g); Protein 14g
% daily value: Vitamin A 50%; Vitamin C 70%; Calcium 8%; Iron 25%   **exchanges:** 3 Starch, 1/2 Other Carbohydrate, 1/2 Very Lean Meat, 2 1/2 Fat   **carbohydrate choices:** 3 1/2

LEMON-PEPPER PASTA and shrimp: **Add 1/2 lb cooked peeled deveined shrimp, thawed if frozen, with the beans in step 3.**

Coconut milk, which is richly flavored and slightly sweet, is made from simmering fresh coconut meat and water. It is used extensively in Indonesian cooking. Don't buy cream of coconut by mistake; that is for making tropical-flavored drinks and desserts.

CURRIED RAVIOLI with spinach

prep time: 20 minutes   **start to finish:** 20 minutes   4 servings

1 package (9 oz) refrigerated cheese-filled ravioli
1 box (9 oz) frozen spinach
2 oz cream cheese, softened
2/3 cup canned coconut milk
1/3 cup vegetable broth
3/4 teaspoon curry powder
1/4 teaspoon salt
3 medium green onions, sliced (1/3 cup)
1/4 cup chopped peanuts

1. Cook and drain ravioli as directed on package. Cook and drain spinach as directed on box.

2. In 1-quart saucepan, mix cream cheese, coconut milk, broth, curry powder and salt. Cook over medium heat, stirring occasionally, until hot.

3. Spoon spinach onto serving plate. Top with ravioli and sauce. Sprinkle with onions and peanuts.

1 serving: Calories 320 (Calories from Fat 190); Total Fat 22g (Saturated Fat 12g; Trans Fat 0g); Cholesterol 80mg; Sodium 890mg; Total Carbohydrate 19g (Dietary Fiber 4g; Sugars 4g); Protein 13g
% daily value: Vitamin A 80%; Vitamin C 6%; Calcium 20%; Iron 15%   **exchanges:** 1 Starch, 1 1/2 High-Fat Meat, 2 Fat
carbohydrate choices: 1

Because curry powder is a mixture of spices, the flavor will vary by brand. Most stores carry regular curry powder, sometimes labeled sweet curry, or Madras, also called hot curry powder. Experimenting can be an exciting culinary adventure!

VEGETABLE CURRY with couscous

prep time: 25 minutes   **start to finish:** 25 minutes   4 servings

2/3 cup uncooked couscous
1 cup water
1 tablespoon vegetable oil
1 medium red bell pepper, cut into thin strips
1/4 cup vegetable broth
1 tablespoon curry powder
1 teaspoon salt
1 bag (1 lb) frozen broccoli, carrots and cauliflower
1/2 cup raisins
1/3 cup chutney
1/4 cup chopped peanuts

1. Cook couscous in water as directed on package.

2. Meanwhile, in 12-inch skillet, heat oil over medium-high heat. Add bell pepper; cook, stirring frequently, until tender.

3. Stir in broth, curry powder, salt and frozen vegetables. Heat to boiling. Boil about 4 minutes, stirring frequently, until vegetables are crisp-tender.

4. Stir in raisins and chutney. Serve over couscous. Sprinkle with peanuts.

1 serving: Calories 330 (Calories from Fat 80); Total Fat 9g (Saturated Fat 1.5g; Trans Fat 0g); Cholesterol 0mg; Sodium 930mg; Total Carbohydrate 53g (Dietary Fiber 7g; Sugars 22g); Protein 9g
% daily value: Vitamin A 100%; Vitamin C 80%; Calcium 6%; Iron 10%   **exchanges:** 2 Starch, 1 Fruit, 2 Vegetable, 1 1/2 Fat
carbohydrate choices: 3 1/2

CHICKEN CURRY with couscous: **Add 2 boneless skinless chicken breasts, cut into 3/4-inch pieces, with the bell pepper in step 2. Cook until chicken is no longer pink in center.**

VEGETABLE CURRY with couscous

Use the frozen vegetable mix suggested in this recipe, or try one of your favorite frozen stir-fry vegetable combinations.

easy vegetable CHOW MEIN

prep time: 15 minutes   **start to finish:** 15 minutes

1 cup vegetable broth
2 tablespoons cornstarch
2 tablespoons stir-fry sauce
1/4 teaspoon red pepper sauce
2 tablespoons vegetable oil
2 cloves garlic, finely chopped
1 bag (1 lb) frozen carrots, sugar snap peas, onions and mushrooms
2 1/2 cups coleslaw mix (shredded cabbage and carrots)
4 cups chow mein noodles

1. In small bowl, mix broth, cornstarch, stir-fry sauce and pepper sauce; set aside.

2. In 12-inch nonstick skillet, heat oil over medium-high heat. Add garlic and frozen vegetables; cook about 5 minutes, stirring frequently, until vegetables are crisp-tender.

3. Stir in coleslaw mix and broth mixture. Cook, stirring constantly, until thickened. Serve over noodles.

1 serving: Calories 380 (Calories from Fat 190); Total Fat 21g (Saturated Fat 3g; Trans Fat 0g); Cholesterol 0mg; Sodium 760mg; Total Carbohydrate 43g (Dietary Fiber 5g; Sugars 4g); Protein 6g
% daily value: Vitamin A 40%; Vitamin C 15%; Calcium 6%; Iron 15%   **exchanges:** 2 Other Carbohydrate, 3 Vegetable, 4 Fat
carbohydrate choices: 3

easy chicken CHOW MEIN: **Add 2 cups cubed cooked chicken or turkey with the frozen vegetables in step 2.**

This is vegetarian comfort food and a delicious way to use up leftover French bread! The bread becomes a toasted crust for this creamy pasta pie. Just add veggies or a salad, and you'll "own" dinner!

ALFREDO PASTA PIE with toasted french bread crust

prep time: 15 minutes   **start to finish:** 40 minutes

4 oz uncooked capellini (angel hair) pasta
18 slices French bread, about 1/4 inch thick
2 tablespoons butter or margarine, softened
3/4 cup shredded Swiss cheese (3 oz)
2 tablespoons chopped fresh or 2 teaspoons dried basil leaves
1 container (10 oz) refrigerated Alfredo sauce
3 medium roma (plum) tomatoes, chopped (1 cup)
2 medium green onions, sliced (1/4 cup)
1 tablespoon grated Romano or Parmesan cheese

1. Heat oven to 400°F. Cook and drain pasta as directed on package.

2. Meanwhile, brush bread with butter. Line bottom and side of 10-inch pie plate with bread, butter sides up and slightly overlapping slices. Bake about 10 minutes or until light brown.

3. Reduce oven temperature to 350°F. In medium bowl, mix Swiss cheese, 1 tablespoon of the basil and the Alfredo sauce. Gently stir in pasta. Spoon into baked crust.

4. In small bowl, mix tomatoes, onions and remaining 1 tablespoon basil. Sprinkle over pasta mixture; lightly press onto surface. Sprinkle with Romano cheese.

5. Bake 15 to 20 minutes or until hot. Let stand 5 minutes before cutting.

1 serving: Calories 410 (Calories from Fat 220); Total Fat 24g (Saturated Fat 14g; Trans Fat 1g); Cholesterol 70mg; Sodium 520mg; Total Carbohydrate 34g (Dietary Fiber 2g; Sugars 2g); Protein 14g
% daily value: Vitamin A 25%; Vitamin C 6%; Calcium 30%; Iron 10%   **exchanges:** 2 Starch, 1 High-Fat Meat, 3 Fat
carbohydrate choices: 2

vegetable TETRAZZINI

prep time: 15 minutes   **start to finish:** 45 minutes   6 servings

7 oz uncooked spaghetti
2 cups vegetable broth
2 cups half-and-half
1/2 cup all-purpose flour
1/4 cup butter or margarine
1/2 teaspoon salt
1/4 teaspoon pepper
2 cups frozen mixed vegetables (from 1-lb bag)
1 can (2 1/4 oz) sliced ripe olives, drained
1/2 cup slivered almonds
1/2 cup shredded Cheddar cheese (2 oz)

1. Heat oven to 350°F. Cook and drain spaghetti as directed on package. Rinse with cold water; drain.

2. In 3-quart saucepan, mix broth, half-and-half, flour, butter, salt and pepper. Heat to boiling over medium heat, stirring constantly. Boil 1 minute, stirring constantly. Stir in spaghetti, frozen vegetables and olives. In ungreased 2-quart casserole, spread mixture. Sprinkle with almonds and cheese.

3. Bake uncovered 25 to 30 minutes or until hot and bubbly.

1 serving: Calories 500 (Calories from Fat 250); Total Fat 27g (Saturated Fat 12g; Trans Fat 1g); Cholesterol 60mg; Sodium 920mg; Total Carbohydrate 50g (Dietary Fiber 7g; Sugars 8g); Protein 14g
% daily value: Vitamin A 70%; Vitamin C 2%; Calcium 20%; Iron 20%   **exchanges:** 3 Starch, 1/2 Other Carbohydrate, 1/2 High-Fat Meat, 4 Fat   **carbohydrate choices:** 3

chicken TETRAZZINI: Omit the frozen mixed vegetables. Add 2 cups diced cooked chicken or turkey with the spaghetti in step 2.

Homemade mac 'n cheese is just about as good as it gets. Here's a little secret: Process American cheese loaf melts much better than natural Cheddar cheese and won't clump up or curdle when cooked, so this classic favorite stays rich, smooth and creamy.

mom's MACARONI AND CHEESE

prep time: 10 minutes   **start to finish:** 40 minutes   5 servings

1 1/2 cups uncooked elbow macaroni (5 oz)
2 tablespoons butter or margarine
1 small onion, chopped (1/4 cup)
1/2 teaspoon salt
1/4 teaspoon pepper
1/4 cup all-purpose flour
1 3/4 cups milk
6 oz process American cheese loaf, cut into 1/2-inch cubes

1. Heat oven to 375°F. Cook and drain macaroni as directed on package.

2. Meanwhile, in 2-quart saucepan, melt butter over medium heat. Add onion, salt and pepper; cook, stirring occasionally, until onion is crisp-tender. In small bowl, mix flour and milk until smooth; stir into onion mixture. Heat to boiling, stirring constantly. Boil 1 minute, stirring constantly. Remove from heat. Stir in cheese until melted.

3. Stir macaroni into cheese mixture. Into ungreased 1 1/2-quart casserole, spoon mixture.

4. Bake uncovered about 30 minutes or until bubbly and light brown.

1 serving: Calories 350 (Calories from Fat 160); Total Fat 18g (Saturated Fat 10g; Trans Fat 0.5g); Cholesterol 50mg; Sodium 900mg; Total Carbohydrate 32g (Dietary Fiber 2g; Sugars 6g); Protein 15g
% daily value: Vitamin A 15%; Vitamin C 0%; Calcium 30%; Iron 10%   **exchanges:** 2 Starch, 1 1/2 High-Fat Meat, 1 Fat
carbohydrate choices: 2

This casserole will soon be a family favorite. Not only is it easy, the kids will love the wagon wheel pasta shape. If the kids don't care for ripe olives, just leave them out. Mafalda pasta, which looks like mini-lasagna noodles, can be used instead of the wagon wheels.

pizza CASSEROLE

prep time: 15 minutes   **start to finish:** 50 minutes   6 servings

4 cups uncooked wagon wheel pasta (8 oz)
1 jar (28 oz) tomato pasta sauce
1 can (8 oz) mushroom pieces and stems, drained
1 can (2 1/4 oz) sliced ripe olives, drained
1 cup shredded mozzarella cheese (4 oz)

1. Heat oven to 350°F. Cook and drain pasta as directed on package.

2. In ungreased 2 1/2-quart casserole, mix pasta and remaining ingredients except cheese.

3. Cover; bake about 30 minutes or until hot and bubbly. Sprinkle with cheese; bake uncovered about 5 minutes longer or until cheese is melted.

1 serving: Calories 370 (Calories from Fat 90); Total Fat 10g (Saturated Fat 3.5g; Trans Fat 0g); Cholesterol 10mg; Sodium 1140mg; Total Carbohydrate 57g (Dietary Fiber 5g; Sugars 11g); Protein 12g
% daily value: Vitamin A 20%; Vitamin C 15%; Calcium 20%; Iron 15%   **exchanges:** 3 Starch, 1 Other Carbohydrate, 1/2 Medium-Fat Meat, 1 Fat   **carbohydrate choices:** 4

pizza turkey CASSEROLE: **Add 1 lb cooked ground turkey with remaining ingredients in step 2.**

This impressive-looking torte is deceptively easy to make and perfect for entertaining. If you like ripe olives, drain a 4-oz can of sliced ripe olives and add to the spaghetti mixture. Serve with whole green beans and warm crusty bread.

spaghetti basil TORTE (LOW fat)

prep time: 15 minutes   **start to finish:** 1 hour   8 servings

1 package (16 oz) spaghetti
1/2 cup grated Parmesan cheese
1/2 cup ricotta cheese
1 tablespoon Italian seasoning
2 eggs, beaten
1/4 cup chopped fresh or 1 1/2 teaspoons dried basil leaves
2 medium tomatoes, each cut into 5 slices
4 slices (1 oz each) provolone cheese, cut in half

1. Heat oven to 350°F. Spray 9-inch springform pan with cooking spray. Cook and drain spaghetti as directed on package. Rinse with cold water; drain.

2. In large bowl, mix Parmesan cheese, ricotta cheese, Italian seasoning and eggs until well blended. Add spaghetti; toss until well coated.

3. Press half of spaghetti mixture in bottom of pan. Sprinkle with half of the basil. Layer with half of the tomato and cheese slices. Press remaining spaghetti mixture on top. Sprinkle with remaining basil. Layer with remaining tomato and cheese slices.

4. Bake uncovered 30 minutes until hot and light brown. Let stand 15 minutes. Remove side of pan. Cut into wedges.

1 serving: Calories 350 (Calories from Fat 80); Total Fat 9g (Saturated Fat 5g; Trans Fat 0g); Cholesterol 70mg; Sodium 510mg; Total Carbohydrate 49g (Dietary Fiber 4g; Sugars 2g); Protein 18g
% daily value: Vitamin A 15%; Vitamin C 6%; Calcium 25%; Iron 15%   **exchanges:** 3 Starch, 1 1/2 Medium-Fat Meat
carbohydrate choices: 3

spinach pasta SALAD

prep time: 30 minutes   **start to finish:** 30 minutes   6 servings

3 cups uncooked farfalle (bow-tie) pasta (6 oz)
1 small tomato, cut into quarters
1/2 cup basil pesto
1/4 teaspoon salt
1/4 teaspoon pepper
4 cups bite-size pieces spinach leaves
2 medium carrots, thinly sliced (1 cup)
1 small red onion, thinly sliced
1 can (14 oz) quartered artichokes hearts, drained, rinsed

1. Cook and drain pasta as directed on package. Rinse with cold water; drain.

2. Meanwhile, in food processor or blender, place tomato, pesto, salt and pepper. Cover; process 30 seconds.

3. Toss pasta, pesto mixture and remaining ingredients.

1 serving: Calories 270 (Calories from Fat 110); Total Fat 12g (Saturated Fat 2.5g; Trans Fat 0g); Cholesterol 0mg; Sodium 540mg; Total Carbohydrate 33g (Dietary Fiber 6g; Sugars 3g); Protein 8g
% daily value: Vitamin A 120%; Vitamin C 25%; Calcium 15%; Iron 15%   **exchanges:** 2 Starch, 1 Vegetable, 2 Fat
carbohydrate choices: 2

spinach pasta SALAD

Couscous is on the most-wanted list because it's versatile, tastes great and is fast to fix—just 5 minutes! This tiniest form of pasta is granular semolina, a staple of North African cuisine.

couscous-vegetable SALAD

prep time: 25 minutes   **start to finish:** 25 minutes   6 servings

1 cup uncooked couscous
2 teaspoons olive or vegetable oil
1 medium zucchini, cut into 1/4-inch slices (2 cups)
1 medium yellow summer squash, cut into 1/4-inch slices (1 1/2 cups)
1 large red bell pepper, cut into 1-inch pieces
1/2 medium red onion, cut into 8 wedges
1 container (7 oz) refrigerated pesto with sun-dried tomatoes or regular basil pesto
2 tablespoons balsamic or cider vinegar

1. Cook couscous as directed on package.

2. In 10-inch nonstick skillet, heat oil over medium-high heat. Add zucchini, yellow squash, bell pepper and onion; cook about 5 minutes, stirring frequently, until crisp-tender.

3. In large bowl, toss couscous, vegetable mixture, pesto and vinegar. Serve warm or cool.

1 serving: Calories 320 (Calories from Fat 180); Total Fat 20g (Saturated Fat 4g; Trans Fat 0g); Cholesterol 5mg; Sodium 300mg; Total Carbohydrate 29g (Dietary Fiber 4g; Sugars 4g); Protein 8g
% daily value: Vitamin A 45%; Vitamin C 50%; Calcium 15%; Iron 8%   **exchanges:** 1 1/2 Starch, 1 Vegetable, 4 Fat
carbohydrate choices: 2

Buying Grains

Look for grains, from whole kernels to finely ground meals and flours, in large supermarkets, ethnic food markets, whole food stores and food co-ops. They're available both in packages and bulk-food bins.

Storing Grains

UNCOOKED: Most grains keep indefinitely but are best used within one to two years. Store them in their original packaging or in airtight glass or plastic containers in a cool (60°F or less), dry place. All grains can be refrigerated or frozen—a good idea if you live in a hot, humid climate. Grains containing oil (brown rice, stone-ground or whole-grain cornmeal, wheat berries, wheat germ and whole wheat flour) can become rancid and *must be stored in the refrigerator or freezer;* store these up to six months.

COOKED: Divide cooked grain into portion sizes you will use in recipes or as a side dish. Tightly cover and refrigerate up to five days, or freeze in airtight containers up to six months.

grain cooking CHART

Grains Cooking and Soaking Chart

1. Use 1 cup uncooked grain. Rinsing grains before cooking isn't necessary with the exception of quinoa. Quinoa has a bitter coating that can be eliminated only by a good rinse.

2. Use 2-quart saucepan for cooking 1 cup of uncooked grain. Use medium bowl for soaking 1 cup of uncooked grain.

3. For cooking liquid besides water, try vegetable broth or half vegetable broth or fruit juice. Adding salt to the water isn't necessary, but if you want to, use 1/2 teaspoon salt per 1 cup of grain.

4. Cook or soak as directed in the following chart. Don't remove the lid or stir during cooking (stirring releases more starch, making grains—especially rice—sticky). After cooking, fluff with fork, lifting grains to release steam.

NOTE: Grains lose moisture with age, so more or less liquid than the chart calls for may be needed. If all the liquid is absorbed but the grain isn't tender, add a little more liquid and cook longer. If the grain is tender but all the liquid hasn't been absorbed, just drain.

Type (1 cup)	Cooking Liquid (in cups)	Directions	Approximate Simmer Time (in minutes)	Approximate Yield (in cups)
RICE				
White Rice				
Regular long-grain	2	Heat rice and liquid to boiling. Reduce heat to low; cover and simmer.	15	3
Parboiled (converted)	2 1/2	Heat liquid to boiling; stir in rice. Reduce heat to low; cover and simmer. Remove from heat; let stand covered 5 minutes.	20 to 25	3 to 4
Precooked (instant)	1	Heat liquid to boiling; stir in rice. Cover and remove from heat; let stand covered 5 minutes.	0	2
Brown Rice				
Regular long-grain	2 3/4	Heat rice and liquid to boiling. Reduce heat to low; cover and simmer.	45 to 50	4
Precooked (instant)	1 1/4	Heat liquid to boiling; stir in rice. Reduce heat to low; cover and simmer.	10	2
Aromatic Rice				
Basmati	1 1/2	Heat rice and liquid to boiling. Reduce heat to low; cover and simmer.	15 to 20	3
Jasmine, Texmati	1 3/4	Heat rice and liquid to boiling. Reduce heat to low; cover and simmer.	15 to 20	3
Wild Rice	2 1/2	Heat rice and liquid to boiling. Reduce heat to low; cover and simmer.	40 to 50	3
OTHER GRAINS—COOKING				
Barley				
Quick-cooking	2	Heat liquid to boiling; stir in barley. Reduce heat to low; cover and simmer. Remove from heat; let stand covered 5 minutes.	10 to 12	3
Regular	4	Heat liquid to boiling; stir in barley. Reduce heat to low; cover and simmer.	45 to 50	4
Millet	2 1/2	Heat millet and liquid to boiling. Reduce heat to low; cover and simmer.	15 to 20	4
Quinoa	2	Heat quinoa and liquid to boiling. Reduce heat to low; cover and simmer.	15	3 to 4
Triticale	2 1/2	Heat water (do not use broth or add salt) to boiling; stir in triticale. Reduce heat to low; cover and simmer.	1 hour 45 minutes	2 1/2
Wheat Berries	2 1/2	Heat wheat berries and liquid to boiling. Reduce heat to low; cover and simmer.	50 to 60	2 3/4 to 3
OTHER GRAINS—SOAKING				
Bulgur	3	Pour boiling liquid over bulgur. Cover and soak (do not cook). Drain if needed. Or cook as directed on package.	Soak 30 to 60 minutes	3
Kasha (roasted buckwheat groats/kernels)	2	Pour boiling liquid over kasha. Cover and soak (do not cook). Drain if needed. Or cook as directed on package.	Soak 10 to 15 minutes	4

Note: Follow manufacturer's directions if using a rice cooker.

zucchini-corn GRATIN *(page 86)*

gratins, casseroles & pot pies

Splurging now and again is what this rich gratin is all about. For a less rich entrée, use half whipping cream and half half-and-half instead of all whipping cream. Along with the gratin, not much more than a very lightly dressed crisp salad is in order.

sweet potato, apple and leek GRATIN

prep time: 30 minutes   **start to finish:** 1 hour 25 minutes   5 servings

1 1/4 cups whipping (heavy) cream
2 large leeks, sliced (2 cups)
2 tablespoons chopped fresh or 2 teaspoons dried thyme leaves
1 teaspoon salt
1/4 teaspoon pepper
1/4 teaspoon ground nutmeg
2 medium dark-orange sweet potatoes (about 3/4 lb), peeled, thinly sliced (2 cups)
4 medium parsnips, peeled, thinly sliced (2 cups)
2 cups shredded white Cheddar cheese (8 oz)
1 large cooking apple, thinly sliced (1 1/2 cups)

1. Heat oven to 375°F. Grease 3-quart casserole with shortening. In heavy 2-quart saucepan, cook whipping cream, leeks, thyme, salt, pepper and nutmeg over low heat, stirring occasionally, until mixture begins to simmer. Stir in sweet potatoes and parsnips. Cover; simmer about 10 minutes or until vegetables are slightly tender.

2. Layer half of vegetable mixture and half of cheese in casserole. Top with apple. Repeat layers of vegetables and cheese.

3. Bake uncovered about 45 minutes or until golden brown and bubbly. Let stand 10 minutes before serving.

1 serving: Calories 500 (Calories from Fat 310); Total Fat 34g (Saturated Fat 21g; Trans Fat 1g); Cholesterol 115mg; Sodium 790mg; Total Carbohydrate 34g (Dietary Fiber 5g; Sugars 16g); Protein 15g
% daily value: Vitamin A 160%; Vitamin C 20%; Calcium 35%; Iron 10%   **exchanges:** 1 1/2 Starch, 1 Other Carbohydrate, 1 1/2 High-Fat Meat, 4 Fat   **carbohydrate choices:** 2

Serve this authentic Italian gratin with extra shredded cheeses. Cooked green beans drizzled with a little olive oil and sprinkled with toasted walnuts would go along nicely with this dish.

CAULIFLOWER au gratin

prep time: 10 minutes   **start to finish:** 40 minutes   4 servings

1 medium head cauliflower (2 lb)
1 medium red onion, cut into 8 wedges
1 tablespoon fresh lemon juice
1 tablespoon olive or vegetable oil
2 large cloves garlic, finely chopped
1 tablespoon chopped fresh parsley
1/2 teaspoon coarsely ground pepper
2 tablespoons freshly grated or shredded Parmesan cheese
2 tablespoons freshly grated or shredded Asiago cheese
1/4 cup shredded provolone cheese (1 oz)

1. Separate cauliflower into florets. In 3-quart saucepan, heat 1 inch salted water (1/2 teaspoon salt to 1 cup water) to boiling. Add cauliflower, onion and lemon juice; cover and heat to boiling. Reduce heat; simmer about 6 minutes or until cauliflower is just tender. Drain.

2. Heat oven to 425°F. In ungreased 9-inch square pan, mix oil, garlic and parsley. Heat uncovered in oven 5 minutes. Spread cauliflower and onion in pan; sprinkle with pepper and cheeses.

3. Bake uncovered about 20 minutes or until cheese is melted and forms a golden brown crust.

1 serving: Calories 140 (Calories from Fat 70); Total Fat 8g (Saturated Fat 3g; Trans Fat 0g); Cholesterol 10mg; Sodium 190mg; Total Carbohydrate 10g (Dietary Fiber 4g; Sugars 5g); Protein 7g
% daily value: Vitamin A 8%; Vitamin C 50%; Calcium 15%; Iron 4%   **exchanges:** 2 Vegetable, 1/2 High-Fat Meat, 1 Fat
carbohydrate choices: 1/2

mediterranean GRATIN

prep time: 15 minutes   **start to finish:** 40 minutes   4 servings

1 box (5.8 oz) roasted garlic and olive oil flavor couscous mix
6 cups fresh baby spinach leaves (5 oz)
2 tablespoons water
1/2 cup roasted red bell peppers (from 7.25-oz jar), drained, chopped
1 1/2 teaspoons grated lemon peel
1/4 teaspoon salt
1 can (15 to 16 oz) garbanzo beans, drained, rinsed
1 cup crumbled feta cheese (4 oz)
1/2 cup coarsely chopped walnuts
1 tablespoon olive or vegetable oil

1. Heat oven to 350°F. Make couscous as directed on box for version without olive oil.

2. Meanwhile, spray 11 × 7-inch (2-quart) glass baking dish or gratin dish with cooking spray. In 12-inch skillet, place spinach and 2 tablespoons water. Cover; cook over medium heat 2 to 4 minutes, stirring occasionally, until spinach is wilted.

3. Stir in cooked couscous, roasted red peppers, lemon peel, salt, beans and 1/2 cup of the cheese. Spread mixture in baking dish.

4. In small bowl, mix remaining cheese, walnuts and oil. Sprinkle over couscous mixture.

5. Bake uncovered 20 to 25 minutes or until heated through.

1 serving: Calories 530 (Calories from Fat 200); Total Fat 23g (Saturated Fat 6g; Trans Fat 0g); Cholesterol 25mg; Sodium 910mg; Total Carbohydrate 61g (Dietary Fiber 11g; Sugars 5g); Protein 21g
% daily value: Vitamin A 90%; Vitamin C 35%; Calcium 25%; Iron 25%   **exchanges:** 3 1/2 Starch, 1 Vegetable, 1 Medium-Fat Meat, 3 Fat
carbohydrate choices: 4

Serve this wonderfully rich and creamy breakfast dish, along with fresh fruit and muffins or scones, for your next brunch.

potato, "sausage" and cheese GRATIN

prep time: 25 minutes   **start to finish:** 1 hour 10 minutes   6 servings

1 can (10 3/4 oz) condensed cream of potato soup
1 container (8 oz) smoked Cheddar cold-pack cheese food
1 container (8 oz) reduced-fat sour cream
4 cups frozen potatoes O'Brien with onions and peppers (from 28-oz bag)
2 cups fresh small broccoli florets
1 package (8 oz) frozen soy-protein breakfast patties, cut into 1/2-inch pieces
1 1/2 cups seasoned croutons, coarsely crushed

1. Heat oven to 350°F. Spray 11 × 7-inch (2-quart) glass baking dish with cooking spray. In 2-quart saucepan, heat soup and cheese product over medium heat, stirring frequently, until cheese is melted. Remove from heat. Stir in sour cream.

2. In large microwavable bowl, microwave potatoes on High 3 to 4 minutes, stirring every minute, until thawed. Stir in broccoli, cut-up patties and soup mixture. Spread evenly in baking dish. Sprinkle with crushed croutons.

3. Bake uncovered 40 to 45 minutes or until mixture is heated through and topping is golden brown.

1 serving: Calories 460 (Calories from Fat 180); Total Fat 20g (Saturated Fat 10g; Trans Fat 1g); Cholesterol 45mg; Sodium 1190mg; Total Carbohydrate 46g (Dietary Fiber 7g; Sugars 7g); Protein 24g
% daily value: Vitamin A 20%; Vitamin C 35%; Calcium 30%; Iron 25%   **exchanges:** 2 1/2 Starch, 1/2 Other Carbohydrate, 2 1/2 Medium-Fat Meat, 1 Fat   **carbohydrate choices:** 3

potato, smoked sausage and cheese GRATIN: **Substitute 8 oz of fully cooked turkey smoked sausage or kielbasa, cut into 1/4-inch slices, for the breakfast patties.**

The term gratin usually refers to baked dishes topped with cheese or some type of crumb topping that gets nice and toasty brown—like this yummy dish.

zucchini-corn GRATIN

prep time: 30 minutes   **start to finish:** 1 hour 5 minutes   6 servings

2 tablespoons butter or margarine
1 medium onion, chopped (1/2 cup)
6 cups sliced zucchini (1 3/4 lb)
1 cup frozen whole kernel corn (from 1-lb bag)
1/2 cup water
1 egg
3/4 cup milk
1/4 teaspoon salt
1/4 teaspoon pepper
1 1/4 cups corn bread stuffing mix
1 cup shredded Cheddar cheese (4 oz)

1. Heat oven to 350°F. Spray 11 × 7-inch (2-quart) glass baking dish with cooking spray. In 12-inch nonstick skillet, melt 1 tablespoon butter over medium–high heat. Add onion; cook 2 minutes, stirring frequently, until onion is crisp–tender.

2. Stir in zucchini, corn and water. Reduce heat to medium; cover and cook 9 to 11 minutes, stirring occasionally, until zucchini is tender. Remove from heat. While still in skillet, mash zucchini slightly with fork.

3. In large bowl, beat egg, milk, salt and pepper with fork until well blended. Stir in zucchini mixture, 3/4 cup of the stuffing mix and 1/2 cup of the cheese. Spoon into baking dish.

4. In small microwavable bowl, microwave remaining 1 tablespoon butter on High 15 to 20 seconds or until melted. Stir in remaining 1/2 cup stuffing mix and 1/2 cup cheese. Sprinkle evenly over zucchini mixture.

5. Bake uncovered 25 to 30 minutes or until set and topping is golden brown. Let stand 5 minutes before serving.

1 serving: Calories 230 (Calories from Fat 110); Total Fat 12g (Saturated Fat 7g; Trans Fat 0g); Cholesterol 70mg; Sodium 400mg; Total Carbohydrate 21g (Dietary Fiber 3g; Sugars 5g); Protein 10g
% daily value: Vitamin A 25%; Vitamin C 10%; Calcium 15%; Iron 8%   **exchanges:** 1 Starch, 1 Vegetable, 1/2 High-Fat Meat, 1 1/2 Fat
carbohydrate choices: 1 1/2

Frozen cooked soybeans would taste great instead of the sweet peas. Give it a try!

creamy tortellini CASSEROLE

prep time: 20 minutes   **start to finish:** 35 minutes   4 servings

2 tablespoons butter or margarine
1/2 cup shredded carrots (3/4 medium)
1 medium onion, chopped (1/2 cup)
1 package (8 oz) sliced fresh mushrooms (3 cups)
2 tablespoons all-purpose flour
1/2 teaspoon salt
2 cups milk
1 cup shredded Gouda cheese (4 oz)
3/4 cup frozen sweet peas (from 1-lb bag), thawed
1 package (9 oz) refrigerated cheese-filled tortellini
1/2 cup finely crushed buttery crackers

1. Heat oven to 350°F. Spray 1 1/2-quart casserole with cooking spray. In 3-quart saucepan, melt butter over medium heat. Add carrots, onion and mushrooms; cook about 5 minutes, stirring occasionally, until mushrooms are tender.

2. Stir in flour and salt. Gradually add milk, stirring constantly. Cook, stirring constantly, until mixture is bubbly. Remove from heat. Stir in cheese, peas and tortellini. Spoon into casserole. Sprinkle with crackers.

3. Bake uncovered about 15 minutes or until edge begins to bubble.

1 serving: Calories 430 (Calories from Fat 210); Total Fat 24g (Saturated Fat 12g; Trans Fat 2g); Cholesterol 110mg; Sodium 760mg; Total Carbohydrate 34g (Dietary Fiber 3g; Sugars 12g); Protein 20g
% daily value: Vitamin A 70%; Vitamin C 6%; Calcium 40%; Iron 15%   **exchanges:** 1 Starch, 1 Other Carbohydrate, 1 Vegetable, 2 High-Fat Meat, 1 1/2 Fat   **carbohydrate choices:** 2

Frozen soy-protein burger crumbles replace the ground beef in this popular casserole.

texas tater CASSEROLE

prep time: 25 minutes   **start to finish:** 1 hour 15 minutes   6 servings

Cooking spray
1 large onion, chopped (1 cup)
1 medium stalk celery, chopped (1/2 cup)
2 cloves garlic, finely chopped
2 cups frozen soy-protein burger crumbles (from 12-oz package)
2 cans (10 3/4 oz each) condensed Cheddar cheese soup
1 can (11 oz) vacuum-packed whole kernel corn
   with red and green peppers, drained
1/2 cup chunky-style salsa
2 teaspoons chili powder
1/4 teaspoon pepper
4 1/2 cups (16 oz) frozen potato nuggets (from 32-oz bag)
1/2 cup shredded taco-seasoned cheese (2 oz)

1. Heat oven to 375°F. Generously spray 12-inch skillet with cooking spray. Add onion, celery and garlic to skillet; spray vegetables with cooking spray. Cook vegetables over medium heat 8 to 10 minutes, stirring occasionally, until crisp-tender.

2. Stir in crumbles, soup, corn, salsa, chili powder and pepper. Spoon into ungreased 2 1/2-quart casserole. Top with frozen potato nuggets.

3. Bake uncovered 40 minutes. Sprinkle with cheese. Bake 5 to 10 minutes longer or until bubbly and cheese is melted.

1 serving: Calories 470 (Calories from Fat 190); Total Fat 21g (Saturated Fat 10g; Trans Fat 4g); Cholesterol 25mg; Sodium 2070mg; Total Carbohydrate 51g (Dietary Fiber 7g; Sugars 8g); Protein 19g
% daily value: Vitamin A 50%; Vitamin C 10%; Calcium 20%; Iron 15%   **exchanges:** 3 Starch, 1/2 Other Carbohydrate, 1 1/2 Lean Meat, 3 Fat   **carbohydrate choices:** 3 1/2

Sausage-style soy-protein crumbles flavor this hearty casserole instead of traditional bulk pork sausage. If you can't find the crumbles, look for soy-protein breakfast sausage links and cut into thin slices or crumble before using.

three-bean CASSEROLE   (LOW fat)

prep time: 20 minutes   **bake:** 1 hour 5 minutes   8 servings

Cooking spray
2 medium stalks celery, sliced (1 cup)
1 medium onion, chopped (1/2 cup)
1 large clove garlic, finely chopped
2 cups frozen sausage-style soy-protein crumbles (from 12-oz package)
2 cans (21 oz each) baked beans (any variety)
1 can (15 to 16 oz) lima or butter beans, drained
1 can (15 to 16 oz) kidney beans, drained
1 can (8 oz) tomato sauce
1 tablespoon ground mustard
2 tablespoons honey or packed brown sugar
1 tablespoon white or cider vinegar
1/4 teaspoon red pepper sauce

1. Heat oven to 400°F. Generously spray 10-inch skillet with cooking spray. Add celery, onion and garlic to skillet; spray vegetables with cooking spray. Cook vegetables over medium heat 8 to 10 minutes, stirring occasionally, until crisp-tender.

2. In ungreased 3-quart casserole, mix vegetable mixture and remaining ingredients.

3. Bake uncovered about 45 minutes, stirring once, until hot and bubbly.

SLOW COOKER DIRECTIONS: Substitute 1/2 cup ketchup for the tomato sauce; decrease honey to 1 tablespoon. Generously spray 10-inch skillet with cooking spray. Add celery, onion and garlic; spray vegetables with cooking spray. Cook vegetables over medium heat 8 to 10 minutes, stirring occasionally, until crisp-tender. In 3 1/2- to 4-quart slow cooker, mix vegetable mixture and remaining ingredients. Cover; cook on High heat setting 2 hours to 2 hours 30 minutes to blend flavors.

1 serving: Calories 350 (Calories from Fat 35); Total Fat 3.5g (Saturated Fat 1g; Trans Fat 0g); Cholesterol 10mg; Sodium 1240mg; Total Carbohydrate 59g (Dietary Fiber 16g; Sugars 15g); Protein 20g
% daily value: Vitamin A 30%; Vitamin C 10%; Calcium 15%; Iron 45%   **exchanges**: 3 Starch, 1 Other Carbohydrate, 1 1/2 Very Lean Meat   **carbohydrate choices**: 4

Kitchen scissors quickly cut the tortillas into bite-size pieces. Shredded lettuce, chopped tomatoes, sour cream and guacamole make darn good "fixin's" to top each serving.

stacked enchilada BAKE

prep time: 10 minutes   **start to finish:** 30 minutes   6 servings

12 corn tortillas (5 or 6 inch), torn into bite-size pieces
2 cans (15 to 16 oz each) chili beans in sauce, undrained
1 can (10 oz) enchilada sauce
1 1/2 cups shredded Monterey Jack cheese (6 oz)
3 medium green onions, sliced (1/4 cup)

1. Heat oven to 400°F. Grease 2-quart casserole with shortening. Arrange half of the tortilla pieces in casserole. Top with 1 can beans. Repeat layers. Pour enchilada sauce oven top. Sprinkle with cheese and onions.

2. Bake uncovered about 20 minutes or until bubbly around edge.

1 serving: Calories 320 (Calories from Fat 90); Total Fat 10g (Saturated Fat 6g; Trans Fat 0g); Cholesterol 25mg; Sodium 1440mg; Total Carbohydrate 41g (Dietary Fiber 8g; Sugars 5g); Protein 17g
% daily value: Vitamin A 25%; Vitamin C 20%; Calcium 35%; Iron 20%   **exchanges:** 3 Starch, 1 High-Fat Meat   **carbohydrate choices:** 3

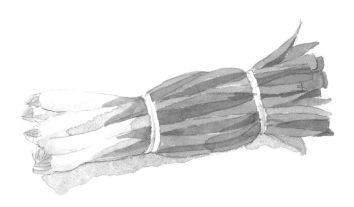

vegetarian menus
FOR THE HOLIDAYS AND MORE!

Stumped about what to make over the holidays for vegetarian family or friends? Many vegetarians are happy to make a meal out of the appetizers and side dishes while skipping the turkey or beef rib roast. But planning a "real" holiday meal is easy with this enticing collection of vegetarian menu ideas, leaving you more time to enjoy friends and great food!

No-Fuss Thanksgiving
Roasted Carrot and Herb Spread, page 24
Savory Pecans, page 33
Chunky Tomato Soup, page 213
Angel Hair Pasta with Autumn Vegetable Ragout, page 63, or Roasted Vegetable Lasagna, page 104
Focaccia
Apple, Pecan or Pumpkin Pie

Home for Christmas
Greek Marinated Roasted Peppers, Olives and Feta, page 27
Assorted Olives
Lasagna Primavera, page 102, or "Meat" Lover's Lasagna, page 100
Tossed Salad
Baguette
Cheesecake and Toppings

Easy Easter Dinner
Asparagus with Creamy Spanish Dip, page 30
Olive and Herb Deviled Eggs, page 31
Cheesy Broccoli-Rice Bake, page 96
Edamame Stir-Fry Salad, page 242
Lemon Bars or Lemon Meringue Pie

Take-It-Easy Sunday Brunch
Italian "Sausage" Egg Bake, page 252
Spinach Pasta Salad, page 76
Muffins and Scones
Fresh Fruit
Coffee and Tea

Casual Gathering with Friends
Southwest Cheese Bread, page 14
Chili Blanco, page 236
Veggie Joes, page 199
Chips
Brownies

Chase Away the Winter Blues
Appetizer Beer-Cheese Fondue, page 16
Zesty Black Bean Soup, page 188
Toasted Cheese, Avocado and Tomato Sandwiches, page 145
Dulce de Leche Ice Cream with Hot Fudge Sauce

Relaxing Summer Supper
Fresh Fruit with Ginger Dip, page 32
Roasted Sesame and Honey Snack Mix, page 34
California Black Bean Burgers, page 128
Hearty Soybean and Cheddar-Pasta Salad, page 251
Sorbet

Kids Lunch Bunch
Chili Dog Wraps, page 134
Brown Rice and Vegetable-Cheese Soup, page 208
Fresh Vegetables
Chocolate Chip Cookies

Garnish this cheesy Mexican bake with sour cream, cherry tomato wedges and cilantro, and sprinkle taco seasoning mix over the sour cream. To make ahead, cover unbaked casserole tightly and refrigerate up to 24 hours. Bake as directed in step 3.

chili con queso BAKE

prep time: 15 minutes   **start to finish:** 55 minutes   6 servings

2 cans (4.5 oz each) mild chopped green chiles, drained
2 large tomatoes, seeded and chopped (2 cups)
1 cup Original Bisquick® mix
1/2 cup sour cream
3 eggs
2 cups shredded Cheddar cheese (8 oz)

1. Heat oven to 375°F. Grease 8-inch square pan with shortening. Sprinkle chiles and tomatoes evenly in pan.

2. In small bowl, beat Bisquick mix, sour cream and eggs with wire whisk or hand beater until blended. Stir in cheese. Spoon evenly over chiles and tomatoes.

3. Bake uncovered 35 to 40 minutes or until knife inserted in center comes out clean.

1 serving: Calories 330 (Calories from Fat 200); Total Fat 22g (Saturated Fat 12g; Trans Fat 1g); Cholesterol 160mg; Sodium 680mg; Total Carbohydrate 18g (Dietary Fiber 2g; Sugars 5g); Protein 15g
% daily value: Vitamin A 25%; Vitamin C 20%; Calcium 30%; Iron 10%   **exchanges:** 1 Starch, 1 1/2 High-Fat Meat, 2 Fat
carbohydrate choices: 1

chili con queso BAKE

Take a walk on the "light" side with our reduced-fat version of this popular casserole.

green chile CASSEROLE

prep time: 10 minutes   **start to finish:** 1 hour   6 servings

12 corn tortillas (5 or 6 inch)
2 cans (4.5 oz each) chopped green chiles, undrained
2 1/2 cups shredded reduced-fat Monterey Jack cheese (10 oz)
1 jalapeño chili, seeded, finely chopped, if desired
1/2 cup shredded sharp Cheddar cheese (2 oz)
2 eggs
3 egg whites
2 cups fat-free (skim) milk
1/2 teaspoon salt
Dash of pepper
3/4 cup chunky-style salsa

1. Heat oven to 375°F. Spray 13 × 9-inch (3-quart) glass baking dish with cooking spray. Tear 6 of the tortillas into bite-size pieces; spread in bottom of baking dish.

2. Layer 1 can of the green chiles and half of the Monterey Jack cheese over tortillas. Sprinkle with jalapeño chili if desired. Repeat with remaining tortillas, green chiles and Monterey Jack cheese. Sprinkle with Cheddar cheese.

3. In small bowl, beat eggs, egg whites, milk, salt and pepper until well blended; pour slowly over casserole.

4. Bake uncovered 45 to 50 minutes or until set and golden brown. Serve with salsa.

1 serving: Calories 370 (Calories from Fat 150); Total Fat 17g (Saturated Fat 9g; Trans Fat 0g); Cholesterol 115mg; Sodium 1080mg; Total Carbohydrate 31g (Dietary Fiber 4g; Sugars 8g); Protein 24g
% daily value: Vitamin A 25%; Vitamin C 15%; Calcium 60%; Iron 10%   **exchanges:** 1 1/2 Starch, 1/2 Other Carbohydrate, 3 Medium-Fat Meat   **carbohydrate choices:** 2

The green beans are added frozen halfway through the cooking time to help keep their bright green color and texture.

lentil and brown rice CASSEROLE

prep time: 10 minutes   **start to finish:** 1 hour 40 minutes   6 servings

3/4 cup dried lentils (6 oz), sorted, rinsed
1/2 cup uncooked brown rice
2 1/2 cups vegetable broth
1 bag (1 lb) frozen cut green beans or broccoli cuts
1 cup shredded Cheddar cheese (4 oz)

1. Heat oven to 375°F. In 2-quart casserole, mix lentils, rice and broth. Cover; bake 1 hour.

2. Stir in frozen green beans. Bake covered about 30 minutes or until liquid is absorbed and rice is tender. Sprinkle with cheese before serving.

1 serving: Calories 250 (Calories from Fat 60); Total Fat 7g (Saturated Fat 4g; Trans Fat 0g); Cholesterol 20mg; Sodium 540mg; Total Carbohydrate 33g (Dietary Fiber 8g; Sugars 3g); Protein 14g
% daily value: Vitamin A 20%; Vitamin C 4%; Calcium 15%; Iron 20%   **exchanges:** 2 Starch, 1 Very Lean Meat, 1 Fat
carbohydrate choices: 2

Try this super recipe as a side dish with your favorite vegetarian burgers.

cheesy broccoli-rice BAKE

prep time: 15 minutes   **start to finish:** 50 minutes   8 servings

1 cup uncooked regular long-grain white rice
2 cups water
1 tablespoon butter or margarine
1 large onion, chopped (1 cup)
1 loaf (16 oz) prepared cheese product, cut into cubes
1 can (10 3/4 oz) condensed cream of mushroom soup
2/3 cup milk
1/4 teaspoon pepper, if desired
2 cups fresh broccoli florets (1/2 inch)
1 cup fine soft bread crumbs (about 1 1/2 slices bread)
1 tablespoon butter or margarine, melted

1. Heat oven to 350°F. Spray 13 × 9-inch (3-quart) glass baking dish with cooking spray. Cook rice in water as directed on package.

2. Meanwhile, in 10-inch skillet, melt 1 tablespoon butter over medium-high heat. Add onion; cook, stirring occasionally, until crisp-tender. Reduce heat to medium. Stir in cheese, soup, milk and pepper if desired. Cook, stirring frequently, until cheese is melted.

3. Stir in broccoli and rice. Spoon into baking dish. In small bowl, mix bread crumbs and 1 tablespoon melted butter; sprinkle over rice mixture.

4. Bake uncovered 30 to 35 minutes or until light brown on top and bubbly around edges.

1 serving: Calories 410 (Calories from Fat 200); Total Fat 22g (Saturated Fat 12g; Trans Fat 1g); Cholesterol 65mg; Sodium 1510mg; Total Carbohydrate 38g (Dietary Fiber 2g; Sugars 9g); Protein 15g
% daily value: Vitamin A 25%; Vitamin C 15%; Calcium 35%; Iron 10%   **exchanges:** 2 Starch, 1/2 Other Carbohydrate, 1 1/2 High-Fat Meat, 1 1/2 Fat   **carbohydrate choices:** 2 1/2

lighter cheesy broccoli-rice BAKE: For 9 grams of fat and 275 calories per serving, omit 1 tablespoon butter for cooking onion; spray skillet with cooking spray. Use reduced-fat pre-pared cheese product loaf, condensed 98% fat-free cream of mushroom soup and fat-free (skim) milk.

On the side, try vegetarian bacon, sausage patties or sausage links; they're widely available and taste remarkably like their animal protein counterparts!

cheesy vegetable STRATA

prep time: 15 minutes   **start to finish:** 3 hours 40 minutes   8 servings

8 slices firm bread
1 bag (1 lb) frozen broccoli, carrots and cauliflower, thawed, drained
2 1/2 cups shredded sharp Cheddar cheese (10 oz)
8 eggs, slightly beaten
4 cups milk
1 teaspoon salt
1 teaspoon ground mustard
1/4 teaspoon pepper
1/4 teaspoon ground red pepper (cayenne)

1. Cut each bread slice diagonally into 4 triangles. In ungreased 13 × 9-inch pan, arrange half of bread triangles. Top with thawed vegetables. Sprinkle with 2 cups of the cheese. Top with remaining bread.

2. In large bowl, beat remaining ingredients with wire whisk until blended; pour over bread. Cover tightly with foil; refrigerate at least 2 hours but no longer than 24 hours.

3. Heat oven to 325°F. Bake covered 30 minutes. Uncover; bake about 40 minutes or until knife inserted in center comes out clean. Top with remaining 1/2 cup cheese; bake 5 minutes longer or until cheese is melted. Let stand 10 minutes before cutting.

1 serving: Calories 360 (Calories from Fat 180); Total Fat 21g (Saturated Fat 10g; Trans Fat 0.5g); Cholesterol 260mg; Sodium 780mg; Total Carbohydrate 22g (Dietary Fiber 2g; Sugars 9g); Protein 23g
% daily value: Vitamin A 50%; Vitamin C 15%; Calcium 40%; Iron 10%   **exchanges:** 1 Starch, 1 Vegetable, 2 1/2 High-Fat Meat
carbohydrate choices: 1 1/2

cheesy vegetable-ham STRATA: Sprinkle 1 cup chopped fully cooked smoked turkey ham over the vegetables in step 1. Decrease the salt to 1/2 teaspoon.

Jazz it up! Offer sides of sour cream and chopped avocado or guacamole. How about crushed red pepper flakes, too?

spanish rice BAKE

prep time: 25 minutes   **start to finish:** 1 hour 10 minutes   6 servings

2 tablespoons vegetable oil
1 cup uncooked regular long-grain white rice
1 medium onion, chopped (1/2 cup)
1 small green bell pepper, chopped (1/2 cup)
1 cup frozen whole kernel corn (from 1-lb bag)
1 can (10 3/4 oz) condensed tomato soup
2 1/2 cups boiling water
1 tablespoon chopped fresh cilantro, if desired
1 teaspoon chili powder
1/2 teaspoon salt
2 cups shredded Colby-Monterey Jack cheese (8 oz)

1. Heat oven to 375°F. Spray 2 1/2-quart casserole with cooking spray. In 10-inch skillet, heat oil over medium heat. Add rice, onion and bell pepper; cook 6 to 8 minutes, stirring frequently, until rice is light brown and onion is tender. Stir in corn.

2. In casserole, mix remaining ingredients except cheese. Stir in rice mixture and 1 cup of the cheese.

3. Cover; bake 20 minutes. Carefully remove casserole from oven; stir. Cover; bake 20 to 25 minutes longer or until rice is tender. Stir; sprinkle with remaining 1 cup cheese. Bake uncovered 2 to 3 minutes or until cheese is melted.

1 serving: Calories 380 (Calories from Fat 160); Total Fat 18g (Saturated Fat 8g; Trans Fat 0g); Cholesterol 35mg; Sodium 720mg; Total Carbohydrate 42g (Dietary Fiber 2g; Sugars 5g); Protein 14g
% daily value: Vitamin A 15%; Vitamin C 15%; Calcium 30%; Iron 10%   **exchanges:** 2 1/2 Starch, 1/2 Other Carbohydrate, 1 High-Fat Meat, 1 1/2 Fat   **carbohydrate choices:** 3

SPANISH RICE BAKE with soy: Increase casserole size to 3-quart. Add 2 cups frozen soy-protein burger crumbles with the corn in step 1.

To make ahead, follow directions through step 3 and then cover and refrigerate up to 24 hours. You may need to add 10 to 15 minutes to the baking time if you put it right from the fridge into the oven.

vegetable MANICOTTI

prep time: 20 minutes   **start to finish:** 1 hour 20 minutes   4 servings

12 uncooked manicotti pasta shells
1 container (15 oz) ricotta cheese
1 small zucchini, coarsely shredded (1 cup)
1 cup coarsely shredded carrots (1 1/2 medium)
1/2 cup shredded mozzarella cheese (2 oz)
2 tablespoons chopped fresh parsley
2 teaspoons sugar
1 egg white, slightly beaten
1 jar (26 to 30 oz) tomato pasta sauce
2 tablespoons grated Parmesan cheese

1. Heat oven to 350°F. Spray 13 × 9-inch (3-quart) glass baking dish with cooking spray. Cook and drain shells as directed on package.

2. Meanwhile, mix remaining ingredients except pasta sauce and Parmesan cheese.

3. Fill each cooked pasta shell with about 2 tablespoons vegetable mixture; place filled sides up in baking dish. Spoon pasta sauce over shells. Sprinkle with Parmesan cheese.

4. Cover tightly with foil; bake 50 to 60 minutes or until hot.

1 serving: Calories 620 (Calories from Fat 180); Total Fat 20g (Saturated Fat 9g; Trans Fat 0g); Cholesterol 45mg; Sodium 1390mg; Total Carbohydrate 84g (Dietary Fiber 7g; Sugars 19g); Protein 27g
% daily value: Vitamin A 140%; Vitamin C 30%; Calcium 50%; Iron 25%   **exchanges:** 4 1/2 Starch, 1 Other Carbohydrate, 2 Medium-Fat Meat, 1 1/2 Fat   **carbohydrate choices:** 5 1/2

For this makeover recipe, a traditional Italian Sausage Lasagna recipe was tweaked not only to make it vegetarian but also to make it quicker and more convenient. Prep time was cut in half! Changes include substituting Italian-style soy-protein sausages for regular Italian sausage, purchased pasta sauce instead of a scratch pasta sauce and mozzarella-style soy cheese instead of dairy mozzarella cheese. Nutritionwise, the vegetarian version slashes 160 calories, 11 grams fat, 20 milligrams cholesterol, 160 milligrams sodium and 12 grams carbohydrate compared to the traditional version.

"meat" lover's LASAGNA

prep time: 30 minutes   **start to finish:** 1 hour 25 minutes   8 servings

6 uncooked lasagna noodles
1 package (10 oz) frozen Italian-style soy-protein sausages
1 container (15 oz) ricotta cheese
1/2 cup grated Parmesan cheese (2 oz)
1 egg
1 jar (26 oz) spicy red pepper pasta sauce
1 teaspoon Italian seasoning
1/3 cup water
8 oz mozzarella-style soy cheese, shredded (2 cups)

1. Heat oven to 350°F. Cook and drain noodles as directed on package.

2. Unwrap sausages; place on large microwavable plate. Microwave uncovered on High 1 to 2 minutes, turning sausages once, until slightly thawed. Cut sausages into 1/4-inch slices.

3. In medium bowl, mix ricotta cheese, 1/4 cup of the Parmesan cheese and the egg. In another medium bowl, mix pasta sauce, Italian seasoning and water.

4. In ungreased 13 × 9-inch (3-quart) glass baking dish, spread about 1/2 cup pasta sauce mixture. Top with 3 noodles, half of the ricotta mixture and half of the sausage pieces. Top with about 1 1/4 cups remaining pasta sauce mixture and half of the soy cheese. Repeat with remaining noodles, ricotta mixture, sausage, pasta sauce mixture and soy cheese. Sprinkle with remaining 1/4 cup Parmesan cheese.

5. Bake uncovered 35 to 45 minutes or until bubbly and cheese is melted. Cover loosely with foil; let stand 10 minutes before serving.

1 serving: Calories 340 (Calories from Fat 140); Total Fat 15g (Saturated Fat 5g; Trans Fat 0g); Cholesterol 50mg; Sodium 1090mg; Total Carbohydrate 24g (Dietary Fiber 3g; Sugars 6g); Protein 26g

% daily value: Vitamin A 20%; Vitamin C 4%; Calcium 35%; Iron 15%   **exchanges:** 1 1/2 Starch, 3 Lean Meat, 1 Fat
carbohydrate choices: 1 1/2

"meat" lover's LASAGNA

Ricotta cheese is smoother and just a tad sweeter than cottage cheese, but the two are almost always interchangeable if you use a small-curd cottage cheese. Ricotta cheese is a good source of calcium and protein.

LASAGNA primavera

prep time: 20 minutes   **start to finish:** 1 hour 35 minutes   8 servings

12 uncooked lasagna noodles
3 cups frozen broccoli florets (from 14-oz bag), thawed, well drained
3 large carrots, coarsely shredded (2 cups)
1 can (14.5 oz) diced tomatoes, well drained
2 medium bell peppers, cut into 1/2-inch pieces
1 container (15 oz) ricotta cheese
1/2 cup grated Parmesan cheese
1 egg
2 containers (10 oz each) refrigerated Alfredo sauce
1 bag (16 oz) shredded mozzarella cheese (4 cups)

1. Cook and drain noodles as directed on package.

2. Meanwhile, cut broccoli florets into bite-size pieces if necessary. In large bowl, mix broccoli, carrots, tomatoes and bell peppers. In small bowl, mix ricotta cheese, Parmesan cheese, and egg.

3. Heat oven to 350°F. In 13 × 9-inch (3-quart) glass baking dish, spoon 2/3 cup of the Alfredo sauce. Place 4 noodles over sauce. Spread with half of cheese mixture and 2 1/2 cups of vegetable mixture; randomly spoon 2/3 cup remaining sauce in dollops over noodles. Sprinkle with 1 cup of the mozzarella cheese. Top with 4 noodles. Spread with remaining cheese mixture and 2 1/2 cups vegetable mixture; randomly spoon 2/3 cup sauce in dollops over vegetables. Sprinkle with 1 cup mozzarella cheese. Top with remaining 4 noodles and vegetable mixture; randomly spoon remaining sauce in dollops over top. Sprinkle with remaining 2 cups mozzarella cheese.

4. Bake uncovered 45 to 60 minutes or until bubbly and hot in center. Let stand 15 minutes before cutting.

1 serving: Calories 730 (Calories from Fat 370); Total Fat 42g (Saturated Fat 24g; Trans Fat 1.5g); Cholesterol 150mg; Sodium 1050mg; Total Carbohydrate 52g (Dietary Fiber 5g; Sugars 6g); Protein 38g
% daily value: Vitamin A 150%; Vitamin C 45%; Calcium 90%; Iron 15%   **exchanges:** 3 Starch, 1 Vegetable, 4 Medium-Fat Meat, 4 Fat
carbohydrate choices: 3 1/2

LASAGNA primavera

For stylish individual servings, top with a spoonful or two of warmed pasta sauce followed by a sprinkle of shredded Parmesan; garnish the plate with fresh basil. The vegetables in this lasagna can be roasted and refrigerated up to 8 hours ahead.

roasted vegetable LASAGNA

prep time: 25 minutes   **start to finish:** 1 hour 45 minutes   8 servings

2 medium red, green or yellow bell peppers, each cut into 8 pieces
1 medium onion, cut into 8 wedges
1 medium zucchini, cut into 2-inch pieces (2 cups)
6 small red potatoes, cut into quarters
1 package (8 oz) whole fresh mushrooms, cut in half
2 tablespoons olive or vegetable oil
1/2 teaspoon peppered seasoned salt
2 teaspoons chopped fresh or 1/2 teaspoon dried basil leaves
9 uncooked lasagna noodles
1 container (15 oz) ricotta cheese
1/2 cup basil pesto
1 egg, slightly beaten
2 cups shredded provolone cheese (8 oz)
1 cup shredded mozzarella cheese (4 oz)

1. Heat oven to 425°F. Grease 15 × 10 × 1-inch pan with shortening. In large bowl, gently toss bell peppers, onion, zucchini, potatoes, mushrooms, oil, peppered seasoned salt and basil to coat. Spread vegetables in pan. Bake uncovered about 30 minutes or until crisp-tender. Cool slightly.

2. Reduce oven temperature to 350°F. Grease 13 × 9-inch (3-quart) glass baking dish. Cook and drain noodles as directed on package. In small bowl, mix ricotta cheese, pesto and egg. Coarsely chop vegetables.

3. Place 3 noodles crosswise in baking dish. Spread with half of ricotta mixture. Top with 2 cups vegetables and 1 cup of the provolone cheese. Repeat layers, starting with noodles. Top with remaining 3 noodles and remaining vegetables. Sprinkle with mozzarella cheese.

4. Bake uncovered 40 to 45 minutes or until hot in center and top is golden brown. Let stand 5 minutes before cutting.

1 serving: Calories 550 (Calories from Fat 250); Total Fat 28g (Saturated Fat 12g; Trans Fat 0g); Cholesterol 75mg; Sodium 750mg; Total Carbohydrate 49g (Dietary Fiber 5g; Sugars 6g); Protein 27g
% daily value: Vitamin A 50%; Vitamin C 60%; Calcium 60%; Iron 20%   **exchanges:** 3 Starch, 1 Vegetable, 2 Medium-Fat Meat, 3 Fat
carbohydrate choices: 3

Eggplant has been called "the vegetarian's beef" because of its meaty texture. Choose firm, even-colored eggplants that are heavy for their size and free of blemishes. Caps and stems should be intact with no mold. Refrigerate unwashed in a plastic bag up to five days.

MOUSSAKA

prep: 30 minutes   **start to finish:** 1 hour 40 minutes   4 servings

4 frozen soy-protein burgers or soy-protein vegetable burgers
1 medium eggplant (about 1 1/4 lb)
1/4 cup all-purpose flour
1/2 teaspoon salt
1/2 teaspoon pepper
1/4 teaspoon ground nutmeg
1/4 teaspoon ground cinnamon
3 cups milk
4 oz fat-free or regular cream cheese (from 8-oz package), softened
1 can (15 oz) tomato sauce
1/2 cup fat-free egg product or 2 eggs

1. Heat oven to 375°F. Grease 3-quart casserole with shortening. On large microwavable plate, microwave burgers uncovered on High 2 to 3 minutes, turning once, until thawed. Cut into 1-inch pieces; set aside.

2. Cut eggplant into 1/4-inch slices. In 2-quart saucepan, cook eggplant in enough boiling water to cover 5 to 8 minutes or until tender. Drain in colander; set aside.

3. In same saucepan, mix flour, salt, pepper, nutmeg, cinnamon and milk. Heat to boiling, stirring constantly. Boil 1 minute, stirring constantly. Remove from heat. Stir in cream cheese until melted and smooth.

4. Place half of the eggplant in casserole. Layer with burger pieces, tomato sauce, 1 1/2 cups of the white sauce and remaining eggplant. To remaining white sauce, stir in egg product; pour over eggplant.

5. Bake uncovered about 1 hour or until firm. Let stand 10 minutes before serving.

1 serving: Calories 330 (Calories from Fat 50); Total Fat 6g (Saturated Fat 2.5g; Trans Fat 0g); Cholesterol 15mg; Sodium 1560mg; Total Carbohydrate 40g (Dietary Fiber 7g; Sugars 21g); Protein 29g
% daily value: Vitamin A 30%; Vitamin C 15%; Calcium 35%; Iron 25%   **exchanges:** 2 Starch, 2 Vegetable, 2 1/2 Very Lean Meat, 1 Fat
carbohydrate choices: 2 1/2

The meaty texture of portabella mushrooms makes them a great animal protein alternative. Not familiar with oil pie crust? It's a bit more fragile to work with than traditional shortening crust, and although not flaky, it's very, very tender.

portabella and vegetable POT PIE

prep time: 40 minutes   **start to finish:** 1 hour 5 minutes   6 servings

1 1/3 cups all-purpose flour
1/2 teaspoon salt
1/4 teaspoon dried thyme leaves
1/3 cup vegetable oil
2 tablespoons cold water
1 tablespoon butter or margarine
8 oz baby portabella mushrooms, each cut into quarters (3 1/2 cups)
1 1/2 cups half-and-half
1 package (1.6 oz) garlic herb sauce mix
1 bag (1 lb) frozen mixed vegetables, thawed
1 teaspoon half-and-half

1. In medium bowl, mix flour, salt, thyme and oil until all flour is moistened. Sprinkle with cold water, 1 tablespoon at a time, tossing with fork until all water is absorbed. Gather pastry into a ball. Place pastry between 2 sheets of waxed paper. With rolling pin, roll into 8 1/2-inch round; set aside, covered with towel.

2. Heat oven to 425°F. In 12-inch skillet, melt butter over medium-high heat. Add mushrooms; cook 5 to 7 minutes, stirring frequently, until mushrooms are tender. Stir in 1 1/2 cups half-and-half and the sauce mix. Heat to boiling over medium-high heat, stirring constantly. Stir in vegetables. Cook 2 to 3 minutes, stirring frequently, until heated through.

3. Spoon vegetable mixture into ungreased 9 1/2-inch deep-dish pie plate. Remove top waxed paper from crust; cut about 1-inch hole in center of crust. Carefully invert crust over filling; remove remaining waxed paper. Cut small slits in several places in crust. Brush crust with 1 teaspoon half-and-half.

4. Bake 25 to 30 minutes or until crust is golden brown. Let stand 10 minutes before cutting.

1 serving: Calories 400 (Calories from Fat 210); Total Fat 23g (Saturated Fat 7g; Trans Fat 0g); Cholesterol 30mg; Sodium 710mg; Total Carbohydrate 39g (Dietary Fiber 5g; Sugars 7g); Protein 9g
% daily value: Vitamin A 70%; Vitamin C 4%; Calcium 10%; Iron 15%   **exchanges:** 2 1/2 Starch, 4 1/2 Fat   **carbohydrate choices:** 2 1/2

The pasta sauce mixture needs to be good and hot before spooning it into the baking dish so the breadsticks will bake through.

"chicken" alfredo POT PIE

prep time: 20 minutes   **start to finish:** 45 minutes   6 servings

1 can (11 oz) refrigerated soft breadsticks
4 frozen grilled chicken-style soy-protein patties
1/3 cup milk
1 jar (16 oz) Alfredo pasta sauce
1 bag (1 lb) frozen broccoli, carrots and cauliflower, thawed, drained
2 tablespoons grated Parmesan cheese
1 teaspoon Italian seasoning

1. Heat oven to 375°F. Unroll dough; separate at perforations into 12 breadsticks. Set aside. On small microwavable plate, microwave patties on High 30 to 45 seconds or until slightly thawed. Cut patties into cubes to make about 2 cups.

2. In 3-quart saucepan, mix patty cubes, milk, pasta sauce and vegetables. Heat to boiling, stirring occasionally. Spoon into ungreased 13 × 9-inch (3-quart) glass baking dish.

3. Twist each breadstick; arrange crosswise over hot patties mixture, gently stretching strips if necessary to fit. Sprinkle with cheese and Italian seasoning.

4. Bake uncovered 20 to 30 minutes or until breadsticks are deep golden brown.

1 serving: Calories 530 (Calories from Fat 280); Total Fat 32g (Saturated Fat 15g; Trans Fat 2g); Cholesterol 75mg; Sodium 1040mg; Total Carbohydrate 42g (Dietary Fiber 4g; Sugars 6g); Protein 21g
% daily value: Vitamin A 60%; Vitamin C 20%; Calcium 30%; Iron 20%   **exchanges:** 2 1/2 Starch, 1 Vegetable, 1 1/2 Medium-Fat Meat, 4 1/2 Fat   **carbohydrate choices:** 3

Sweet potatoes with darker-colored skins are generally more moist and flavorful than the lighter ones. Two medium sweet potatoes or half of a small butternut squash will give you 2 cups cubed.

southwestern POT PIE

prep time: 15 minutes   **start to finish:** 55 minutes   4 servings

1 tablespoon vegetable oil
1 large onion, chopped (1 cup)
2 cups cubed sweet potatoes or butternut squash
2 cups chunky-style salsa
1/2 cup water
1/4 teaspoon ground cinnamon
1 cup frozen whole kernel corn (from 1-lb bag)
1 can (15 to 16 oz) garbanzo beans, drained
1 pouch (6.5 oz) golden corn muffin and bread mix
1/2 cup milk
1 tablespoon vegetable oil
1 tablespoon roasted sunflower nuts, if desired

1. In 4-quart Dutch oven, heat 1 tablespoon oil over medium-high heat. Add onion; cook about 5 minutes, stirring occasionally, until crisp-tender.

2. Stir in sweet potatoes, salsa, water and cinnamon. Heat to boiling. Reduce heat; cover and simmer 20 to 25 minutes or until squash is tender. Stir in corn and beans.

3. In medium bowl, mix corn muffin mix, milk and 1 tablespoon oil. Stir in nuts if desired. Drop by large spoonfuls onto vegetable mixture. Cover; simmer about 15 minutes or until toothpick inserted into center of dumplings comes out clean.

1 serving: Calories 590 (Calories from Fat 140); Total Fat 16g (Saturated Fat 3g; Trans Fat 0.5g); Cholesterol 0mg; Sodium 1230mg; Total Carbohydrate 94g (Dietary Fiber 15g; Sugars 28g); Protein 17g
% daily value: Vitamin A 220%; Vitamin C 35%; Calcium 15%; Iron 30%   **exchanges:** 5 Starch, 1 Other Carbohydrate, 2 1/2 Fat
carbohydrate choices: 6

Vegetarian beans are saucy and delicious and sold right alongside regular baked beans.

"beef" and bean POT PIE (LOW fat)

prep time: 25 minutes   **start to finish:** 50 minutes   4 servings

2 cups frozen soy-protein burger crumbles (from 12-oz package)
2 teaspoons dried minced onion
1 can (16 oz) vegetarian baked beans, undrained
1 can (8 oz) tomato sauce
3 tablespoons packed brown sugar
1 cup Original Bisquick® mix
3 tablespoons boiling water
1 tablespoon ketchup

1. Heat oven to 375°F. Spray 1 1/2-quart round casserole with cooking spray. In casserole, mix crumbles, onion, baked beans, tomato sauce and brown sugar; set aside.

2. In medium bowl, stir remaining ingredients until soft dough forms; beat vigorously 20 strokes. On surface dusted with Bisquick mix, gently roll dough in Bisquick mix to coat. Shape into ball; knead about 10 times or until smooth. Pat ball into 7 1/2-inch round or a round the size of top of casserole; place on bean mixture in casserole.

3. Bake uncovered 20 to 25 minutes or until crust is light brown.

1 serving: Calories 390 (Calories from Fat 50); Total Fat 5g (Saturated Fat 1g; Trans Fat 0.5g); Cholesterol 0mg; Sodium 1540mg; Total Carbohydrate 63g (Dietary Fiber 10g; Sugars 24g); Protein 21g
% daily value: Vitamin A 30%; Vitamin C 10%; Calcium 20%; Iron 20%   **exchanges:** 2 1/2 Starch, 1 1/2 Other Carbohydrate, 2 Very Lean Meat, 1/2 Fat   **carbohydrate choices:** 4

Puff pastry is made of hundreds of layers of chilled butter and pastry dough. As it bakes, the moisture in the butter creates steam, causing the dough to puff and separate into hundreds of flaky layers. The golden flaky layers are the perfect texture contrast for the creamy vegetable filling.

CABBAGE-RICE POT PIE
with basil–tomato sauce

prep time: 20 minutes   **start to finish:** 45 minutes   6 servings

PIE
1 1/2 cups water
1 extra-large vegetarian vegetable bouillon cube
3 cups coleslaw mix (from 16-oz bag)
2 cups refrigerated or frozen shredded hash brown potatoes
1 1/4 cups uncooked instant rice
1 package (8 oz) cream cheese, softened
2 tablespoons chopped fresh or 1 teaspoon dried basil leaves
1 sheet frozen puff pastry (half of 17 1/4-oz package), thawed

SAUCE
1 can (10 3/4 oz) condensed tomato soup
2 tablespoons chopped fresh or 1 teaspoon dried basil leaves
1/4 cup water

1. Heat oven to 400°F. Grease 9-inch deep-dish pie plate with shortening. In 3-quart saucepan, heat 1 1/2 cups water to boiling. Stir in bouillon cube, coleslaw mix and potatoes. Return to boiling. Reduce heat to medium; cover and cook 5 minutes.

2. Stir in rice, cream cheese and 2 tablespoons basil. Remove from heat; cover and let stand 5 minutes. Stir cabbage mixture; spoon into pie plate.

3. Unfold puff pastry sheet; place over coleslaw mixture. Trim pastry to fit pie plate; with fork, press edge of pastry onto edge of pie plate.

4. Bake uncovered about 25 minutes or until golden brown. During last 5 minutes of baking, in 1-quart saucepan, heat sauce ingredients over medium-low heat. Serve pie with warm sauce.

1 serving: Calories 530 (Calories from Fat 250); Total Fat 28g (Saturated Fat 13g; Trans Fat 2g); Cholesterol 85mg; Sodium 920mg; Total Carbohydrate 60g (Dietary Fiber 3g; Sugars 6g); Protein 10g
% daily value: Vitamin A 20%; Vitamin C 20%; Calcium 8%; Iron 20%   **exchanges:** 4 Starch, 5 Fat   **carbohydrate choices:** 4

Leftover mashed potatoes, instant mashed potatoes or mashed potatoes from the deli are all options for topping this hearty vegetable and bean pie.

vegetarian SHEPHERD'S PIE (LOW fat)

prep time: 10 minutes   **start to finish:** 35 minutes   6 servings

2 cans (15 to 16 oz each) kidney beans, drained, rinsed
1 jar (16 oz) chunky-style salsa (2 cups)
1 cup frozen whole kernel corn (from 1-lb bag)
1 medium carrot, chopped (1/2 cup)
1 1/4 cups water
1/4 cup milk
2 tablespoons butter or margarine
1/4 teaspoon salt
1 1/4 cups plain mashed potato mix (dry)
2 tablespoons grated Parmesan cheese
Chopped fresh chives or parsley, if desired

1. In 10-inch nonstick skillet, heat beans, salsa, corn and carrot to boiling. Reduce heat to low; cover and simmer about 15 minutes or until carrot is tender.

2. In 2-quart saucepan, heat water, milk, butter and salt to boiling. Remove from heat. Stir in mashed potato mix just until moistened. Let stand about 30 seconds or until liquid is absorbed. Whip mashed potatoes with fork until fluffy.

3. Spoon mashed potatoes onto bean mixture around edge of skillet. Cover; simmer 5 minutes. Sprinkle with cheese and chives if desired before serving.

1 serving: Calories 300 (Calories from Fat 50); Total Fat 6g (Saturated Fat 2.5g; Trans Fat 0g); Cholesterol 15mg; Sodium 560mg; Total Carbohydrate 48g (Dietary Fiber 11g; Sugars 5g); Protein 15g
% daily value: Vitamin A 60%; Vitamin C 20%; Calcium 10%; Iron 25%   **exchanges:** 3 Starch, 1 Very Lean Meat, 1/2 Fat
carbohydrate choices: 3

easy mushroom PIZZA PIE

prep time: 10 minutes   **start to finish:** 55 minutes   6 servings

1 can (4 oz) mushroom pieces and stems, drained
1 cup chopped onion (2 medium)
1/3 cup grated Parmesan cheese
1 1/2 cups milk
3 eggs
3/4 cup Original Bisquick® mix
1/2 cup pizza sauce
1/4 cup grated Parmesan cheese
1/2 cup chopped green bell pepper
1 to 1 1/2 cups shredded mozzarella cheese (4 to 6 oz)

1. Heat oven to 425°F. Grease 10-inch pie plate with shortening. Sprinkle mushrooms, 2/3 cup of the onion and 1/3 cup Parmesan cheese in pie plate.

2. In blender or bowl with wire whisk or hand beater, beat milk, eggs and Bisquick mix 15 seconds on high speed or 1 minute with whisk until smooth. Pour over vegetable mixture.

3. Bake uncovered 20 minutes. Spread pizza sauce over top. Top with remaining ingredients. Bake 15 to 20 minutes longer or until cheese is light brown. Let stand 5 minutes before cutting.

1 serving: Calories 260 (Calories from Fat 110); Total Fat 13g (Saturated Fat 6g; Trans Fat 0.5g); Cholesterol 130mg; Sodium 720mg; Total Carbohydrate 19g (Dietary Fiber 2g; Sugars 8g); Protein 16g
% daily value: Vitamin A 10%; Vitamin C 10%; Calcium 40%; Iron 8%   **exchanges:** 1/2 Starch, 1 Other Carbohydrate, 2 Medium-Fat Meat, 1/2 Fat   **carbohydrate choices:** 1

easy mushroom PIZZA PIE

Make soft bread crumbs by tearing fresh slices of bread by hand or using a food processor. Serve this pie with slices of dark pumpernickel or caraway rye bread.

eggplant and gouda cheese PIE

prep: 20 minutes   **start to finish:** 50 minutes   6 servings

2 small eggplants (about 1 lb each), peeled, cut into 3/4-inch pieces
1 cup shredded smoked Gouda cheese (4 oz)
1/2 cup ricotta cheese
1/4 cup fine soft bread crumbs
1 tablespoon chopped fresh or 1 teaspoon dried basil leaves
1/2 teaspoon salt
1/8 teaspoon pepper
1 clove garlic, finely chopped
3 eggs, beaten

1. Heat oven to 350°F. Grease 9-inch pie plate with shortening. In 3-quart saucepan, place steamer basket in 1/2 inch water (water should not touch bottom of basket). Place eggplant in steamer basket. Cover tightly; heat to boiling. Reduce heat; steam 5 to 7 minutes or until tender.

2. In large bowl, place eggplant; mash with fork. Stir in 3/4 cup of the Gouda cheese and the remaining ingredients. Spoon mixture into pie plate. Sprinkle with remaining 1/4 cup Gouda cheese.

3. Bake uncovered about 30 minutes or until knife inserted in center comes out clean.

1 serving: Calories 190 (Calories from Fat 90); Total Fat 10g (Saturated Fat 5g; Trans Fat 0g); Cholesterol 135mg; Sodium 450mg; Total Carbohydrate 13g (Dietary Fiber 3g; Sugars 6g); Protein 12g
% daily value: Vitamin A 10%; Vitamin C 0%; Calcium 20%; Iron 6%   **exchanges:** 1/2 Starch, 1 Vegetable, 1 Medium-Fat Meat, 1 Fat
carbohydrate choices: 1

This pie is somewhere between a spinach soufflé and crustless quiche. It makes a good main dish for casual entertaining. Serve it with your favorite pasta sauce or cheese sauce and add a salad of fresh orange and red onion slices sprinkled with toasted almonds.

easy spinach PIE

prep time: 20 minutes   **start to finish:** 50 minutes   4 servings

2 tablespoons butter or margarine
1 bag (10 oz) washed fresh spinach, finely chopped
1 small red bell pepper, chopped (1/2 cup)
3/4 cup milk
2 tablespoons all-purpose flour
1/2 teaspoon salt
1/8 teaspoon ground nutmeg
3 eggs
2 tablespoons grated Parmesan cheese

1. Heat oven to 350°F. Grease 9-inch pie plate with shortening. In 12-inch skillet, melt butter over medium heat. Add spinach and bell pepper; cook about 5 minutes, stirring occasionally, until spinach is wilted and bell pepper is crisp-tender.

2. In small bowl, beat remaining ingredients except cheese with wire whisk until smooth. Pour over vegetables in skillet; stir to mix. Pour into pie plate.

3. Bake uncovered about 30 minutes or until center is set. Sprinkle with cheese. Serve immediately.

1 serving: Calories 190 (Calories from Fat 110); Total Fat 12g (Saturated Fat 5g; Trans Fat 0g); Cholesterol 180mg; Sodium 520mg; Total Carbohydrate 9g (Dietary Fiber 3g; Sugars 4g); Protein 10g
% daily value: Vitamin A 160%; Vitamin C 45%; Calcium 20%; Iron 15%   **exchanges:** 2 Vegetable, 1 Medium-Fat Meat, 1 1/2 Fat
carbohydrate choices: 1/2

Regular yellow or white onions can be used in this pie, but try one of the juicy sweet onion varieties like Maui, Walla Walla, Oso Sweet or Rio Sweet. Check with your grocer to find out which variety is available.

onion and cheese PIE

prep time: 20 minutes   **start to finish:** 1 hour 5 minutes   6 servings

1 1/4 cups finely crushed saltine crackers (36 squares)
1/4 cup butter or margarine, melted
2 tablespoons butter or margarine
2 large onions, chopped (2 cups)
1 1/2 cups shredded sharp Cheddar cheese (6 oz)
1 cup milk
1/2 teaspoon salt
1/4 teaspoon pepper
3 eggs

1. Heat oven to 325°F. Grease 9-inch pie plate with shortening. In small bowl, mix cracker crumbs and 1/4 cup melted butter. Press evenly in bottom and up side of pie plate.

2. In 10-inch skillet, melt 2 tablespoons butter over medium-high heat. Add onions; cook 5 to 6 minutes, stirring frequently, until light brown. Spread onions in crust. Sprinkle with cheese.

3. In small bowl, beat milk, salt, pepper and eggs with wire whisk until well blended; pour over cheese.

4. Bake uncovered 40 to 45 minutes or until knife inserted in center comes out clean. Serve immediately.

1 serving: Calories 380 (Calories from Fat 240); Total Fat 27g (Saturated Fat 14g; Trans Fat 1.5g); Cholesterol 170mg; Sodium 710mg; Total Carbohydrate 20g (Dietary Fiber 2g; Sugars 9g); Protein 14g
% daily value: Vitamin A 20%; Vitamin C 2%; Calcium 25%; Iron 8%   **exchanges:** 1 Starch, 1/2 Other Carbohydrate, 1 1/2 High-Fat Meat, 3 Fat
carbohydrate choices: 1

fajita POT PIE

prep time: 15 minutes   **start to finish:** 45 minutes   4 servings

4 frozen grilled chicken-style soy-protein patties
1 teaspoon vegetable oil
1/2 medium bell pepper, cut into 1/2-inch strips
1 3/4 cups chunky-style salsa
1/4 cup water
1 cup Original Bisquick® mix
1/3 cup shredded Monterey Jack cheese (1 1/3 oz)
1/2 cup milk

1. Heat oven to 400°F. On small microwavable plate, microwave patties on High 30 to 45 seconds or until slightly thawed. Cut patties into cubes to make about 2 cups; set aside.

2. In 10-inch skillet, heat oil over medium heat. Add bell pepper; cook, stirring occasionally, until crisp–tender. Stir in patty cubes, salsa and water. Cook 1 to 2 minutes, stirring occasionally, until bubbly. Pour into ungreased 1 1/2-quart casserole; set aside.

3. In small bowl, stir remaining ingredients with fork until blended. Pour over patty mixture; carefully spread almost to edge of casserole.

4. Bake uncovered about 30 minutes or until light golden brown. If desired, with squeezable ketchup, write a message on top.

1 serving: Calories 360 (Calories from Fat 140); Total Fat 15g (Saturated Fat 4.5g; Trans Fat 1.5g); Cholesterol 10mg; Sodium 1410mg; Total Carbohydrate 39g (Dietary Fiber 3g; Sugars 8g); Protein 18g
% daily value: Vitamin A 20%; Vitamin C 25%; Calcium 25%; Iron 25%   **exchanges:** 2 Starch, 1/2 Other Carbohydrate, 1 1/2 Lean Meat, 2 Fat   **carbohydrate choices:** 2 1/2

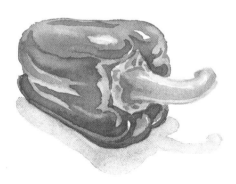

Toss together a simple salad of mixed greens, sliced roma (plum) tomatoes and your favorite dressing. Dessert can be as easy as chocolate chip cookies or brownies from the grocery store.

lasagna POT PIE

prep time: 15 minutes   **start to finish:** 55 minutes   6 servings

2 cups frozen sausage-style soy-protein crumbles (from 12-oz package)
1 cup tomato pasta sauce
1 cup ricotta cheese
1/3 cup grated Parmesan cheese
1 egg
1 cup Original Bisquick® mix
1/2 cup milk
1 egg
1 cup shredded mozzarella cheese (4 oz)

1. Heat oven to 400°F. In 10-inch skillet, mix crumbles and pasta sauce. Heat to boiling, stirring occasionally. Spoon into 8-inch square (2-quart) glass baking dish.

2. In small bowl, mix ricotta cheese, Parmesan cheese and 1 egg until well mixed. Drop by heaping tablespoonfuls onto crumbles mixture.

3. In another small bowl, stir Bisquick mix, milk and 1 egg with fork until blended. Pour over ricotta cheese mixture.

4. Spray sheet of foil large enough to cover baking dish with cooking spray; place sprayed side down on dish and seal tightly. Bake 23 to 28 minutes or until light golden brown. Uncover; sprinkle with mozzarella cheese. Bake uncovered 5 to 10 minutes longer or until cheese is melted.

TO FREEZE AND BAKE: Spray sheet of foil large enough to cover baking dish with cooking spray. Place sprayed side down on unbaked casserole; seal tightly. Freeze up to 2 months. Bake covered at 400°F 1 hour to 1 hour 15 minutes or until golden brown. Sprinkle with mozzarella cheese. Bake uncovered 5 to 10 minutes longer or until cheese is melted.

1 serving: Calories 340 (Calories from Fat 150); Total Fat 16g (Saturated Fat 7g; Trans Fat 0.5g); Cholesterol 100mg; Sodium 990mg; Total Carbohydrate 27g (Dietary Fiber 1g; Sugars 7g); Protein 22g
% daily value: Vitamin A 15%; Vitamin C 6%; Calcium 40%; Iron 10%   **exchanges:** 1 1/2 Starch, 1/2 Other Carbohydrate, 2 1/2 Medium-Fat Meat, 1/2 Fat   **carbohydrate choices:** 2

lasagna POT PIE

ROASTED VEGETABLE WRAPS with garlic aioli *(page 133)*

CHAPTER 4   burgers, wraps & pizzas

Stir-fry sauce is available in many flavors from sweet-and-sour to teriyaki. Use your favorite to make this nutritious supper dish; if you don't have stir-fry sauce, try bottled sweet-and-sour sauce instead.

asian rice and lentil BURGERS

prep time: 25 minutes **start to finish:** 1 hour 15 minutes **4 servings**

PATTIES
1/2 cup uncooked brown rice
1/4 cup dried lentils (2 oz), sorted, rinsed
1 1/2 cups water
1/4 cup finely chopped cashews
2 tablespoons unseasoned dry bread crumbs
2 tablespoons stir-fry sauce
4 medium green onions, finely chopped (1/2 cup)
1 egg, beaten

VEGETABLE SAUCE
1 cup frozen mixed vegetables (from 16-oz bag)
1/2 cup water
2 tablespoons stir-fry sauce
Noodles or Rice, if desired

1. In 2-quart saucepan, heat rice, lentils and 1 1/2 cups water to boiling. Reduce heat to low; cover and simmer 30 to 40 minutes, stirring occasionally, until lentils are tender and water is absorbed. Cool slightly.

2. In saucepan, mash rice mixture slightly with fork. Stir in remaining patty ingredients. Shape mixture into 4 patties, about 1/2 inch thick.

3. Spray 10-inch skillet with cooking spray. Cook patties in skillet about 10 minutes, turning once, until golden brown. Remove from skillet; keep warm.

4. In same skillet, mix sauce ingredients; heat to boiling. Reduce heat to medium; add patties. Cover; cook 5 to 8 minutes until patties are hot and vegetables are crisp-tender. Serve sauce and patties over Chinese noodles.

1 serving: Calories 240 (Calories from Fat 60); Total Fat 6g (Saturated Fat 1.5g; Trans Fat 0g); Cholesterol 55mg; Sodium 590mg; Total Carbohydrate 38g (Dietary Fiber 6g; Sugars 6g); Protein 9g
% daily value: Vitamin A 10%; Vitamin C 4%; Calcium 4%; Iron 15% **exchanges:** 2 Starch, 1/2 Other Carbohydrate, 1/2 Medium-Fat Meat
carbohydrate choices: 2 1/2

asian rice and lentil BURGERS

Cream-colored butter beans are big lima beans, but unlike the chewier green limas, they are very soft and creamy in texture.

BUTTER BEAN BURGERS
with southwestern sauce (LOW fat)

prep time: 35 minutes   **start to finish:** 35 minutes   4 servings

PATTIES
1 can (15 to 16 oz) butter beans, drained, rinsed
1 egg, beaten
10 round buttery crackers, crushed (1/3 cup)
2 tablespoons chili sauce
2 tablespoons finely chopped onion

SAUCE
1 cup frozen mixed vegetables (from 1-lb bag)
1/4 cup raisins
1/4 teaspoon ground cumin
1 can (14 1/2 oz) Mexican-style stewed tomatoes with jalapeño peppers,
    garlic and onion, undrained

1. In medium bowl, mash beans with fork. Stir in remaining patty ingredients. Shape mixture into 4 patties, about 1/2 inch thick.

2. Spray 10-inch skillet with cooking spray. Cook patties in skillet 8 to 10 minutes, turning once, until golden brown. Remove from skillet; keep warm.

3. In same skillet, mix sauce ingredients. Cook over medium-low heat 5 to 8 minutes, stirring occasionally, until vegetables are tender. Serve sauce over patties.

1 serving: Calories 260 (Calories from Fat 35); Total Fat 4g (Saturated Fat 1g; Trans Fat 0.5g); Cholesterol 55mg; Sodium 700mg; Total Carbohydrate 44g (Dietary Fiber 9g; Sugars 14g); Protein 11g
% daily value: Vitamin A 15%; Vitamin C 15%; Calcium 6%; Iron 20%   **exchanges:** 2 Starch, 1 Other Carbohydrate, 1/2 Medium-Fat Meat
carbohydrate choices: 3

Beef burgers, beware! These "burgers" are absolutely delicious served in sandwich buns with cranberry sauce. On the side, try steamed broccoli with melted butter and fresh fruit for dessert.

wild rice–pecan BURGERS

prep time: 20 minutes   **start to finish:** 1 hour 10 minutes   4 servings (2 burgers each)

2/3 cup uncooked wild rice
1 1/2 cups water
1 cup soft bread crumbs (about 1 1/2 slices bread)
1/3 cup chopped pecans
1/2 teaspoon garlic salt
2 eggs
1 jar (2.5 oz) sliced mushrooms, drained, finely chopped
1 jar (2 oz) diced pimientos, drained
2 tablespoons vegetable oil

1. Cook wild rice in water as directed on package.

2. In medium bowl, mix rice and remaining ingredients except oil.

3. In 10-inch skillet, heat oil over medium heat. Scoop wild rice mixture by 1/3 cupfuls into skillet; flatten to 1/2 inch. Cook about 3 minutes on each side or until light brown. Remove patties from skillet; cover and keep warm while cooking remaining burgers.

1 serving: Calories 360 (Calories from Fat 160); Total Fat 18g (Saturated Fat 2.5g; Trans Fat 0g); Cholesterol 105mg; Sodium 450mg; Total Carbohydrate 40g (Dietary Fiber 4g; Sugars 3g); Protein 11g
% daily value: Vitamin A 8%; Vitamin C 8%; Calcium 8%; Iron 15%   **exchanges:** 2 1/2 Starch, 1 Vegetable, 3 Fat   **carbohydrate choices:** 2 1/2

If soybeans are missing from your supermarket shelves, canned pinto beans, drained and rinsed, are a tasty bean backup for these low-fat bean burgers.

cheesy soy BURGERS

prep time: 25 minutes   **start to finish:** 25 minutes   4 servings

HORSERADISH SAUCE
1/2 cup plain fat-free yogurt
2 teaspoons prepared horseradish

PATTIES
1 can (15 oz) soybeans, drained, rinsed
1/2 cup shredded reduced-fat Cheddar cheese (2 oz)
1/4 cup unseasoned dry bread crumbs
2 medium green onions, finely chopped (2 tablespoons)
1 teaspoon Worcestershire sauce
1/4 teaspoon pepper
1/8 teaspoon salt
2 tablespoons fat-free egg product or 1 egg white

BUNS
4 burger buns, split, toasted

TOPPINGS
4 slices tomato
4 lettuce leaves

1. In small bowl, mix sauce ingredients; set aside.

2. In medium bowl, mash beans with fork. Stir in remaining patty ingredients. Shape mixture into 4 patties.

3. Spray 10-inch nonstick skillet with cooking spray. Cook patties in skillet over medium heat about 10 minutes, turning once, until light brown.

4. Top bottom halves of buns with patties, sauce, tomato and lettuce. Cover with top halves of buns.

1 serving: Calories 380 (Calories from Fat 110); Total Fat 12g (Saturated Fat 2.5g; Trans Fat 0g); Cholesterol 0mg; Sodium 790mg; Total Carbohydrate 41g (Dietary Fiber 7g; Sugars 6g); Protein 26g
% daily value: Vitamin A 8%; Vitamin C 6%; Calcium 35%; Iron 40%   **exchanges:** 2 1/2 Starch, 1/2 Other Carbohydrate, 2 1/2 Lean Meat, 1/2 Fat   **carbohydrate choices:** 3

Counting carbs? Drop the bun, and serve these homemade veggie burgers between leaves of crisp iceberg lettuce.

veggie and bean BURGERS

prep time: 25 minutes   **start to finish:** 25 minutes   4 sandwiches

PATTIES
1/4 cup uncooked instant rice
1/4 cup boiling water
1/2 cup fresh broccoli florets
2 oz fresh whole mushrooms (about 4 medium)
1/2 small red bell pepper, cut up
1 can (15 to 16 oz) garbanzo beans, drained, rinsed
1 egg
1 clove garlic
1/2 teaspoon seasoned salt

1 teaspoon dried chopped onion
1/3 cup Italian-style dry bread crumbs
3 tablespoons vegetable oil

BUNS
4 whole wheat burger buns, split

TOPPINGS, IF DESIRED
Cheddar cheese slices, lettuce, tomato slices, onion slices and/or mayonnaise

1. In medium bowl, stir rice and boiling water. Cover; let stand 5 minutes. Drain if necessary.

2. Meanwhile, in food processor, place broccoli, mushrooms and bell pepper. Cover; process, using quick on-and-off motions, to finely chop vegetables (do not puree).

3. Stir chopped vegetables into rice. In food processor, place beans, egg, garlic and seasoned salt. Cover; process until smooth. Stir bean mixture, onion and bread crumbs into vegetable-rice mixture. Using about 1/2 cup vegetable-rice mixture for each patty, shape into four 1/2-inch-thick patties.

4. In 10-inch nonstick skillet, heat oil over medium-high heat. Add patties; cook 8 to 10 minutes, turning once, until brown and crisp.

5. Top bottom halves of buns with patties and desired toppings. Cover with top halves of buns.

1 sandwich: Calories 440 (Calories from Fat 140); Total Fat 16g (Saturated Fat 2.5g; Trans Fat 0g); Cholesterol 55mg; Sodium 580mg; Total Carbohydrate 58g (Dietary Fiber 8g; Sugars 4g); Protein 16g
% daily value: Vitamin A 15%; Vitamin C 25%; Calcium 10%; Iron 25%   **exchanges:** 3 Starch, 2 Vegetable, 3 Fat   **carbohydrate choices:** 4

veggie and bean "MEATBALLS": Heat oven to 400°F. Generously spray 15 × 10 × 1-inch pan with cooking spray. Shape vegetable mixture into 16 balls; place in pan. Generously spray tops of balls with cooking spray. Bake about 20 minutes or until crisp. Serve with pasta sauce (any flavor) or cheese sauce.

Coating the patties with cornmeal gives them a crispy crunch. If the seasoned black beans aren't available, use unseasoned black beans and add a teaspoon of chili powder.

california black bean BURGERS

prep time: 30 minutes   **start to finish:** 30 minutes   5 sandwiches

1 can (15 oz) black beans with cumin and chili spices, undrained
1 can (4.5 oz) chopped green chiles, undrained
1 cup unseasoned dry bread crumbs
1 egg, beaten
1/4 cup yellow cornmeal
2 tablespoons vegetable oil
5 burger buns, split, toasted
1 tablespoon mayonnaise or salad dressing
1 1/4 cups shredded lettuce
3 tablespoons chunky-style salsa

1. In food processor or blender, place beans. Cover; process until slightly mashed. Remove from food processor; place in medium bowl. Stir in chiles, bread crumbs and egg. Shape mixture into 5 patties, about 1/2 inch thick. Coat each patty with cornmeal.

2. In 10-inch skillet, heat oil over medium heat. Add patties; cook 10 to 15 minutes, turning once, until crisp and thoroughly cooked on both sides.

3. Spread bottom halves of buns with mayonnaise. Top with lettuce, patties and salsa. Cover with top halves of buns.

1 sandwich: Calories 410 (Calories from Fat 120); Total Fat 13g (Saturated Fat 2.5g; Trans Fat 0g); Cholesterol 45mg; Sodium 1110mg; Total Carbohydrate 60g (Dietary Fiber 8g; Sugars 5g); Protein 14g
% daily value: Vitamin A 20%; Vitamin C 2%; Calcium 20%; Iron 30%   **exchanges:** 4 Starch, 2 Fat   **carbohydrate choices:** 4

california black bean **BURGERS**

Want a little more zing? Add about 1/4 cup chopped pickled okra to the bean mixture. Make an easy side dish by using a box or packet of Spanish rice mix.

cajun bean PATTIES (LOW fat)

prep time: 20 minutes   **start to finish:** 20 minutes   4 servings

2 cans (15 to 16 oz each) dark red kidney beans, drained, rinsed
1 egg
1/4 cup unseasoned dry bread crumbs
2 teaspoons Cajun or Creole seasoning
1 tablespoon vegetable oil
Sour cream, if desired

1. In medium bowl, mash beans with fork. Stir in egg, bread crumbs and Cajun seasoning. With wet hands, shape mixture into 4 patties, 1/2 inch thick.

2. In 10-inch skillet, heat oil over medium-high heat. Add patties; cook 6 to 8 minutes, turning once, until hot. Serve with sour cream if desired.

1 serving: Calories 320 (Calories from Fat 50); Total Fat 6g (Saturated Fat 1g; Trans Fat 0g); Cholesterol 55mg; Sodium 780mg; Total Carbohydrate 47g (Dietary Fiber 12g; Sugars 2g); Protein 18g
% daily value: Vitamin A 0%; Vitamin C 0%; Calcium 8%; Iron 35%   **exchanges:** 3 Starch, 1 Medium-Fat Meat   **carbohydrate choices:** 3

It's easy to make hard-cooked eggs just right! Put eggs in cold water in saucepan with water at least 1 inch above eggs. Heat to boiling; immediately remove from heat. Cover and let stand 20 minutes. Immediately run cold water over eggs to prevent further cooking. Tap egg to crack shell; roll egg between hands to loosen shell, then peel.

caesar salad WRAPS

prep time: 35 minutes   **start to finish:** 35 minutes   4 wraps

4 eggs
16 small romaine lettuce leaves
1/4 cup chopped red onion
2 tablespoons shredded Parmesan or Romano cheese
1/4 cup Caesar dressing
4 garden vegetable–flavored flour tortillas (6 to 8 inch)
2 roma (plum) tomatoes, sliced

1. In 2-quart saucepan, place eggs in single layer; add enough cold water to cover eggs by 1 inch. Cover; heat to boiling. Remove from heat; let stand covered 15 minutes. Drain. Immediately place eggs in cold water with ice cubes or run cold water over eggs until completely cooled.

2. Meanwhile, in large bowl, toss lettuce, onion, cheese and dressing to coat. Place lettuce mixture evenly down center of each tortilla. Top with tomatoes.

3. To remove shell from each egg, crackle it by tapping gently all over; roll between hands to loosen. Peel, starting at large end. Cut eggs into slices; place over lettuce mixture with tomatoes.

4. Fold up one end of each tortilla up about 1 inch over filling; fold right and left sides over folded end, overlapping. Fold remaining end down; secure with toothpick if necessary.

1 wrap: Calories 330 (Calories from Fat 160); Total Fat 18g (Saturated Fat 4.5g; Trans Fat 0.5g); Cholesterol 215mg; Sodium 490mg; Total Carbohydrate 29g (Dietary Fiber 2g; Sugars 3g); Protein 12g
% daily value: Vitamin A 25%; Vitamin C 25%; Calcium 15%; Iron 15%   **exchanges:** 2 Starch, 1 Medium-Fat Meat, 2 Fat
carbohydrate choices: 2

chicken caesar salad WRAPS: **Add 2 cups chopped cooked chicken to the lettuce mixture.**

Hoisin sauce is a sweet, reddish brown sauce made of soybeans, chilies and spices. If you love hoisin, spread extra on each pancake before adding vegetables.

mou shu VEGETABLE WRAPS (LOW fat)

prep time: 30 minutes   **start to finish:** 30 minutes   6 servings (2 wraps each)

1 tablespoon vegetable oil
1 bag (16 oz) coleslaw mix
1 cup canned drained bean sprouts or 1 bag (8 oz) fresh bean sprouts
1 package (8 oz) sliced fresh mushrooms (3 cups)
1 tablespoon grated gingerroot
3 tablespoons hoisin sauce
1 1/4 cups Original Bisquick® mix
1 1/4 cups milk
1 egg
8 green onions, chopped (1/2 cup)
Additional hoisin sauce, if desired

1. In 4-quart Dutch oven, heat oil over medium-high heat. Add coleslaw mix, bean sprouts, mushrooms and gingerroot; cook about 10 minutes, stirring frequently, until vegetables are tender. Stir in 3 tablespoons hoisin sauce. Reduce heat; keep warm.

2. In medium bowl, beat Bisquick mix, milk and egg with wire whisk or hand beater until well blended. Stir in onions.

3. Spray 10-inch skillet with cooking spray; heat over medium-high heat. For each pancake, pour slightly less than 1/4 cup batter into skillet; rotate skillet to make a thin pancake, 5 to 6 inches in diameter. Cook until bubbles break on surface. Turn; cook other side until golden brown. Keep warm while making remaining pancakes.

4. Spoon about 1/3 cup vegetable mixture onto each pancake; roll up. Serve with additional hoisin sauce if desired.

1 serving: Calories 220 (Calories from Fat 80); Total Fat 8g (Saturated Fat 2g; Trans Fat 0.5g); Cholesterol 40mg; Sodium 570mg; Total Carbohydrate 29g (Dietary Fiber 4g; Sugars 11g); Protein 8g
% daily value: Vitamin A 45%; Vitamin C 25%; Calcium 15%; Iron 15%   **exchanges:** 1 1/2 Starch, 1/2 Other Carbohydrate, 1/2 Lean Meat, 1 Fat   **carbohydrate choices:** 2

If you love garlic but hate to chop it, keep those handy little jars of chopped garlic on hand.

ROASTED VEGETABLE WRAPS
with garlic aioli

prep time: 30 minutes   start to finish: 30 minutes   6 sandwiches

ROASTED VEGETABLES
1 medium bell pepper, cut into 3/4-inch pieces
1 medium red onion, cut into 1/2-inch wedges
1 medium zucchini, cut in half lengthwise,
    cut crosswise into 1/4-inch slices
4 oz fresh whole mushrooms, cut into quarters
3 tablespoons olive or vegetable oil
1/2 teaspoon dried basil leaves
1/4 teaspoon salt
1/4 teaspoon coarsely ground pepper

GARLIC MAYONNAISE
1/4 cup mayonnaise or salad dressing
1 tablespoon finely chopped fresh parsley
1 teaspoon chopped garlic or 1/4 teaspoon
    garlic powder

TORTILLAS AND LETTUCE
6 flour tortillas (8 to 10 inch)
1 1/2 cups shredded lettuce

1. Heat oven to 450°F. In ungreased 15 × 10 × 1-inch pan, spread bell pepper, onion, zucchini and mushrooms. In small bowl, mix oil, basil, salt and pepper; brush over vegetables. Bake uncovered 12 to 15 minutes or until crisp-tender. Cool slightly.

2. Meanwhile, in another small bowl, mix mayonnaise ingredients. Spread about 2 teaspoons mayonnaise mixture down center of each tortilla to within 2 inches of bottom.

3. Top each tortilla evenly with roasted vegetables, spreading to within 2 inches of bottom. Top each with 1/4 cup lettuce.

4. Fold one end of each tortilla up about 1 inch over filling; fold right and left sides over folded end, overlapping. Fold remaining end down.

1 sandwich: Calories 290 (Calories from Fat 160); Total Fat 17g (Saturated Fat 3g; Trans Fat 0g); Cholesterol 5mg; Sodium 360mg; Total Carbohydrate 29g (Dietary Fiber 3g; Sugars 3g); Protein 5g
% daily value: Vitamin A 10%; Vitamin C 20%; Calcium 8%; Iron 10%   **exchanges:** 1 1/2 Starch, 1 Vegetable, 3 Fat   **carbohydrate choices:** 2

GRILLED CHICKEN AND ROASTED VEGETABLE WRAPS with garlic mayonnaise: Use 8 tortillas. Thinly slice 2 warm or chilled grilled boneless skinless chicken breast halves. Arrange chicken on vegetables in step 3.

Serve this easy, kid-approved meal with carrot and celery sticks and apple wedges. Look for vegetarian hot dogs in both the freezer and refrigerated sections of the store.

chili dog WRAPS

prep time: 10 minutes   **start to finish:** 40 minutes   5 servings (2 wraps each)

10 corn tortillas (5 or 6 inch)
10 vegetarian hot dogs
1 can (15 oz) or 1 box (14.3 oz) vegetarian chili
1 jar (16 oz) chunky-style salsa (2 cups)
1 cup shredded Cheddar cheese (4 oz)

1. Heat oven to 350°F. Spray 13 × 9-inch (3-quart) glass baking dish with cooking spray. Soften tortillas as directed on package.

2. Place 1 hot dog and 2 tablespoons chili on each tortilla. Roll up tortillas; place seam sides down in baking dish. Spoon salsa over tortillas.

3. Spray sheet of foil large enough to cover baking dish with cooking spray; place sprayed side down on dish and seal tightly. Bake 25 minutes. Uncover; sprinkle with cheese. Bake uncovered about 5 minutes longer or until cheese is melted.

1 serving: Calories 540 (Calories from Fat 210); Total Fat 24g (Saturated Fat 8g; Trans Fat 0g); Cholesterol 35mg; Sodium 1800mg; Total Carbohydrate 50g (Dietary Fiber 8g; Sugars 7g); Protein 31g
% daily value: Vitamin A 20%; Vitamin C 4%; Calcium 25%; Iron 20%   **exchanges:** 3 Starch, 1/2 Other Carbohydrate, 3 Medium-Fat Meat, 1 Fat   **carbohydrate choices:** 3

For a refreshing and light dessert, arrange jarred mango slices and sliced kiwifruit on a serving platter or individual serving plates. Drizzle with a mixture of equal parts honey and frozen (thawed) limeade concentrate.

portabella mushroom FAJITAS

prep time: 30 minutes   **start to finish:** 30 minutes   6 fajitas

1 tablespoon vegetable oil
1 clove garlic, finely chopped
1 teaspoon ground cumin
1/2 teaspoon salt
12 oz fresh baby portabella or crimini mushrooms, thinly sliced (6 cups)
2 cups frozen bell pepper and onion stir-fry (from 1-lb bag)
1/4 cup chopped fresh cilantro
2 tablespoons lime juice
6 flour tortillas (8 to 10 inch)
Guacamole or sour cream, if desired
Chunky-style salsa, if desired

1. In 10-inch nonstick skillet, heat oil, garlic, cumin and salt over medium-high heat. Add mushrooms and bell pepper and onion stir-fry; cook 4 to 6 minutes, stirring frequently, until vegetables are crisp-tender. Sprinkle with cilantro and lime juice.

2. Spoon about 1/2 cup mushroom mixture onto each tortilla; roll up. Serve with guacamole and salsa if desired.

1 fajita: Calories 190 (Calories from Fat 50); Total Fat 6g (Saturated Fat 1g; Trans Fat 0g); Cholesterol 0mg; Sodium 420mg; Total Carbohydrate 29g (Dietary Fiber 2g; Sugars 2g); Protein 6g
% daily value: Vitamin A 0%; Vitamin C 2%; Calcium 6%; Iron 15%   **exchanges:** 1 1/2 Starch, 1 Vegetable, 1 Fat   **carbohydrate choices:** 2

For a family fiesta, serve with tortilla chips, purchased salsa con queso dip, watermelon wedges and brownie sundaes for dessert.

salsa rice ENCHILADAS

prep time: 25 minutes   **start to finish:** 25 minutes   4 servings (2 enchiladas each)

1 1/2 cups chunky-style salsa
1 1/2 teaspoons chili powder
1 cup uncooked instant rice
1 can (15 oz) black beans, drained, rinsed
1 can (11 oz) whole kernel corn with red and green peppers, undrained
1 1/2 cups shredded Cheddar cheese (6 oz)
8 flour tortillas (8 inch)
Additional chunky-style salsa, if desired

1. In 10-inch skillet, heat 1 1/2 cups salsa and the chili powder to boiling. Stir in rice. Remove from heat; cover and let stand 5 minutes. Stir in beans, corn and cheese.

2. Spoon about 1/2 cup rice mixture onto center of each tortilla. Fold up bottom of each tortilla; fold over sides. Secure with toothpick if necessary. Serve with salsa if desired.

1 serving: Calories 780 (Calories from Fat 190); Total Fat 21g (Saturated Fat 11g; Trans Fat 1.5g); Cholesterol 45mg; Sodium 1730mg; Total Carbohydrate 117g (Dietary Fiber 10g; Sugars 8g); Protein 30g

% daily value: Vitamin A 25%; Vitamin C 8%; Calcium 40%; Iron 40%   **exchanges:** 7 Starch, 1/2 Other Carbohydrate, 1 Vegetable, 1 High-Fat Meat, 1 1/2 Fat   **carbohydrate choices:** 8

salsa rice ENCHILADAS

Here's a useful item to have on hand for quick meals: flour tortillas! These handy wrappers can be stuffed, rolled and folded for a super-easy meal. Look for regular, whole wheat, fat-free and flavored varieties.

cheesy green chile QUESADILLAS

prep time: 10 minutes   **start to finish:** 15 minutes   6 quesadillas

2 cups shredded Cheddar or Monterey Jack cheese (8 oz)
6 flour tortillas (8 to 10 inch)
1 small tomato, seeded, chopped (1/2 cup)
4 medium green onions, chopped (1/4 cup)
1 can (4.5 oz) chopped green chiles, drained
Chopped fresh cilantro, if desired

1. Heat oven to 350°F. Sprinkle 1/3 cup cheese evenly over half of each tortilla. Sprinkle tomato, onions, chiles and cilantro if desired over cheese. Fold tortillas over filling; sprinkle with additional cilantro. Place on ungreased cookie sheet.

2. Bake about 5 minutes or just until cheese is melted. Serve quesadillas whole, or cut each into 3 wedges, beginning cuts from center of folded sides.

1 quesadilla: Calories 300 (Calories from Fat 140); Total Fat 16g (Saturated Fat 9g; Trans Fat 1g); Cholesterol 40mg; Sodium 520mg; Total Carbohydrate 27g (Dietary Fiber 2g; Sugars 2g); Protein 14g
% daily value: Vitamin A 15%; Vitamin C 10%; Calcium 25%; Iron 10%   **exchanges:** 2 Starch, 1 1/2 High-Fat Meat
carbohydrate choices: 2

Hummus is a thick Middle Eastern sauce made from mashed garbanzo beans seasoned with lemon juice, garlic and olive oil. Prepared hummus is available in plain and flavored varieties in the refrigerated deli or dairy section of your supermarket.

middle east vegetable TACOS

prep time: 25 minutes   **start to finish:** 25 minutes   6 servings (2 tacos each)

1 tablespoon olive or vegetable oil
1 medium eggplant (1 lb), peeled and cut into 1/2-inch cubes
1 medium red bell pepper, cut into 1/2-inch strips
1 medium onion, cut into 1/2-inch wedges
1 can (14 1/2 oz) diced tomatoes with basil, garlic and oregano, undrained
1/4 teaspoon salt
1 container (8 oz) refrigerated hummus
12 taco shells
Plain yogurt or sour cream, if desired

1. In 10-inch nonstick skillet, heat oil over medium-high heat. Add eggplant, bell pepper and onion; cook 5 to 7 minutes, stirring occasionally, until vegetables are crisp-tender.

2. Stir in tomatoes and salt. Reduce heat to medium; cover and cook about 5 minutes or until eggplant is tender.

3. Spread slightly less than 2 tablespoons hummus on half of inside of each taco shell. Spoon about 1/2 cup vegetable mixture over hummus in each shell. Serve with yogurt if desired.

1 serving: Calories 290 (Calories from Fat 110); Total Fat 12g (Saturated Fat 1.5g; Trans Fat 2g); Cholesterol 0mg; Sodium 600mg; Total Carbohydrate 40g (Dietary Fiber 7g; Sugars 10g); Protein 7g
% daily value: Vitamin A 30%; Vitamin C 40%; Calcium 10%; Iron 15%   **exchanges:** 2 Starch, 2 Vegetable, 2 Fat   **carbohydrate choices:** 2 1/2

crunchy "chicken" nugget TACOS

prep time: 20 minutes   **start to finish:** 20 minutes   4 tacos

12 frozen chicken-style breaded soy-protein nuggets
(from 10- or 10.5-oz package)
1/4 cup creamy Caesar dressing
4 flour tortillas (8 to 10 inch)
2 cups shredded iceberg lettuce
1 medium tomato, cut into 8 slices
1/2 cup chow mein noodles

1. Bake or microwave nuggets as directed on package.

2. Meanwhile, spread 1 tablespoon dressing over each tortilla; sprinkle each evenly with 1/2 cup lettuce.

3. Arrange 2 tomato slices and 3 nuggets down center of each tortilla; sprinkle nuggets with 2 tablespoons chow mein noodles. Fold sides of tortillas over filling, slightly overlapping.

1 taco: Calories 400 (Calories from Fat 170); Total Fat 19g (Saturated Fat 3g; Trans Fat 0g); Cholesterol 0mg; Sodium 760mg; Total Carbohydrate 43g (Dietary Fiber 3g; Sugars 2g); Protein 14g
% daily value: Vitamin A 6%; Vitamin C 10%; Calcium 8%; Iron 20%   **exchanges:** 3 Starch, 1 Medium-Fat Meat, 2 Fat
carbohydrate choices: 3

Can't resist the aroma and flavor of a meatball sandwich slathered in spaghetti sauce and adorned with peppers and onions? The solution is at hand. Frozen soy-protein burgers mixed with just a few ingredients create memorable "meatless" meatballs.

italian GRINDERS

prep time: 25 minutes   **start to finish:** 25 minutes   4 sandwiches

4 frozen soy-protein burgers or soy-protein vegetable burgers
3 tablespoons grated Parmesan cheese
1 teaspoon Italian seasoning
4 teaspoons olive or vegetable oil
1 small onion, cut in half, sliced
1 small red bell pepper, cut into 1/4-inch strips
1 small green bell pepper, cut into 1/4-inch strips
4 hot dog buns, split
1/2 cup tomato pasta sauce, heated

1. On large microwavable plate, microwave burgers uncovered on High 2 to 3 minutes, turning once, until thawed. In medium bowl, mix thawed burgers, cheese and Italian seasoning. Shape mixture into 16 balls.

2. In 10-inch nonstick skillet, heat 2 teaspoons of the oil over medium heat. Add burger balls; cook, turning frequently, until brown. Remove from skillet; keep warm.

3. In same skillet, heat remaining 2 teaspoons oil over medium heat. Add onion and bell peppers; cook, stirring frequently, until crisp-tender.

4. Place 4 burger balls in each bun. Top with vegetable mixture. Serve with pasta sauce.

1 sandwich: Calories 320 (Calories from Fat 90); Total Fat 10g (Saturated Fat 2.5g; Trans Fat 0g); Cholesterol 0mg; Sodium 1080mg; Total Carbohydrate 40g (Dietary Fiber 6g; Sugars 6g); Protein 17g
% daily value: Vitamin A 40%; Vitamin C 60%; Calcium 15%; Iron 15%   **exchanges:** 2 1/2 Starch, 1 1/2 Lean Meat, 1 Fat
carbohydrate choices: 2 1/2

The peak season for eggplant is generally August and September, but they usually are available all year. Choose eggplants that are firm and smooth skinned with no soft or wrinkled spots.

pesto-eggplant SANDWICHES

prep time: 20 minutes **start to finish:** 20 minutes   4 open-face sandwiches

4 slices unpeeled eggplant (1/2 inch thick)
1 egg, beaten
1/3 cup Italian-style dry bread crumbs
2 tablespoons olive or vegetable oil
4 thin slices red onion
4 slices (1 oz each) provolone cheese
2 tablespoons basil pesto
4 slices Italian bread (1/2 inch thick), toasted
8 thin slices cucumber
4 thin slices tomato

1. Dip eggplant slices into egg, then coat with bread crumbs. In 10-inch skillet, heat oil over medium heat. Add eggplant; cook 3 to 4 minutes, turning once, until golden brown and crisp.

2. Top each eggplant slice with onion and cheese. Cover; cook 1 to 2 minutes or until cheese is melted.

3. Spread pesto on each slice of bread. Top with cucumber, tomato and eggplant.

1 open-face sandwich: Calories 340 (Calories from Fat 190); Total Fat 21g (Saturated Fat 7g; Trans Fat 0g); Cholesterol 75mg; Sodium 590mg; Total Carbohydrate 23g (Dietary Fiber 3g; Sugars 4g); Protein 13g
% daily value: Vitamin A 10%; Vitamin C 4%; Calcium 30%; Iron 10%   **exchanges:** 1 1/2 Starch, 1 Vegetable, 1 Medium-Fat Meat, 3 Fat
carbohydrate choices: 1 1/2

In 1906, the Central Grocery in New Orleans created the muffuletta, a wonderful specialty sandwich. It combines meats and cheeses, but it's the olive salad that makes it unique. Our vegetarian version keeps the olive salad but replaces the meat with a spicy, mashed black-eyed pea mixture.

cajun MUFFULETTAS

prep time: 25 minutes   **start to finish:** 1 hour 25 minutes   4 sandwiches

OLIVE SALAD
1/4 cup chopped pimiento-stuffed olives
1/4 cup chopped Kalamata or ripe olives
1/4 cup sliced hot pickled okra (from 16-oz jar)
1 tablespoon chopped fresh parsley
1 tablespoon olive or vegetable oil
1/4 teaspoon dried oregano leaves, crumbled
1/8 teaspoon pepper
1 small clove garlic, finely chopped

SANDWICHES
1 can (15 to 16 oz) black-eyed peas, drained, rinsed
1/4 cup water
1 teaspoon red pepper sauce
4 large kaiser rolls, split
4 slices (1 oz each) provolone cheese
4 slices tomato

1. In small bowl, mix salad ingredients. Cover; refrigerate at least 1 hour to blend flavors.

2. In blender or food processor, place peas, water and pepper sauce. Cover; blend or process until smooth.

3. Cut 1/2-inch slice from top of each roll; set aside. Remove soft bread from inside of each roll to within 1/2 inch of edge; reserve bread trimmings for another use.

4. Spread about 1/4 cup pea mixture in each roll. Top pea mixture in each with cheese slice, tomato slice and scant 2 tablespoons salad. Spoon remaining pea mixture and salad evenly into each. Cover with tops of rolls.

1 sandwich: Calories 410 (Calories from Fat 140); Total Fat 16g (Saturated Fat 6g; Trans Fat 0.5g); Cholesterol 20mg; Sodium 940mg; Total Carbohydrate 47g (Dietary Fiber 6g; Sugars 2g); Protein 19g
% daily value: Vitamin A 10%; Vitamin C 10%; Calcium 30%; Iron 25%   **exchanges:** 3 Starch, 1 Medium-Fat Meat, 2 Fat
carbohydrate choices: 3

Yummy! Warm, creamy peanut butter and bananas are tucked between slices of crispy bread. Peanut butter is a good source of protein, but if allergies are a problem, just substitute another type of nut butter like almond or cashew.

grilled peanut butter and banana
SANDWICHES

prep time: 15 minutes   **start to finish:** 15 minutes   4 sandwiches

8 slices English muffin bread
1/2 cup peanut butter
2 medium bananas
3 tablespoons butter or margarine, softened

1. Spread 4 slices of bread with peanut butter. Slice bananas; arrange on peanut butter. Top with remaining slices of bread to make 4 sandwiches. Spread top bread slice of each sandwich with about 1 teaspoon butter.

2. Place sandwiches, butter sides down, in skillet. Spread top bread slices with remaining butter. Cook uncovered over medium heat about 4 minutes or until bottoms are golden brown. Turn; cook 2 to 3 minutes longer or until bottoms are golden brown and peanut butter is melted.

1 sandwich: Calories 480 (Calories from Fat 240); Total Fat 26g (Saturated Fat 8g; Trans Fat 0.5g); Cholesterol 25mg; Sodium 470mg; Total Carbohydrate 46g (Dietary Fiber 5g; Sugars 17g); Protein 13g
% daily value: Vitamin A 6%; Vitamin C 4%; Calcium 10%; Iron 10%   **exchanges:** 2 Starch, 1 Other Carbohydrate, 1 High-Fat Meat, 3 1/2 Fat   **carbohydrate choices:** 3

Colby-Monterey Jack cheese is also known as marble cheese or Co-Jack; it has a fairly mild flavor. For an all-American favorite, use American cheese slices instead of the Colby-Monterey Jack.

toasted cheese, avocado and tomato
SANDWICHES

prep time: 15 minutes   **start to finish:** 15 minutes   4 sandwiches

8 slices pumpernickel bread
2 to 3 tablespoons creamy Dijon mustard-mayonnaise spread
1 medium avocado, pitted, peeled and thinly sliced
1 medium tomato, thinly sliced
4 slices (1 oz each) Colby-Monterey Jack cheese blend
2 tablespoons butter or margarine

1. Spread each slice of bread with mustard–mayonnaise spread. Top 4 slices with avocado, tomato and cheese. Top with remaining bread slices, spread side down.

2. In 12-inch skillet, melt butter over medium heat. Add sandwiches; cover and cook 4 to 5 minutes, turning once, until both sides are crisp and cheese is melted.

1 sandwich: Calories 380 (Calories from Fat 210); Total Fat 23g (Saturated Fat 10g; Trans Fat 0.5g); Cholesterol 40mg; Sodium 660mg; Total Carbohydrate 32g (Dietary Fiber 5g; Sugars 3g); Protein 13g
% daily value: Vitamin A 15%; Vitamin C 8%; Calcium 25%; Iron 15%   **exchanges:** 2 Starch, 1 High-Fat Meat, 2 1/2 Fat
carbohydrate choices: 2

FLAVOR it up!

Up the flavor of soy protein products, pasta, rice, beans and vegetables with these taste-bud-tingling salsas and sauces. Every recipe offers serving suggestions, but these are just food for thought—create your own tasty options!

spicy chimichurri SAUCE

prep time: 5 minutes   **start to finish:** 5 minutes
2/3 cup; 10 servings (1 tablespoon each)

1/4 cup olive or vegetable oil
2 tablespoons chopped fresh parsley
3 tablespoons red wine vinegar
1 tablespoon lemon juice
1 teaspoon chopped fresh or 1/2 teaspoon dried oregano leaves
1/2 teaspoon crushed red pepper flakes
2 cloves garlic, finely chopped

1. In tightly covered container, shake all ingredients.
2. Serve with grilled or steamed vegetables, soy-protein burgers or bean burgers or use as a dipping sauce for bread and raw vegetables.

1 serving: Calories 50 (Calories from Fat 50); Total Fat 5g (Saturated Fat 0.5g; Trans Fat 0g); Cholesterol 0mg; Sodium 0mg; Total Carbohydrate 0g (Dietary Fiber 0g; Sugars 0g); Protein 0g
% daily value: Vitamin A 2%; Vitamin C 2%; Calcium 0%; Iron 0%   **exchanges:** 1 Fat
carbohydrate choices: 0

herbed butter SAUCE

prep time: 10 minutes   **start to finish:** 10 minutes
1/2 cup; 8 servings (1 tablespoon each)

1/2 cup butter or margarine
2 tablespoons chopped fresh or 1 teaspoon dried herb leaves (such as basil, chives, oregano, savory, tarragon or thyme)
2 teaspoons lemon juice

1. In 1-quart heavy saucepan or 8-inch skillet, melt butter over medium heat. Stir in herbs and lemon juice.
2. Toss with hot cooked pasta, rice or beans or serve over hot cooked vegetables.

1 serving: Calories 100 (Calories from Fat 100); Total Fat 12g (Saturated Fat 6g; Trans Fat 0.5g); Cholesterol 30mg; Sodium 75mg; Total Carbohydrate 0g (Dietary Fiber 0g; Sugars 0g); Protein 0g
% daily value: Vitamin A 10%; Vitamin C 0%; Calcium 0%; Iron 0%   **exchanges:** 2 1/2 Fat
carbohydrate choices: 0

chipotle MAYONNAISE

prep time: 5 minutes   **start to finish:** 1 hour 5 minutes
1 cup; 16 servings (1 tablespoon each)

2 canned chipotle chiles in adobo sauce, finely chopped
1/2 cup mayonnaise or salad dressing
1/2 cup sour cream
1/8 teaspoon dried oregano leaves, if desired

1. In small bowl, mix all ingredients. Cover; refrigerate at least 1 hour to blend flavors.
2. Serve with soy-protein burgers, chicken-style breaded soy-protein patties and nuggets, grilled chicken–style soy-protein patties, bean burgers and vegetable burgers.

1 serving: Calories 60 (Calories from Fat 60); Total Fat 7g (Saturated Fat 1.5g; Trans Fat 0g); Cholesterol 10mg; Sodium 45mg; Total Carbohydrate 0g (Dietary Fiber 0g; Sugars 0g); Protein 0g
% daily value: Vitamin A 0%; Vitamin C 0%; Calcium 0%; Iron 0%   **exchanges:** 1 1/2 Fat
carbohydrate choices: 0

peanut SAUCE

prep time: 10 minutes   **start to finish:** 10 minutes
1 cup; 16 servings (1 tablespoon each)

1/2 cup creamy peanut butter
1/2 cup water
2 tablespoons lime juice
1/2 teaspoon ground coriander
1/2 teaspoon ground cumin
1/8 teaspoon salt
1/8 teaspoon ground red pepper (cayenne), if desired
2 cloves garlic, finely chopped

1. In 1-quart saucepan, mix all ingredients with wire whisk. Heat over medium heat, stirring occasionally, until smooth and warm. Use sauce immediately, or cover and refrigerate up to 3 days or freeze up to 2 months.
2. Serve as a dipping sauce with baked tofu cut into cubes, grilled chicken-style soy-protein patties cut into wedges, chicken-style breaded soy-protein nuggets or grilled vegetables. Also use as a sauce for a vegetable pizza.

1 serving: Calories 50 (Calories from Fat 35); Total Fat 4g (Saturated Fat 1g; Trans Fat 0g); Cholesterol 0mg; Sodium 55mg; Total Carbohydrate 2g (Dietary Fiber 0g; Sugars 0g); Protein 2g
% daily value: Vitamin A 0%; Vitamin C 0%; Calcium 0%; Iron 0%   **exchanges:** 1 Fat
carbohydrate choices: 0

So tasty, and so easy.

garbanzo bean SANDWICHES

prep time: 15 minutes   **start to finish:** 15 minutes   8 sandwiches

1 can (15 to 16 oz) garbanzo beans, drained, rinsed
1/2 cup water
2 tablespoons chopped fresh parsley
2 tablespoons chopped walnuts
1 tablespoon finely chopped onion
1 clove garlic, finely chopped
1/2 medium cucumber, sliced
4 whole wheat pita breads (6 inch)
Lettuce leaves
1 medium tomato, seeded, chopped (3/4 cup)
1/2 cup cucumber ranch dressing

1. In food processor or blender, place beans, water, parsley, walnuts, onion and garlic. Cover; process until smooth.

2. Cut cucumber slices into quarters. Cut each pita bread in half crosswise to form 2 pockets; line with lettuce leaves. Spoon 2 tablespoons bean mixture into each pita half. Add tomato and cucumber; drizzle with dressing.

1 sandwich: Calories 260 (Calories from Fat 100); Total Fat 11g (Saturated Fat 1.5g; Trans Fat 0g); Cholesterol 0mg; Sodium 360mg; Total Carbohydrate 33g (Dietary Fiber 6g; Sugars 4g); Protein 8g

% daily value: Vitamin A 6%; Vitamin C 10%; Calcium 4%; Iron 15%   **exchanges:** 2 Starch, 1 Vegetable, 2 Fat   **carbohydrate choices:** 2

Focaccia is an Italian bread shaped into a large, flat round that's drizzled with olive oil and sometimes topped with rosemary, Parmesan cheese or other goodies like tomatoes or onions. It can be found in the bakery, deli and frozen-food sections of the grocery store.

italian vegetable focaccia SANDWICH

prep time: 5 minutes   **start to finish:** 20 minutes   4 servings

1 focaccia bread (10 to 12 inch), cut in half horizontally
1 1/2 cups shredded mozzarella or smoked provolone cheese (6 oz)
1 bag (1 lb) frozen broccoli, carrots and cauliflower, thawed, drained
3 tablespoons fat-free Italian dressing

1. Heat oven to 400°F. Place bottom half of focaccia on ungreased cookie sheet.

2. Sprinkle with 3/4 cup of the cheese. Spread vegetables over cheese; drizzle with dressing. Sprinkle with remaining 3/4 cup cheese. Cover with top half of focaccia.

3. Bake 12 to 15 minutes or until golden brown. Cut into wedges to serve.

1 serving: Calories 590 (Calories from Fat 200); Total Fat 22g (Saturated Fat 7g; Trans Fat 0g); Cholesterol 25mg; Sodium 1550mg; Total Carbohydrate 75g (Dietary Fiber 6g; Sugars 3g); Protein 23g
% daily value: Vitamin A 70%; Vitamin C 30%; Calcium 35%; Iron 30%   **exchanges:** 4 Starch, 2 Vegetable, 1 Medium-Fat Meat, 3 Fat
carbohydrate choices: 5

italian vegetable focaccia SANDWICH

You won't miss the sausage when you make "mini-meatballs" using roasted garlic or regular frozen soy-protein burgers. It tastes just like Italian sausage pizza!

meatless meatball PIZZA

prep time: 15 minutes   **start to finish:** 35 minutes   6 servings

2 frozen roasted garlic or regular soy-protein burgers
1 package (14 oz) prebaked original Italian pizza crust
    or other 12-inch prebaked pizza crust
3/4 cup pizza sauce
2 tablespoons sliced ripe olives
1 cup shredded mozzarella cheese (4 oz)
1 cup shredded provolone cheese (4 oz)

1. Heat oven to 425°F. On medium microwavable plate, microwave burgers uncovered on High 1 to 1 1/2 minutes, turning once, until thawed. Shape into 1/2-inch balls.

2. On ungreased cookie sheet, place pizza crust. Spread pizza sauce over crust. Top with burger balls and olives. Sprinkle with both cheeses.

3. Bake 18 to 20 minutes or until cheese is melted and light golden brown.

1 serving: Calories 360 (Calories from Fat 120); Total Fat 14g (Saturated Fat 6g; Trans Fat 0g); Cholesterol 25mg; Sodium 880mg; Total Carbohydrate 41g (Dietary Fiber 3g; Sugars 2g); Protein 18g
% daily value: Vitamin A 8%; Vitamin C 6%; Calcium 30%; Iron 15%   **exchanges:** 2 1/2 Starch, 1 1/2 Lean Meat, 1 1/2 Fat
carbohydrate choices: 3

Vegetarian Substitutions

Here is a quick at-a-glance substitution guide for replacing meat, poultry, fish, seafood and animal by-products with a vegetarian option.

Meat, poultry, fish or seafood	Cheese, eggs, legumes, mushrooms, nut butters (almond, cashew, peanut, sesame), nuts, seeds, seitan, soy-protein products, tempeh, tofu
Meat, poultry, fish or seafood broth	Fruit juices, miso, vegetable broth and juices, wine
Cheese	Rice cheese, soy cheeses
Eggs	Egg replacer, tofu
Milk	Nut milk, rice milk, soy milk
Honey	Barley malt syrup, brown rice syrup, real maple syrup
Gelatin	Agar-agar, arrowroot, ground nuts, ground peanuts, ground seeds, kudzu

Artichoke hearts add distinctive flavor to this easy pizza. Serve the pizza for a light supper, or cut into small squares for a great meatless appetizer. If roasted red bell peppers aren't available, use jarred pimiento.

sharp cheddar, artichoke and red onion PIZZA

prep time: 10 minutes   **start to finish:** 20 minutes   4 servings

2 teaspoons butter or margarine
1 large red onion, sliced (2 cups)
1 package (14 oz) prebaked original Italian pizza crust
    or other 12-inch prebaked pizza crust
1/2 cup marinated artichoke hearts (from 6- to 7-oz jar), drained, sliced
3 tablespoons sliced drained roasted red bell peppers (from a jar)
1 cup shredded sharp Cheddar cheese (4 oz)

1. Heat oven to 400°F. In 8-inch skillet, melt butter over medium heat. Add onion; cook 3 to 5 minutes, stirring occasionally, until crisp-tender.

2. Spread onion over pizza crust. Top with artichokes, roasted peppers and cheese.

3. Bake 8 to 10 minutes or until cheese is melted. Cut into wedges to serve.

1 serving: Calories 440 (Calories from Fat 140); Total Fat 16g (Saturated Fat 8g; Trans Fat 0g); Cholesterol 35mg; Sodium 690mg; Total Carbohydrate 59g (Dietary Fiber 4g; Sugars 3g); Protein 16g
% daily value: Vitamin A 15%; Vitamin C 15%; Calcium 20%; Iron 20%   **exchanges:** 4 Starch, 1/2 High-Fat Meat, 1 1/2 Fat
carbohydrate choices: 4

chicken, artichoke and red onion PIZZA: **Add 1 cup cubed cooked chicken or turkey with the artichokes in step 2.**

Keep prebaked pizza crusts or pita bread on hand for impromptu meals and snacks. Why? You can top them a thousand ways to satisfy even the pickiest eaters.

cheesy tomato and bell pepper PIZZAS

prep time: 10 minutes   **start to finish:** 25 minutes   6 pizzas

3 packages (10 oz each) prebaked Italian pizza crusts (6 inch)
    or 6 pita breads (6 inch)
6 oz 1/3-less-fat cream cheese (Neufchâtel) or regular cream cheese,
    softened (from 8-oz package)
6 tablespoons basil pesto
4 roma (plum) tomatoes, sliced
3/4 cup 1/2-inch pieces yellow bell pepper
4 medium green onions, sliced (1/4 cup)
1 tablespoon chopped fresh or 1/2 teaspoon dried basil leaves
1 cup shredded mozzarella cheese (4 oz)
2 tablespoons freshly grated Parmesan cheese

1. Heat oven to 450°F. On ungreased large cookie sheet, place pizza crusts.

2. Spread cream cheese on pizza crusts to within 1/4 inch of edges. Gently spread pesto over cream cheese. Top with tomatoes, bell pepper and onions. Sprinkle with basil and both cheeses.

3. Bake 7 to 12 minutes or until cheeses are melted.

1 pizza: Calories 640 (Calories from Fat 230); Total Fat 25g (Saturated Fat 10g; Trans Fat 0g); Cholesterol 35mg; Sodium 1010mg; Total Carbohydrate 82g (Dietary Fiber 5g; Sugars 3g); Protein 22g
% daily value: Vitamin A 25%; Vitamin C 40%; Calcium 30%; Iron 30%   **exchanges:** 5 1/2 Starch, 1 High-Fat Meat, 2 Fat
carbohydrate choices: 5 1/2

Refrigerated pizza dough and frozen vegetables let you make this pizza very quickly! If the vegetable mixture listed doesn't excite your taste buds, go ahead and use the combination you love—the recipe will work just fine.

PIZZA monterey

prep time: 15 minutes   **start to finish:** 40 minutes   6 servings

1 can (13.8 oz) refrigerated pizza crust
2 cups shredded reduced-fat Monterey Jack cheese (8 oz)
1 bag (1 lb) frozen broccoli, carrots and cauliflower, thawed, drained
1/2 cup reduced-fat ranch dressing

1. Heat oven to 425°F. Lightly grease 12-inch pizza pan or 13 × 9-inch pan with shortening.

2. Unroll pizza crust dough; place in pan. Starting at center, press dough evenly in pan. Bake about 10 minutes or until light golden brown.

3. Sprinkle 1 cup of the cheese over crust. If necessary, cut large pieces of vegetables into bite-size pieces; spread vegetables over cheese. Drizzle with dressing. Sprinkle with remaining 1 cup cheese.

4. Bake 12 to 15 minutes longer or until crust is deep golden brown and cheese is melted.

1 serving: Calories 340 (Calories from Fat 120); Total Fat 14g (Saturated Fat 6g; Trans Fat 0g); Cholesterol 30mg; Sodium 1000mg; Total Carbohydrate 39g (Dietary Fiber 3g; Sugars 6g); Protein 16g
% daily value: Vitamin A 50%; Vitamin C 20%; Calcium 30%; Iron 15%   **exchanges:** 2 Starch, 1/2 Other Carbohydrate, 1 1/2 Medium-Fat Meat, 1 Fat   **carbohydrate choices:** 2 1/2

Salade Niçoise is a salad from the French city of Nice, perched on the glamorous French Riviera. The salad is often served with crusty French bread, so a French bread pizza is a perfect adaptation. For do-ahead convenience, bake the vegetables and refrigerate them up to 2 days before preparing the pizza.

niçoise FRENCH BREAD PIZZA

prep time: 25 minutes   **start to finish:** 40 minutes   4 servings

2 eggs
4 roma (plum) tomatoes, cut into 1/4-inch slices
1 medium green bell pepper, cut into 1/4-inch rings
1 large onion, thinly sliced
1/2 cup Italian dressing
1/2 loaf (1-lb size) French bread, cut in half horizontally
1/4 cup sliced ripe olives
1 cup finely shredded mozzarella cheese (4 oz)

1. Place eggs in 1-quart saucepan; add enough cold water to cover eggs by 1 inch. Cover; heat to boiling. Remove from heat; let stand covered 15 minutes. Drain. Immediately place eggs in cold water with ice cubes or run cold water over eggs until completely cooled.

2. Meanwhile, heat oven to 450°F. Line 15 × 10 × 1-inch pan with foil. Spread tomatoes, bell pepper and onion on foil. Brush both sides of vegetables with about half of the dressing. Bake uncovered 12 to 15 minutes or until onion is crisp-tender.

3. Reduce oven temperature to 375°F. Remove vegetables and foil from pan. Place bread halves, cut sides up, in pan. Brush with remaining dressing. Top evenly with roasted vegetables. To remove shell from each egg, crackle it by tapping gently all over; roll between hands to loosen. Peel, starting at large end; cut into slices. Place eggs over roasted vegetables. Top with olives and cheese.

4. Bake 8 to 10 minutes or until cheese is melted. Cut into 2-inch slices to serve.

1 serving: Calories 460 (Calories from Fat 220); Total Fat 24g (Saturated Fat 6g; Trans Fat 0.5g); Cholesterol 125mg; Sodium 860mg; Total Carbohydrate 43g (Dietary Fiber 4g; Sugars 8g); Protein 18g
% daily value: Vitamin A 25%; Vitamin C 40%; Calcium 30%; Iron 15%   **exchanges:** 2 1/2 Starch, 1/2 Other Carbohydrate, 1 1/2 Medium-Fat Meat, 2 1/2 Fat   **carbohydrate choices:** 3

niçoise tuna FRENCH BREAD PIZZA: Add a 6-oz can of white tuna in water, drained, with the roasted vegetables in step 3.

niçoise FRENCH BREAD PIZZA

Purchased peanut sauce, found in the ethnic-foods section of your grocery store, can be used in place of the peanut butter spread, soy sauce, vinegar and sugar. Use a scant 1 cup of purchased sauce.

thai vegetable PIZZA

prep time: 15 minutes   **start to finish:** 30 minutes   6 pizzas

6 fat-free flour tortillas (8 to 10 inch)
2/3 cup reduced-fat peanut butter spread
1/4 cup soy sauce
2 tablespoons seasoned rice vinegar
2 teaspoons sugar
2 cups shredded mozzarella cheese (8 oz)
2 cups fresh bean sprouts
1 bag (1 lb) frozen stir-fry vegetables, thawed, drained

1. Heat oven to 400°F. On ungreased large cookie sheet, place tortillas. Bake 5 minutes.

2. Meanwhile, in small bowl, mix peanut butter spread, soy sauce, vinegar and sugar.

3. Spread peanut butter mixture on warm tortillas. Top each with 1/4 cup cheese. Spread bean sprouts and stir-fry vegetables evenly on tortillas. Sprinkle with remaining 1/2 cup cheese.

4. Bake 10 to 15 minutes or until cheese is melted.

1 pizza: Calories 500 (Calories from Fat 170); Total Fat 19g (Saturated Fat 7g; Trans Fat 0g); Cholesterol 20mg; Sodium 1620mg; Total Carbohydrate 54g (Dietary Fiber 7g; Sugars 10g); Protein 27g
% daily value: Vitamin A 20%; Vitamin C 25%; Calcium 35%; Iron 20%   **exchanges:** 3 Starch, 1/2 Other Carbohydrate, 2 1/2 Medium-Fat Meat, 1 Fat   **carbohydrate choices:** 3 1/2

thai chicken PIZZA: **Omit bean sprouts. Add 2 cups chopped cooked chicken with the stir-fry vegetables in step 3.**

These individual pizzas are great for a snack or light lunch, and the recipe doubles easily.

santa fe nacho PIZZAS

prep time: 15 minutes   **start to finish:** 40 minutes   5 pizzas

1 can (10.2 oz) large refrigerated flaky biscuits (5)
3 tablespoons black bean dip
1/3 cup chunky-style salsa
2 tablespoons chopped canned green chiles (from 4.5-oz can)
2 medium green onions, chopped (2 tablespoons)
2 tablespoons sliced ripe olives
3/4 cup shredded Monterey Jack and Cheddar marble cheese (3 oz)
1 tablespoon chopped fresh cilantro

1. Heat oven to 350°F. Separate dough into 5 biscuits. On ungreased cookie sheet, press or roll each into 5-inch round.

2. Spread bean dip evenly over dough. Top with salsa, chiles, onions and olives. Sprinkle with cheese and cilantro.

3. Bake 20 to 25 minutes or until crust is deep golden brown and cheese is melted.

1 pizza: Calories 290 (Calories from Fat 140); Total Fat 16g (Saturated Fat 7g; Trans Fat 3g); Cholesterol 20mg; Sodium 970mg; Total Carbohydrate 28g (Dietary Fiber 0g; Sugars 6g); Protein 9g
% daily value: Vitamin A 8%; Vitamin C 0%; Calcium 20%; Iron 10%   **exchanges:** 2 Starch, 1/2 Medium-Fat Meat, 2 Fat
carbohydrate choices: 2

santa fe chicken nacho PIZZAS: Sprinkle 1 cup chopped cooked chicken or turkey over the bean dip in step 2.

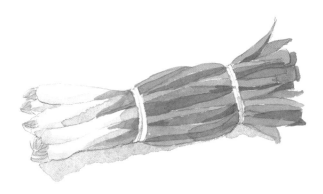

Pepperoncini peppers, also called Tuscan peppers, are a pickled variety of chili pepper; they give a slightly sweet and spicy-hot flavor to this pizza. They are most often sold next to pickles or specialty pickled items.

mediterranean PIZZA

prep time: 15 minutes   **start to finish:** 25 minutes   6 servings

1 package (14 oz) prebaked original Italian pizza crust
 or other 12-inch prebaked pizza crust
1 1/2 cups shredded mozzarella cheese (6 oz)
1 jar (7 or 7.25 oz) roasted red bell peppers, drained, diced (3/4 cup)
1 jar (7 oz) sun-dried tomatoes in oil, drained, chopped
2 roma (plum) tomatoes, sliced
1 small red onion, sliced
2 pepperoncini peppers (bottled Italian peppers), drained, sliced
2 tablespoons sliced pimiento-stuffed olives
2 tablespoons sliced ripe olives
1 tablespoon chopped fresh or 1 teaspoon dried basil leaves

1. Heat oven to 450°F. On ungreased cookie sheet, place pizza crust.

2. Sprinkle 1 cup of the cheese over crust. Top with remaining ingredients except basil. Sprinkle with remaining 1/2 cup cheese and the basil.

3. Bake about 10 minutes or until cheese is melted. Cut into wedges to serve.

1 serving: Calories 360 (Calories from Fat 110); Total Fat 13g (Saturated Fat 4.5g; Trans Fat 0g); Cholesterol 15mg; Sodium 590mg; Total Carbohydrate 47g (Dietary Fiber 4g; Sugars 7g); Protein 14g
% daily value: Vitamin A 45%; Vitamin C 60%; Calcium 25%; Iron 20%   **exchanges:** 2 1/2 Starch, 1/2 Other Carbohydrate, 1 Medium-Fat Meat, 1 Fat   **carbohydrate choices:** 3

mediterranean shrimp PIZZA: Add 1 can (4 oz) medium shrimp, drained and rinsed, with the remaining ingredients in step 2.

Tangy feta cheese is Greek in origin and is traditionally made from sheep or goat milk. It's sometimes referred to as "pickled" cheese because it is cured and stored in its own salty whey brine.

middle eastern pita PIZZAS

prep time: 10 minutes   **start to finish:** 20 minutes   4 pizzas

4 pita breads (6 inch)
1/2 cup roasted garlic–flavored or regular hummus
1 cup crumbled feta cheese (4 oz)
1 small onion, sliced
2 cups shredded fresh spinach
1 large tomato, seeded, chopped (1 cup)
1/4 cup sliced ripe or Kalamata olives

1. Heat oven to 400°F. In ungreased 15 × 10 × 1-inch pan, place pita breads.

2. Spread hummus on each pita bread. Sprinkle with cheese.

3. Bake 8 to 10 minutes or until cheese is melted. Top each pizza with onion, spinach, tomato and olives before serving.

1 pizza: Calories 330 (Calories from Fat 90); Total Fat 11g (Saturated Fat 5g; Trans Fat 0g); Cholesterol 25mg; Sodium 840mg; Total Carbohydrate 46g (Dietary Fiber 5g; Sugars 4g); Protein 13g
% daily value: Vitamin A 40%; Vitamin C 10%; Calcium 25%; Iron 20%   **exchanges:** 3 Starch, 1 Medium-Fat Meat, 1/2 Fat
carbohydrate choices: 3

What a deal! Pizzeria-style pizza made super easy at home! Using string cheese makes stuffing the edge of the crust very simple.

deluxe stuffed-crust PIZZA

prep time: 25 minutes   **start to finish:** 45 minutes   6 servings

Yellow cornmeal
1 loaf (1 lb) frozen wheat bread dough, thawed
4 sticks (1 oz each) string cheese, cut in half lengthwise
1/4 cup tomato paste with Italian seasonings (from 6-oz can)
1 small onion, cut lengthwise in half, then thinly sliced
1 medium bell pepper, thinly sliced
1 can (4 oz) mushroom pieces and stems, drained
1 oz soy-protein pepperoni-style slices, coarsely chopped (1/4 cup)*
12 pitted Kalamata or Greek olives, coarsely chopped (1/3 cup)
2 cups shredded mozzarella cheese (8 oz)

1. Heat oven to 400°F. Grease large cookie sheet with shortening or spray with cooking spray. Sprinkle cornmeal over cookie sheet.

2. On cookie sheet, press or roll dough into 13-inch round. Arrange string cheese sticks in circle around edge of dough. Carefully roll edge of dough up over cheese; seal well.

3. Spread tomato paste evenly over dough. Top with onion, bell pepper, mushrooms, pepperoni-style slices and olives. Sprinkle with cheese.

4. Bake 15 to 17 minutes or until crust is golden brown and cheese is melted. Cut into wedges to serve.

*Two frozen soy-protein burgers, thawed and cut into 1/4-inch pieces, or 1/2 cup frozen soy-protein burger crumbles, thawed, can be substituted for the veggie pepperoni.

1 serving: Calories 400 (Calories from Fat 130); Total Fat 15g (Saturated Fat 7g; Trans Fat 0g); Cholesterol 30mg; Sodium 880mg; Total Carbohydrate 43g (Dietary Fiber 6g; Sugars 7g); Protein 25g
% daily value: Vitamin A 15%; Vitamin C 20%; Calcium 45%; Iron 15%   **exchanges:** 2 1/2 Starch, 1/2 Other Carbohydrate, 2 Medium-Fat Meat, 1/2 Fat   **carbohydrate choices:** 3

deluxe stuffed-crust PIZZA

layered PIZZA PIE

prep time: 10 minutes   **start to finish:** 50 minutes   6 servings

2 cans (13.8 oz each) refrigerated pizza crust
1 can (8 oz) pizza sauce (1 cup)
1 jar (4.5 oz) sliced mushrooms, drained
1/4 cup sliced ripe olives
1 1/2 cups shredded mozzarella cheese (6 oz)
2 boxes (9 oz each) frozen spinach, thawed, squeezed to drain
1 teaspoon olive or vegetable oil
1 tablespoon grated Parmesan cheese

1. Heat oven to 400°F. Lightly grease 9-inch pie plate. Unroll 1 can of dough; place in pie plate. Starting at center, press dough in bottom and up side of pie plate to form crust.

2. In small bowl, mix pizza sauce and mushrooms; spoon onto dough. Layer with olives, 3/4 cup of the mozzarella cheese, the spinach and remaining 3/4 cup mozzarella cheese.

3. Unroll remaining can of dough on work surface. Starting at center, press dough into 9-inch round; place dough over filling. Pinch edges of dough together to seal; roll up edge of dough or flute to form rim. Cut several slits in dough. Brush with oil; sprinkle with Parmesan cheese.

4. Bake 35 to 40 minutes or until deep golden brown.

1 serving: Calories 480 (Calories from Fat 120); Total Fat 13g (Saturated Fat 5g; Trans Fat 0.5g); Cholesterol 15mg; Sodium 1450mg; Total Carbohydrate 70g (Dietary Fiber 5g; Sugars 10g); Protein 20g
% daily value: Vitamin A 100%; Vitamin C 10%; Calcium 30%; Iron 25%   **exchanges:** 4 Starch, 1/2 Other Carbohydrate, 1 Medium-Fat Meat, 1 Fat   **carbohydrate choices:** 4 1/2

layered italian sausage PIZZA PIE: Cook 1/2 lb bulk Italian turkey sausage until no longer pink. Add sausage with the olives in step 2.

A calzone is a stuffed pizza that looks like a big turnover. To give these calzones shiny tops, brush them with a slightly beaten egg white before baking.

broccoli-cheese CALZONES (LOW fat)

prep time: 15 minutes   **start to finish:** 35 minutes   6 servings

1 container (15 oz) fat-free ricotta cheese
1 box (9 oz) frozen cut broccoli, thawed
1/3 cup grated Parmesan cheese
1/4 cup fat-free egg product or 2 egg whites
1 tablespoon chopped fresh or 1 teaspoon dried basil leaves
1/4 teaspoon garlic powder
1 loaf (1 lb) frozen wheat or white bread dough, thawed
1 can (8 oz) pizza sauce

1. Heat oven to 375°F. Grease 2 cookie sheets with shortening. In medium bowl, mix all ingredients except bread dough and pizza sauce.

2. Divide bread dough into 6 equal pieces. On lightly floured surface using floured rolling pin, roll each piece into 7-inch round.

3. Top half of each dough round with cheese mixture to within 1 inch of edge. Carefully fold dough over filling; pinch edge or press with fork to seal securely. Place calzones on cookie sheets.

4. Bake about 20 minutes or until golden brown. Cool 5 minutes.

5. In 1-quart saucepan, heat pizza sauce over medium heat about 2 minutes, stirring occasionally, until hot. Serve warm sauce over calzones.

1 serving: Calories 320 (Calories from Fat 50); Total Fat 6g (Saturated Fat 1.5g; Trans Fat 0g); Cholesterol 10mg; Sodium 650mg; Total Carbohydrate 45g (Dietary Fiber 6g; Sugars 11g); Protein 23g
% daily value: Vitamin A 20%; Vitamin C 20%; Calcium 25%; Iron 15%   **exchanges:** 2 Starch, 1/2 Other Carbohydrate, 1 Vegetable, 2 Lean Meat   **carbohydrate choices:** 3

mediterranean minestrone CASSEROLE *(page 171)*

CHAPTER 5 slow cooker

How wonderful to come home to delicious lasagna! This hearty meat-free version will please everyone and is also great for casual entertaining—just add a green salad and some garlic bread. Mangia!

slow cooker LASAGNA

prep time: 35 minutes   **start to finish:** 6 hours 45 minutes   6 servings

1 medium onion, chopped (1/2 cup)
2 cups frozen sausage-style soy-protein crumbles (from 12-oz package)
2 cans (15 oz each) Italian-style tomato sauce
2 teaspoons dried basil leaves
1/2 teaspoon salt
3 cups shredded mozzarella cheese (12 oz)
1 container (15 oz) part-skim ricotta cheese
1 cup grated Parmesan cheese
12 uncooked lasagna noodles

1. Spray 10-inch skillet with cooking spray. Add onion; cook over medium heat about 3 minutes, stirring occasionally, until crisp-tender. Stir in crumbles, tomato sauce, basil and salt.

2. In medium bowl, mix 2 cups of the mozzarella cheese and the ricotta and Parmesan cheeses.

3. Into 3 1/2- to 4-quart slow cooker, spoon one-fourth of the crumbles mixture; top with 4 noodles, broken into pieces to fit. Top with half of the cheese mixture and one-fourth of the crumbles mixture. Top with 4 noodles, remaining cheese mixture and one-fourth of the crumbles mixture. Top with remaining 4 noodles and remaining crumbles mixture.

4. Cover; cook on Low heat setting 6 to 8 hours. (If slow cooker has black liner, do not cook longer than 8 hours or mixture may burn around edge.)

5. Sprinkle top of lasagna with remaining 1 cup mozzarella cheese. Cover; let stand about 10 minutes or until cheese is melted. Cut into pieces.

1 serving: Calories 590 (Calories from Fat 220); Total Fat 24g (Saturated Fat 14g; Trans Fat 0.5g); Cholesterol 65mg; Sodium 1970mg; Total Carbohydrate 52g (Dietary Fiber 5g; Sugars 9g); Protein 43g
% daily value: Vitamin A 35%; Vitamin C 15%; Calcium 90%; Iron 20%   **exchanges:** 3 Starch, 1/2 Other Carbohydrate, 5 Lean Meat, 1 1/2 Fat
carbohydrate choices: 3 1/2

cheesy ravioli CASSEROLE

prep time: 15 minutes   **start to finish:** 5 hours 45 minutes   10 servings

1 tablespoon olive or vegetable oil
1 medium onion, chopped (1/2 cup)
1 large clove garlic, finely chopped
2 jars or cans (26 oz each) four cheese-flavored tomato pasta sauce
1 can (15 oz) tomato sauce
1 teaspoon Italian seasoning
2 bags (25 oz each) frozen cheese-filled ravioli
2 cups shredded mozzarella cheese (8 oz)
1/4 cup chopped fresh parsley, if desired

1. In 4-quart Dutch oven or 12-inch skillet, heat oil over medium heat. Cook onion and garlic in oil about 4 minutes, stirring occasionally, until onion is tender. Stir in pasta sauce, tomato sauce and Italian seasoning.

2. Spray 5- to 6-quart slow cooker with cooking spray. Place 1 cup of the sauce mixture in cooker. Add 1 bag frozen ravioli; top with 1 cup of the cheese. Top with remaining bag of ravioli and 1 cup cheese. Pour remaining sauce mixture over top.

3. Cover; cook on Low heat setting 5 hours 30 minutes to 6 hours 30 minutes. Sprinkle with parsley before serving if desired. Ravioli will hold on Low heat setting up to 30 minutes.

1 serving: Calories 460 (Calories from Fat 190); Total Fat 22g (Saturated Fat 9g; Trans Fat 0g); Cholesterol 160mg; Sodium 1700mg; Total Carbohydrate 40g (Dietary Fiber 3g; Sugars 9g); Protein 26g
% daily value: Vitamin A 25%; Vitamin C 6%; Calcium 50%; Iron 15%   **exchanges:** 2 Starch, 1/2 Other Carbohydrate, 3 Medium-Fat Meat, 1 Fat   **carbohydrate choices:** 2 ½

cheesy chicken ravioli CASSEROLE: **Substitute any chicken-filled ravioli for the cheese-filled ravioli.**

Can't find diced tomatoes with green chilies? Mix a 14.5-ounce can of plain diced tomatoes with an undrained 4.5-ounce can of chopped green chiles.

taco CASSEROLE

prep time: 15 minutes   **start to finish:** 4 hours 20 minutes   4 servings

3 cups frozen soy-protein burger crumbles (from 12-oz package)
1 can (14.5 oz) diced tomatoes with green chilies, undrained
1 can (10 3/4 oz) condensed tomato soup
1 package (1.25 oz) taco seasoning mix
1/2 cup water
6 corn tortillas (5 or 6 inch), cut into 1/2-inch strips
1/2 cup sour cream
1 cup shredded Cheddar cheese (4 oz)
3 medium green onions, sliced (3 tablespoons)

1. Spray 3- to 3 1/2-quart slow cooker with cooking spray. In slow cooker, mix crumbles, tomatoes, soup, seasoning mix (dry) and water. Gently stir in tortilla strips.

2. Cover; cook on Low heat setting 4 to 5 hours. (If slow cooker has black liner, do not cook longer than 5 hours or mixture may burn around edge.)

3. Spread sour cream over casserole; sprinkle with cheese. Cover; let stand about 5 minutes or until cheese is melted. Sprinkle with onions.

1 serving: Calories 470 (Calories from Fat 160); Total Fat 18g (Saturated Fat 10g; Trans Fat 0g); Cholesterol 50mg; Sodium 1750mg; Total Carbohydrate 44g (Dietary Fiber 9g; Sugars 15g); Protein 32g
% daily value: Vitamin A 40%; Vitamin C 20%; Calcium 40%; Iron 25%   **exchanges:** 1 1/2 Starch, 1 Other Carbohydrate, 1 Vegetable, 3 1/2 Lean Meat, 1 1/2 Fat   **carbohydrate choices:** 3

Sweet and crunchy jicama that has been cut into thin strips, drizzled with lime juice and sprinkled with a little salt and paprika would make a nice little side dish for this satisfying meatless meal.

tamale PIE

prep time: 15 minutes   **start to finish:** 4 hours 45 minutes   4 servings

1 medium onion, chopped (1/2 cup)
2 cups frozen soy-protein burger crumbles (from 12-oz package)
1 can (15 to 16 oz) kidney beans, drained, rinsed
1 can (10 oz) enchilada sauce
1 pouch (6.5 oz) golden corn muffin and bread mix
1/3 cup milk
2 tablespoons butter or margarine, melted
1 egg
1/2 cup shredded Colby-Monterey Jack cheese blend (2 oz)
1 can (4.5 oz) chopped green chiles, undrained
1/4 cup sour cream
4 medium green onions, chopped (1/4 cup)

1. Generously spray 8-inch skillet with cooking spray. Add onion; cook over medium heat about 3 minutes, stirring occasionally, until crisp-tender. In 3- to 3 1/2-quart slow cooker, mix crumbles, onion, beans and enchilada sauce.

2. In medium bowl, stir corn bread mix, milk, butter and egg just until moistened (batter will be lumpy). Stir in cheese and chiles. Spoon over mixture in slow cooker.

3. Cover; cook on Low heat setting 4 hours 30 minutes to 5 hours 30 minutes or until toothpick inserted in center of corn bread comes out clean. (If slow cooker has black liner, do not cook longer than 5 hours 30 minutes or mixture may burn around edge.)

4. Serve tamale pie with sour cream and green onions.

1 serving: Calories 590 (Calories from Fat 190); Total Fat 22g (Saturated Fat 10g; Trans Fat 1g); Cholesterol 95mg; Sodium 1360mg; Total Carbohydrate 69g (Dietary Fiber 14g; Sugars 16g); Protein 32g
% daily value: Vitamin A 25%; Vitamin C 15%; Calcium 30%; Iron 40%   **exchanges:** 3 1/2 Starch, 1 Other Carbohydrate, 3 Lean Meat, 2 Fat   **carbohydrate choices:** 4 1/2

This Mexican version of hash is great on its own and is also terrific as a filling for tacos, enchiladas and tostadas.

PICADILLO

prep time: 20 minutes   **start to finish:** 3 hours 20 minutes   12 servings

**4 cups frozen soy-protein burger crumbles
(from two 12-oz packages)**
1 large onion, chopped (1 cup)
1 cup raisins
2 teaspoons chili powder
1 teaspoon salt
3/4 teaspoon ground cinnamon
1/2 teaspoon ground cumin
1/2 teaspoon pepper
2 cloves garlic, finely chopped
2 medium apples, peeled, chopped (2 cups)
**2 cans (10 oz each) diced tomatoes with green chilies,
undrained**
1/2 cup slivered almonds, toasted*

1. In 3- to 4-quart slow cooker, mix all ingredients except almonds.

2. Cover; cook on Low heat setting 3 to 4 hours. (If slow cooker has black liner, do not cook longer than 4 hours or mixture may burn around edge.)

3. Stir in almonds before serving.

★To toast nuts, bake uncovered in ungreased shallow pan in 350°F oven 6 to 10 minutes, stirring occasionally, until golden brown. Or cook in ungreased heavy skillet over medium-low heat 5 to 7 minutes, stirring frequently until browning begins, then stirring constantly until golden brown.

1 serving: Calories 160 (Calories from Fat 30); Total Fat 3g (Saturated Fat 0g; Trans Fat 0g); Cholesterol 0mg; Sodium 520mg; Total Carbohydrate 22g (Dietary Fiber 5g; Sugars 12g); Protein 11g
% daily value: Vitamin A 6%; Vitamin C 6%; Calcium 8%; Iron 10%   **exchanges:** 1/2 Starch, 1 Fruit, 1 1/2 Very Lean Meat, 1/2 Fat
carbohydrate choices: 1 1/2

Get a leg up with legumes—they're an excellent source of protein, each serving of this casserole provides a delicious 17 grams of protein.

mediterranean minestrone
CASSEROLE (LOW fat)

prep time: 20 minutes   **start to finish:** 6 hours 40 minutes   5 servings

3 medium carrots, sliced (1 1/2 cups)
1 medium onion, chopped (1/2 cup)
1 cup water
2 teaspoons sugar
1 teaspoon Italian seasoning
1/2 teaspoon salt
1/4 teaspoon pepper
1 can (28 oz) diced tomatoes, undrained
1 can (15 to 16 oz) garbanzo beans, drained, rinsed
1 can (6 oz) Italian-style tomato paste
2 cloves garlic, finely chopped
1 1/2 cups frozen cut green beans (from 1-lb bag), thawed
1 cup uncooked elbow macaroni (3 1/2 oz)
1/2 cup shredded Parmesan cheese (2 oz)

1. In 3- to 4-quart slow cooker, mix all ingredients except green beans, macaroni and cheese.

2. Cover; cook on Low heat setting 6 to 8 hours.

3. Stir in green beans and macaroni. Increase heat setting to High. Cover; cook about 20 minutes or until beans and macaroni are tender. Sprinkle with cheese.

1 serving: Calories 360 (Calories from Fat 50); Total Fat 6g (Saturated Fat 2g; Trans Fat 0g); Cholesterol 10mg; Sodium 1050mg; Total Carbohydrate 59g (Dietary Fiber 11g; Sugars 10g); Protein 17g

% daily value: Vitamin A 170%; Vitamin C 35%; Calcium 25%; Iron 30%   **exchanges:** 3 Starch, 1/2 Other Carbohydrate, 2 Vegetable, 1/2 Lean Meat, 1/2 Fat   **carbohydrate choices:** 4

Barley is the perfect grain to cook in the slow cooker. The long, slow cooking makes the barley tender but not gummy, and more good news—barley packs a big fiber punch. Serve this casserole with steamed edamame for a great side dish, as well as extra protein.

barley–pine nut CASSEROLE (LOW fat)

prep time: 15 minutes   **start to finish:** 6 hours 15 minutes   5 servings

1 cup uncooked pearl barley
1 1/2 cups vegetable juice
1/2 teaspoon salt
1/4 teaspoon pepper
2 medium stalks celery, sliced (1 cup)
1 medium bell pepper, chopped (1 cup)
1 medium onion, chopped (1/2 cup)
1 can (14 oz) vegetable broth
4 medium green onions, sliced (1/4 cup)
1/4 cup pine nuts, toasted*

1. In 3- to 4-quart slow cooker, mix all ingredients except green onions and nuts.

2. Cover; cook on Low heat setting 6 to 8 hours.

3. Stir in green onions and nuts.

To toast nuts, bake uncovered in ungreased shallow pan in 350°F oven 6 to 10 minutes, stirring occasionally, until golden brown. Or cook in ungreased heavy skillet over medium-low heat 5 to 7 minutes, stirring frequently until browning begins, then stirring constantly until golden brown.

1 serving: Calories 230 (Calories from Fat 35); Total Fat 4g (Saturated Fat 0.5g; Trans Fat 0g); Cholesterol 0mg; Sodium 790mg; Total Carbohydrate 41g (Dietary Fiber 9g; Sugars 6g); Protein 7g
% daily value: Vitamin A 30%; Vitamin C 40%; Calcium 4%; Iron 15%   **exchanges:** 2 Starch, 1/2 Other Carbohydrate, 1 Vegetable, 1/2 Fat
carbohydrate choices: 3

If you're a salt watcher, by all means use the reduced-sodium, reduced-fat variety of condensed cream of mushroom soup in this tasty Asian dish.

easy CHOP SUEY

prep time: 15 minutes   **start to finish:** 6 hours 30 minutes   8 servings

Cooking spray
1 medium onion, chopped (1/2 cup)
2 medium stalks celery, coarsely chopped (1 cup)
2 cups frozen sausage-style soy-protein crumbles (from 12-oz package)
1/3 cup uncooked regular long-grain rice
1/4 teaspoon pepper
1/4 cup reduced-sodium soy sauce
2 cups water
1 can (10 3/4 oz) condensed cream of mushroom soup
1 bag (1 lb) frozen seven-vegetable stir-fry, thawed
4 cups crisp chow mein noodles

1. Spray 4- to 5-quart slow cooker with cooking spray. Generously spray 12-inch skillet with cooking spray. Add onion and celery; generously spray with cooking spray. Cook about 5 minutes, stirring frequently, until crisp-tender. Stir in remaining ingredients except stir-fry vegetables and noodles. Spoon into slow cooker.

2. Cover; cook on Low heat setting 6 to 7 hours. (If slow cooker has black liner, do not cook longer than 7 hours or mixture may burn around edge.)

3. Stir in stir-fry vegetables. Increase heat setting to High. Cover; cook about 15 minutes longer or until vegetables are tender. Serve with noodles.

1 serving: Calories 260 (Calories from Fat 90); Total Fat 10g (Saturated Fat 1.5g; Trans Fat 0g); Cholesterol 0mg; Sodium 910mg; Total Carbohydrate 31g (Dietary Fiber 4g; Sugars 3g); Protein 12g
% daily value: Vitamin A 10%; Vitamin C 20%; Calcium 8%; Iron 20%   **exchanges:** 1 1/2 Starch, 1 Vegetable, 1 Very Lean Meat, 2 Fat
carbohydrate choices: 2

Here's an easy idea for an after-work party on a Friday night! Cook the potatoes all day in the slow cooker. When you get home, put out additional hearty toppings, like drained and rinsed canned beans, edamame or chopped flavored tofu or tempeh. TGIF!

baked potato BAR

prep time: 10 minutes   **start to finish:** 6 hours 10 minutes   12 servings

12 unpeeled russet potatoes (6 to 8 oz each)
2 tablespoons olive or vegetable oil
1 1/2 teaspoons salt
1 teaspoon coarse black pepper
1 cup sour cream
1/4 cup bacon flavor bits
1 1/2 cups shredded cheese (6 oz)
4 medium green onions, sliced (1/4 cup)

1. Pierce potatoes with fork. In large plastic food-storage bag, place potatoes and oil; toss to coat potatoes with oil. Sprinkle with salt and pepper. Wrap potatoes individually in foil. In 5- to 6-quart slow cooker, place wrapped potatoes.

2. Cover; cook on Low heat setting 6 to 8 hours.

3. Serve potatoes with remaining ingredients as toppings. Potatoes will hold on Low heat setting up to 2 hours.

1 serving: Calories 230 (Calories from Fat 100); Total Fat 11g (Saturated Fat 6g; Trans Fat 0g); Cholesterol 30mg; Sodium 420mg; Total Carbohydrate 24g (Dietary Fiber 2g; Sugars 2g); Protein 7g
% daily value: Vitamin A 6%; Vitamin C 10%; Calcium 10%; Iron 4%   **exchanges:** 1 1/2 Starch, 1/2 High-Fat Meat, 1 Fat
carbohydrate choices: 1 1/2

baked potato BAR

Serve with bowls of chopped red onion and hard-cooked eggs to sprinkle on top for traditional black beans and rice. Or instead of rice, top each serving of beans with a poached egg and sprinkle with shredded Cheddar cheese and chopped fresh cilantro.

cuban BLACK BEANS AND RICE

prep time: 20 minutes   **start to finish:** 6 hours 20 minutes   6 servings

1 lb dried black beans (2 cups), sorted, rinsed
1 large onion, chopped (1 cup)
1 large bell pepper, chopped (1 1/2 cups)
5 cloves garlic, finely chopped
2 dried bay leaves
1 can (14.5 oz) diced tomatoes, undrained
5 cups water
2 tablespoons olive or vegetable oil
4 teaspoons ground cumin
2 teaspoons finely chopped jalapeño chili
1 teaspoon salt
3 cups hot cooked rice

1. In 3- to 4-quart slow cooker, mix all ingredients except rice.

2. Cover; cook on High heat setting 6 to 8 hours.

3. Remove bay leaves. Serve beans over rice.

1 serving: Calories 430 (Calories from Fat 60); Total Fat 6g (Saturated Fat 1g; Trans Fat 0g); Cholesterol 0mg; Sodium 510mg; Total Carbohydrate 73g (Dietary Fiber 18g; Sugars 9g); Protein 20g
% daily value: Vitamin A 8%; Vitamin C 30%; Calcium 10%; Iron 35%   **exchanges:** 4 Starch, 1/2 Other Carbohydrate, 1 Vegetable, 1 Very Lean Meat, 1/2 Fat   **carbohydrate choices:** 5

Our test kitchen has good results using instant rice in slow cooker recipes. Instant rice is fully or partially cooked before dehydration and packaging. It produces less starch, so the finished dish is not as sticky as in some dishes using regular long-grain rice, and it's easier to cook everything all in one pot! The beans are great topped with chopped avocado and sliced green onion.

RED BEANS AND RICE (LOW fat)

prep time: 20 minutes   **start to finish:** 4 hours 40 minutes   8 servings

1 lb dried kidney beans (2 cups), sorted, rinsed
1 large green bell pepper, chopped (1 1/2 cups)
1 large onion, chopped (1 cup)
2 cloves garlic, finely chopped
7 cups water
1 1/2 teaspoons salt
1/4 teaspoon pepper
2 cups uncooked instant rice
Red pepper sauce

1. In 4- to 5-quart slow cooker, mix all ingredients except rice and pepper sauce.

2. Cover; cook on High heat setting 4 to 5 hours.

3. Stir in rice. Cover; cook on High heat setting 15 to 20 minutes or until rice is tender. Serve with pepper sauce.

1 serving: Calories 300 (Calories from Fat 10); Total Fat 1g (Saturated Fat 0g; Trans Fat 0g); Cholesterol 0mg; Sodium 450mg; Total Carbohydrate 57g (Dietary Fiber 10g; Sugars 3g); Protein 14g
% daily value: Vitamin A 0%; Vitamin C 20%; Calcium 6%; Iron 30%   **exchanges:** 4 Starch   **carbohydrate choices:** 4

On the side, how about a large tossed crisp green salad dressed with an olive oil–balsamic vinaigrette, slices of French baguette and a great red wine?

WHITE BEANS with sun-dried tomatoes (LOW fat)

prep time: 10 minutes   **start to finish:** 4 hours 10 minutes   4 servings

1 lb dried great northern beans (2 cups), sorted, rinsed
2 cloves garlic, finely chopped
6 cups water
1 1/2 teaspoons dried basil leaves
1 teaspoon salt
1/4 teaspoon pepper
3/4 cup finely chopped sun-dried tomatoes in olive oil
1 can (2 1/4 oz) sliced ripe olives, drained

1. In 3- to 4-quart slow cooker, mix all ingredients except tomatoes and olives.

2. Cover; cook on High heat setting 4 to 5 hours.

3. Stir in tomatoes and olives.

1 serving: Calories 470 (Calories from Fat 50); Total Fat 6g (Saturated Fat 1g; Trans Fat 0g); Cholesterol 0mg; Sodium 810mg; Total Carbohydrate 77g (Dietary Fiber 20g; Sugars 4g); Protein 29g
% daily value: Vitamin A 8%; Vitamin C 20%; Calcium 30%; Iron 60%   **exchanges:** 5 Starch, 2 Very Lean Meat, 1/2 Fat
carbohydrate choices: 5

Mmm, serve with corn bread slathered with butter, coleslaw and tall glasses of lemonade.

tex-mex PINTO BEANS (LOW fat)

prep time: 10 minutes   **start to finish:** 7 hours 10 minutes   4 servings

1 lb dried pinto beans (2 cups), sorted, rinsed
1 large onion, chopped (1 cup)
2 cloves garlic, finely chopped
6 1/2 cups water
1 tablespoon chili powder
1 1/2 teaspoons salt
1/2 teaspoon pepper

1. In 3- to 4-quart slow cooker, mix all ingredients.

2. Cover; cook on High heat setting 7 to 9 hours.

1 serving: Calories 400 (Calories from Fat 15); Total Fat 2g (Saturated Fat 0g; Trans Fat 0g); Cholesterol 0mg; Sodium 920mg; Total Carbohydrate 73g (Dietary Fiber 24g; Sugars 5g); Protein 23g
% daily value: Vitamin A 15%; Vitamin C 8%; Calcium 15%; Iron 40%   **exchanges:** 5 Starch, 1 Very Lean Meat   **carbohydrate choices:** 5

Cooked greens, like spinach, mustard or collards, are perfect mates for black-eyed peas. Serve the greens with red wine vinegar to splash on top. Add a special touch to the black-eyed peas by topping each serving with sour cream and salsa.

spicy BLACK-EYED PEAS (LOW fat)

prep time: 5 minutes   **start to finish:** 3 hours 15 minutes   8 servings

1 lb dried black-eyed peas (2 cups), sorted, rinsed
1 medium onion, chopped (1/2 cup)
6 cups water
1 teaspoon salt
1/2 teaspoon pepper
3/4 cup medium or hot chunky-style salsa

1. In 3- to 4-quart slow cooker, mix all ingredients except salsa.

2. Cover; cook on High heat setting 3 to 4 hours.

3. Stir in salsa. Cover; cook on High heat setting about 10 minutes or until hot.

1 serving: Calories 200 (Calories from Fat 10); Total Fat 1g (Saturated Fat 0g; Trans Fat 0g); Cholesterol 0mg; Sodium 480mg; Total Carbohydrate 36g (Dietary Fiber 11g; Sugars 4g); Protein 12g
% daily value: Vitamin A 0%; Vitamin C 0%; Calcium 4%; Iron 20%   **exchanges:** 2 1/2 Starch, 1/2 Very Lean Meat
carbohydrate choices: 2 1/2

Want to make this even easier? Use a drained 8-ounce can of sliced mushrooms instead of the fresh mushrooms. Skip the sautéing in step 3 and just add the canned mushrooms, carrots, onions and garlic to the cooked beans. Stir in a tablespoon of olive oil for added flavor.

SAVORY GARBANZO BEANS
with vegetables (LOW fat)

prep time: 15 minutes **start to finish:** 4 hours 30 minutes 8 servings

1 lb dried garbanzo beans (2 cups), sorted, rinsed
5 1/2 cups water
1 teaspoon salt
1/2 teaspoon pepper
2 tablespoons olive or vegetable oil
2 cups sliced fresh mushrooms
1 cup shredded carrots (1 1/2 medium)
4 medium green onions, thinly sliced (1/4 cup)
2 cloves garlic, finely chopped
2 tablespoons lemon juice
1 to 2 tablespoons prepared horseradish
2 teaspoons yellow mustard

1. In 4- to 5-quart slow cooker, place beans, water, salt and pepper.

2. Cover; cook on High heat setting 4 to 5 hours.

3. In 12-inch skillet, heat oil over medium heat. Cook mushrooms, carrots, onions and garlic in oil about 5 minutes, stirring occasionally, until vegetables are tender. Stir vegetables into beans. Stir in remaining ingredients.

4. Cover; cook on High heat setting 15 minutes to blend flavors.

1 serving: Calories 250 (Calories from Fat 60); Total Fat 7g (Saturated Fat 1g; Trans Fat 0g); Cholesterol 0mg; Sodium 330mg; Total Carbohydrate 36g (Dietary Fiber 10g; Sugars 3g); Protein 11g
% daily value: Vitamin A 50%; Vitamin C 6%; Calcium 8%; Iron 20% **exchanges:** 2 1/2 Starch, 1/2 Very Lean Meat, 1 Fat
carbohydrate choices: 2 1/2

Baked beans can be eaten as an entrée or served alongside a grilled veggie burger. To serve these beans as a side dish, you may want to cut the recipe in half and cook it in a 2- to 3 1/2-quart slow cooker.

old-fashioned BAKED BEANS (LOW fat)

prep time: 10 minutes   **start to finish:** 20 hours 10 minutes   6 servings

2 lb dried navy beans (4 cups), sorted, rinsed
9 cups water
2/3 cup packed brown sugar
2/3 cup molasses
1 tablespoon yellow mustard
1 teaspoon salt
1 large onion, chopped (1 cup)

1. In 4- to 5-quart slow cooker, place beans and water.

2. Cover; cook on High heat setting 2 hours. Turn off heat; let stand 8 hours to 24 hours.

3. Stir in remaining ingredients.

4. Cover; cook on Low heat setting 10 to 12 hours.

1 serving: Calories 720 (Calories from Fat 20); Total Fat 2g (Saturated Fat 0.5g; Trans Fat 0g); Cholesterol 0mg; Sodium 460mg; Total Carbohydrate 145g (Dietary Fiber 23g; Sugars 55g); Protein 31g
% daily value: Vitamin A 0%; Vitamin C 4%; Calcium 35%; Iron 60%   **exchanges:** 5 1/2 Starch, 4 Other Carbohydrate, 2 Very Lean Meat
carbohydrate choices: 9

Whip up a bowl of cooling yogurt-mint sauce to dollop on each serving. To make, stir together an 8-ounce container of plain yogurt and 1 tablespoon chopped fresh or 1 1/2 teaspoons dried mint leaves.

mediterranean BULGUR AND LENTILS

prep time: 15 minutes   **start to finish:** 3 hours 30 minutes   8 servings

1 cup uncooked bulgur or cracked wheat
1/2 cup dried lentils, sorted, rinsed
1 teaspoon ground cumin
1/4 teaspoon salt
3 cloves garlic, finely chopped
1 can (15.25 oz) whole kernel corn, drained
2 cans (14 oz each) vegetable broth
2 medium tomatoes, chopped (1 1/2 cups)
1 can (2 1/4 oz) sliced ripe olives, drained
1 cup crumbled feta cheese

1. In 3- to 4-quart slow cooker, mix all ingredients except tomatoes, olives and cheese.

2. Cover; cook on Low heat setting 3 to 4 hours.

3. Stir in tomatoes and olives. Increase heat setting to High. Cover; cook 15 minutes. Sprinkle each serving with cheese.

1 serving: Calories 220 (Calories from Fat 50); Total Fat 6g (Saturated Fat 3g; Trans Fat 0g); Cholesterol 15mg; Sodium 880mg; Total Carbohydrate 33g (Dietary Fiber 7g; Sugars 4g); Protein 10g
% daily value: Vitamin A 15%; Vitamin C 10%; Calcium 10%; Iron 15%   **exchanges:** 2 Starch, 1/2 Medium-Fat Meat, 1/2 Fat
carbohydrate choices: 2

Lentils are often used as a meat substitute—delicious, easy to cook and so versatile. They're also a good source of iron and phosphorus and contain calcium and vitamins A and B. If you'd like, sprinkle 1 cup shredded cheese on top of the casserole during the last 5 minutes of cooking.

lentil and mixed-vegetable
CASSEROLE (LOW fat)

prep time: 5 minutes **start to finish:** 2 hours 35 minutes 8 servings

1 lb dried lentils (2 cups), sorted, rinsed
2 cans (14 oz each) vegetable broth
1/2 teaspoon salt
1/4 teaspoon pepper
1 bag (1 lb) frozen broccoli, carrots and cauliflower, thawed, drained
1 can (10 3/4 oz) condensed golden mushroom soup

1. In 3- to 4-quart slow cooker, mix lentils, broth, salt and pepper.

2. Cover; cook on Low heat setting 2 hours to 2 hours 30 minutes.

3. Stir in vegetables and soup. Cover; cook on Low heat setting about 30 minutes or until vegetable are tender.

1 serving: Calories 220 (Calories from Fat 10); Total Fat 1g (Saturated Fat 0g; Trans Fat 0g); Cholesterol 0mg; Sodium 700mg; Total Carbohydrate 37g (Dietary Fiber 11g; Sugars 3g); Protein 16g
% daily value: Vitamin A 40%; Vitamin C 20%; Calcium 4%; Iron 30% **exchanges:** 2 Starch, 1 Vegetable, 1 Very Lean Meat
carbohydrate choices: 2 1/2

lentil and mixed-vegetable CASSEROLE

This all-purpose sauce is so easy to make that you'll want to cook it often and keep a few extra containers in the freezer. Ladle the cooked sauce into airtight freezer containers; cover and freeze up to 1 month.

MARINARA SAUCE with spaghetti

prep time: 25 minutes   **start to finish:** 8 hours 25 minutes   12 servings

2 cans (28 oz each) crushed tomatoes with Italian herbs, undrained
1 can (6 oz) tomato paste
1 large onion, chopped (1 cup)
8 cloves garlic, finely chopped
1 tablespoon olive or vegetable oil
2 teaspoons sugar
2 teaspoons dried basil leaves
1 teaspoon dried oregano leaves
1 teaspoon salt
1 teaspoon pepper
24 oz uncooked spaghetti
Shredded Parmesan cheese, if desired

1. In 3 1/2- to 4-quart slow cooker, mix all ingredients except spaghetti and cheese.

2. Cover; cook on Low heat setting 8 to 10 hours.

3. Cook and drain spaghetti as directed on package. Serve sauce over spaghetti. Sprinkle with cheese if desired.

1 serving: Calories 260 (Calories from Fat 20); Total Fat 2.5g (Saturated Fat 0g; Trans Fat 0g); Cholesterol 0mg; Sodium 510mg; Total Carbohydrate 51g (Dietary Fiber 5g; Sugars 5g); Protein 9g
% daily value: Vitamin A 15%; Vitamin C 20%; Calcium 6%; Iron 20%   **exchanges:** 3 Starch, 1 Vegetable   **carbohydrate choices:** 3 1/2

Parsnips are root vegetables that look like a creamy white carrot but have a slightly sweet flavor. Go ahead and substitute carrots if you don't have parsnips. Sprinkle the stew with chopped fresh chives or thyme leaves or shredded Parmesan cheese for extra zip.

winter vegetable STEW

(LOW fat)

prep time: 20 minutes   **start to finish:** 8 hours 40 minutes   6 servings

1 can (28 oz) Italian-style peeled whole tomatoes
4 medium red potatoes, cut into 1/2-inch pieces
4 medium stalks celery, cut into 1/2-inch pieces (2 cups)
3 medium carrots, cut into 1/2-inch pieces (1 1/2 cups)
2 medium parsnips, peeled, cut into 1/2-inch pieces
2 medium leeks, cut into 1/2-inch pieces
1 can (14 oz) vegetable broth
1/2 teaspoon salt
1/2 teaspoon dried thyme leaves
1/2 teaspoon dried rosemary leaves
3 tablespoons cornstarch
3 tablespoons cold water

1. Drain tomatoes, reserving liquid. Cut up tomatoes. In 4- to 5-quart slow cooker, mix tomatoes, tomato liquid and remaining ingredients except cornstarch and water.

2. Cover; cook on Low heat setting 8 to 10 hours.

3. In small bowl, mix cornstarch and water; gradually stir into stew until blended. Increase heat setting to High. Cover; cook about 20 minutes, stirring occasionally, until thickened.

1 serving: Calories 180 (Calories from Fat 0); Total Fat 0.5g (Saturated Fat 0g; Trans Fat 0g); Cholesterol 0mg; Sodium 720mg; Total Carbohydrate 39g (Dietary Fiber 7g; Sugars 9g); Protein 4g
% daily value: Vitamin A 130%; Vitamin C 40%; Calcium 10%; Iron 15%   **exchanges:** 1/2 Starch, 1 1/2 Other Carbohydrate, 2 Vegetable
carbohydrate choices: 2 1/2

Black beans, also called turtle beans, have long been popular in Latin American and Caribbean cooking. Black on the outside and a creamy color inside, these beans have a sweet flavor. Pinched for time? Soak the beans in cold water overnight rather than using the quick-soak method in the recipe.

zesty black bean SOUP (LOW fat)

prep time: 10 minutes   **start to finish:** 11 hours 35 minutes   9 servings

1 lb dried black beans (2 cups), sorted, rinsed
10 cups water
8 cups vegetable broth
2 cans (14.5 oz each) no-salt-added stewed tomatoes, undrained
2 medium carrots, coarsely chopped (1 cup)
2 medium onions, coarsely chopped (1 cup)
1/4 cup chopped fresh cilantro
2 teaspoons finely chopped garlic
1/4 teaspoon pepper
1/8 teaspoon ground red pepper (cayenne)
Reduced-fat sour cream, if desired
Additional chopped fresh cilantro, if desired

1. In 4-quart Dutch oven, heat beans and water to boiling; reduce heat. Simmer uncovered 10 minutes; remove from heat. Cover and let stand 1 hour.

2. Drain beans. In 6-quart slow cooker, place beans and remaining ingredients except sour cream and additional cilantro.

3. Cover; cook on Low heat setting 10 to 12 hours.

4. Serve soup topped with sour cream and additional cilantro if desired.

1 serving: Calories 220 (Calories from Fat 5); Total Fat 0.5g (Saturated Fat 0g; Trans Fat 0g); Cholesterol 0mg; Sodium 920mg; Total Carbohydrate 42g (Dietary Fiber 12g; Sugars 12g); Protein 13g
% daily value: Vitamin A 70%; Vitamin C 10%; Calcium 8%; Iron 20%   **exchanges:** 1 1/2 Starch, 1 Other Carbohydrate, 1 Vegetable, 1 Very Lean Meat   **carbohydrate choices:** 3

SLOW COOKER tips

Slow cookers require almost no clock watching. For the most part, you can make the recipe, turn on the cooker and forget about it until it's ready. For the best slow cooker meals, use these tips:

Spray the inside of your slow cooker with cooking spray for easy cleanup.

Recipes using soy-protein crumbles absorb liquids, take less time to cook than traditional meat-based recipes (most recipes in this book cook in the slow cooker in less than 6 hours) and can begin to burn around the edges if cooked longer than the times given in the recipe. Follow slow cooker recipes developed specifically for using soy-protein crumbles for best results.

Root vegetables, like potatoes and carrots, take longer to cook than other vegetables, so cut them into smaller pieces and put at the bottom of the cooker.

Use dried herb leaves instead of ground because they keep their flavor better during long cook times.

Ground red pepper (cayenne) and red pepper sauce tend to become bitter during long, slow cooking. Use small amounts and taste during the last hour of cooking to decide whether you need to add more.

A Low setting is frequently used because longer cooking times fit well into workday schedules. Fast-forward the cooking time by turning the slow cooker to High for 1 hour, which equals 2 hours on Low (except for recipes using soy-protein crumbles—follow recipe directions for best results).

Don't peek! Removing the cover lets heat escape, adding 15 to 20 minutes to the cooking time. Can't wait to see inside? Try spinning the cover until the condensation and steam clears.

Stir in fresh herbs during the last hour of cooking so they stay flavorful. Some herbs, like oregano and basil, lose flavor with an extended cooking time.

Add tender vegetables, like fresh tomatoes, mushrooms and zucchini, during the last 30 minutes of cooking so they don't become overcooked and mushy.

Frozen vegetables that have been thawed will keep their bright color and crisp-tender texture by adding them during the last 30 minutes of cooking.

Dairy products, like milk, sour cream and cheese, tend to curdle. To help prevent curdling, add them during the last 30 minutes of cooking.

Most cooked food can be held up to an hour on the "low" heat setting without overcooking.

For more texture and a little extra flavor, sprinkle slow cooker meals with chopped fresh herbs, grated cheese, crushed croutons or corn chips, chopped tomatoes or sliced green onions just before serving.

An Indian method of cooking the spices together before they are added to the other ingredients is used here and gives this curry its wonderful flavor.

curried sweet potato and lentil STEW

LOW fat

prep time: 15 minutes   **start to finish:** 5 hours 30 minutes   6 servings

3 cups pieces (1 inch) peeled dark-orange sweet potatoes
1 1/2 cups ready-to-eat baby-cut carrots
1 small onion, finely chopped (1/4 cup)
3/4 cup dried lentils, sorted, rinsed
2 teaspoons olive or vegetable oil
1 tablespoon curry powder
1 teaspoon ground cumin
1/2 teaspoon salt
1/4 teaspoon pepper
1 teaspoon finely chopped gingerroot
1 clove garlic, finely chopped
1 can (14 oz) vegetable broth
2 cups frozen cut green beans (from 1-lb bag), thawed
1/2 cup plain fat-free yogurt

1. In 3 1/2- to 4-quart slow cooker, mix sweet potatoes, carrots, onion and lentils.

2. In 8-inch skillet, heat oil over medium heat. Add curry powder, cumin, salt, pepper, gingerroot and garlic. Cook 1 minute, stirring constantly. Stir in broth. Pour mixture into slow cooker; stir.

3. Cover; cook on Low heat setting 5 to 6 hours.

4. Increase heat setting to High. Stir in green beans. Cover; cook about 15 minutes or until green beans are crisp-tender.

5. Serve topped with yogurt.

1 serving: Calories 220 (Calories from Fat 20); Total Fat 2g (Saturated Fat 0g; Trans Fat 0g); Cholesterol 0mg; Sodium 720mg; Total Carbohydrate 39g (Dietary Fiber 9g; Sugars 15g); Protein 10g
% daily value: Vitamin A 330%; Vitamin C 20%; Calcium 10%; Iron 20%   **exchanges:** 1 1/2 Starch, 1 Other Carbohydrate, 1 Very Lean Meat   **carbohydrate choices:** 2 1/2

curried sweet potato and lentil STEW

Many shapes of pasta are available, so use any short-cut pasta in place of the elbow macaroni. For a different "twist," try rotini, gemelli or fusilli.

two-bean MINESTRONE

prep time: 10 minutes   **start to finish:** 8 hours 25 minutes   6 servings

1 can (15 to 16 oz) dark red kidney beans, drained
1 can (15 to 16 oz) garbanzo beans, drained
1 bag (1 lb) frozen mixed vegetables
1 can (14.5 oz) diced tomatoes with basil, garlic and oregano, undrained
1 large vegetarian vegetable bouillon cube
1 can (11 oz) vegetable juice
1 cup water
1/2 cup uncooked elbow macaroni
1 container (7 oz) refrigerated basil pesto

1. In 3 1/2- to 4-quart slow cooker, mix all ingredients except macaroni and pesto.

2. Cover; cook on Low heat setting 8 to 10 hours.

3. Stir in macaroni. Cover; cook on Low heat setting about 15 minutes or until macaroni is tender. Top each serving with spoonful of pesto.

1 serving: Calories 450 (Calories from Fat 180); Total Fat 20g (Saturated Fat 4g; Trans Fat 0g); Cholesterol 5mg; Sodium 970mg; Total Carbohydrate 51g (Dietary Fiber 12g; Sugars 5g); Protein 18g
% daily value: Vitamin A 70%; Vitamin C 45%; Calcium 25%; Iron 30%   **exchanges:** 3 Starch, 1 Vegetable, 1 Very Lean Meat, 3 1/2 Fat
carbohydrate choices: 3 1/2

Aprés-ski, or aprés sledding anyone? Put everything in the slow cooker in the morning and then go play! A mixed fresh fruit salad splashed with a little honey and lime or lemon juice and crusty hard rolls would taste great next to this rich soup.

creamy split pea SOUP (LOW fat)

prep time: 20 minutes   **start to finish:** 10 hours 50 minutes   8 servings

1 lb dried green split peas (2 cups), sorted, rinsed
6 cups water
1/2 cup dry sherry or apple juice
1 large dark-orange sweet potato, peeled, cubed (2 cups)
1 large onion, chopped (1 cup)
4 cloves garlic, finely chopped
2 teaspoons salt
3 cups firmly packed chopped fresh spinach leaves
1 cup whipping (heavy) cream
2 tablespoons chopped fresh dill weed
Freshly ground pepper to taste

1. In 3 1/2- to 4-quart slow cooker, mix split peas, water, sherry, sweet potato, onion, garlic and salt.

2. Cover; cook on Low heat setting 10 to 11 hours.

3. Stir in spinach, whipping cream and dill weed. Cover; cook on Low heat setting about 30 minutes or until spinach is wilted. Season with pepper.

1 serving: Calories 300 (Calories from Fat 90); Total Fat 10g (Saturated Fat 6g; Trans Fat 0g); Cholesterol 35mg; Sodium 620mg; Total Carbohydrate 39g (Dietary Fiber 16g; Sugars 7g); Protein 13g
% daily value: Vitamin A 100%; Vitamin C 10%; Calcium 6%; Iron 15%   **exchanges:** 2 Starch, 1/2 Other Carbohydrate, 1 Very Lean Meat, 1 1/2 Fat   **carbohydrate choices:** 2 1/2

CREAMY SPLIT PEA SOUP with ham: Add 1 cup diced fully cooked turkey ham with the peas. Decrease salt to 1 teaspoon.

This wonderfully rich and flavorful soup became a staff favorite while being tested in our kitchens! Try sprinkling with chopped toasted walnuts, pecans or pumpkin seeds. Adding grilled cheese sandwiches is a nice way to round out the meal—for dessert think apple pie or comforting baked apples.

butternut squash SOUP

prep time: 15 minutes   **start to finish:** 6 hours 45 minutes   6 servings

2 tablespoons butter or margarine
1 medium onion, chopped (1/2 cup)
1 butternut squash (2 lb), peeled, cubed
2 cups water
1/2 teaspoon dried marjoram leaves
1/4 teaspoon ground black pepper
1/8 teaspoon ground red pepper (cayenne)
2 extra-large vegetarian vegetable bouillon cubes
1 package (8 oz) cream cheese, cubed

1. In 10-inch skillet, melt butter over medium heat. Cook onion in butter, stirring occasionally, until crisp-tender.

2. In 3 1/2- to 4-quart slow cooker, mix onion and remaining ingredients except cream cheese.

3. Cover; cook on Low heat setting 6 to 8 hours.

4. In blender or food processor, place one-third to one-half of the soup mixture at a time. Cover; blend on high speed until smooth. Return mixture to slow cooker. Using wire whisk, stir in cream cheese. Cover; cook on Low heat setting about 30 minutes, stirring occasionally with wire whisk, until cheese is melted and soup is smooth.

1 serving: Calories 240 (Calories from Fat 160); Total Fat 17g (Saturated Fat 10g; Trans Fat 0.5g); Cholesterol 50mg; Sodium 1220mg; Total Carbohydrate 15g (Dietary Fiber 2g; Sugars 6g); Protein 5g
% daily value: Vitamin A 210%; Vitamin C 15%; Calcium 10%; Iron 8%   **exchanges:** 1 Starch, 3 1/2 Fat   **carbohydrate choices:** 1

butternut squash SOUP

This hearty vegetarian soup needs only thick slices of a whole-grain bread to complete the meal. It wouldn't hurt to add a little hummus to spread on the bread, or to serve a nice wedge of cheese such as Swiss or Gouda.

tomato-rotini SOUP (LOW fat)

prep time: 15 minutes   **start to finish:** 8 hours 35 minutes   12 servings

4 cups vegetable broth
4 cups tomato juice
1 tablespoon dried basil leaves
1 teaspoon salt
1/2 teaspoon dried oregano leaves
1/4 teaspoon pepper
2 medium carrots, sliced (1 cup)
2 medium stalks celery, chopped (1 cup)
1 medium onion, chopped (1/2 cup)
1 cup sliced fresh mushrooms
2 cloves garlic, finely chopped
1 can (28 oz) diced tomatoes, undrained
1 1/2 cups uncooked rotini pasta (4 1/2 oz)
Shredded Parmesan cheese, if desired

1. In 4- to 5-quart slow cooker, mix all ingredients except pasta and cheese.

2. Cover; cook on Low heat setting 8 to 9 hours.

3. Stir in pasta. Increase heat setting to High. Cover; cook 15 to 20 minutes or until pasta is tender. Sprinkle each serving with cheese if desired.

1 serving: Calories 90 (Calories from Fat 0); Total Fat 0g (Saturated Fat 0g; Trans Fat 0g); Cholesterol 0mg; Sodium 930mg; Total Carbohydrate 18g (Dietary Fiber 2g; Sugars 6g); Protein 3g
% daily value: Vitamin A 60%; Vitamin C 20%; Calcium 4%; Iron 8%   **exchanges:** 1 Starch, 1 Vegetable   **carbohydrate choices:** 1

Traditional French onion soup uses beef broth, giving it a rich, deep brown color but making it off limits for vegetarians, This equally appealing version uses vegetable broth so Golden French Onion Soup is a more appropriate name. Bon appétit!

golden french onion SOUP (LOW fat)

prep time: 20 minutes   **start to finish:** 7 hours 20 minutes   8 servings

SOUP
3 large onions, sliced (3 cups)
3 tablespoons butter or margarine, melted
3 tablespoons all-purpose flour
1 tablespoon Worcestershire sauce
1 teaspoon sugar
1/4 teaspoon pepper
4 cans (14 oz each) vegetable broth

CHEESY BROILED FRENCH BREAD
8 slices French bread, 1 inch thick
3/4 cup shredded mozzarella cheese (3 oz)
2 tablespoons grated or shredded Parmesan cheese

1. In 3 1/2- to 4-quart slow cooker, mix onions and butter. In small bowl, mix flour, Worcestershire sauce, sugar and pepper. Stir flour mixture and broth into onions.

2. Cover; cook on Low heat setting 7 to 9 hours.

3. Set oven control to broil. On rack in broiler pan, place bread slices. Sprinkle with cheeses. Broil with tops 5 to 6 inches from heat about 3 minutes or until cheese is melted. Place 1 slice bread on top of each bowl of soup. Serve immediately.

1 serving: Calories 220 (Calories from Fat 80); Total Fat 8g (Saturated Fat 4g; Trans Fat 0.5g); Cholesterol 20mg; Sodium 1190mg; Total Carbohydrate 29g (Dietary Fiber 2g; Sugars 6g); Protein 8g
% daily value: Vitamin A 20%; Vitamin C 4%; Calcium 15%; Iron 8%   **exchanges:** 1 1/2 Starch, 1/2 Other Carbohydrate, 1/2 Medium-Fat Meat, 1 Fat   **carbohydrate choices:** 2

Pinquitos are small, tender, pink beans and are great in this chili—however, if you can't find them, just substitute pinto beans.

VEGETARIAN CHILI
with spicy tortilla strips (LOW fat)

prep time: 10 minutes   **start to finish:** 6 hours 10 minutes   6 servings

CHILI
1 can (15 to 16 oz) dark red kidney beans, drained
1 can (15 to 16 oz) spicy chili beans, undrained
1 can (15 oz) pinquito beans, undrained
1 can (14.5 oz) chili-style chunky tomatoes, undrained
1 large onion, chopped (1 cup)
2 to 3 teaspoons chili powder
1/8 teaspoon ground red pepper (cayenne)

SPICY TORTILLAS STRIPS
3 corn tortillas (6 inch)
1 tablespoon vegetable oil
Dash ground red pepper (cayenne)

1. In 3 1/2- to 4-quart slow cooker, mix chili ingredients.

2. Cover; cook on Low heat setting 5 to 6 hours.

3. Meanwhile, heat oven to 375°F. Brush both sides of tortillas with oil. Lightly sprinkle red pepper on one side of tortillas. Cut into 1/2-inch strips. Place in single layer on ungreased cookie sheet. Bake 10 to 12 minutes or until strips are crisp and edges are light brown.

4. Stir chili well. Top individual servings with tortilla strips.

1 serving: Calories 300 (Calories from Fat 35); Total Fat 4g (Saturated Fat 0.5g; Trans Fat 0g); Cholesterol 0mg; Sodium 890mg; Total Carbohydrate 52g (Dietary Fiber 14g; Sugars 6g); Protein 16g
% daily value: Vitamin A 15%; Vitamin C 20%; Calcium 10%; Iron 30%   **exchanges:** 3 1/2 Starch, 1/2 Very Lean Meat, 1/2 Fat
carbohydrate choices: 3 1/2

The perfect crowd-pleasing dish! Go ahead, bring it to a potluck, it will be a hit. For some variety, try spooning the veggie joes over tortilla chips (the kids will cheer), pasta or rice instead of filling sandwich buns. Got leftovers? Freeze them in a freezer container up to 4 months. To thaw, put the container in the fridge for about 8 hours or defrost in the microwave.

veggie JOES  LOW fat

prep time: 10 minutes   **start to finish:** 4 hours 10 minutes   16 servings

4 cups frozen soy-protein burger crumbles (from two 12-oz packages)
1 small onion, finely chopped (1/2 cup)
1/2 cup water
1 1/2 cups ketchup
2 tablespoons packed brown sugar
2 tablespoons white vinegar
1 tablespoon yellow mustard
1/2 teaspoon pepper
1/4 teaspoon salt
16 sandwich buns, split

1. In 3- to 3 1/2-quart slow cooker, mix all ingredients except buns.

2. Cover; cook on Low heat setting 4 to 6 hours. (If slow cooker has black liner, do not cook longer than 6 hours or mixture may burn around edge.)

3. Fill each bun with 1/3 cup mixture.

1 serving: Calories 190 (Calories from Fat 25); Total Fat 3g (Saturated Fat 0.5g; Trans Fat 0g); Cholesterol 0mg; Sodium 640mg; Total Carbohydrate 30g (Dietary Fiber 3g; Sugars 10g); Protein 10g

% daily value: Vitamin A 6%; Vitamin C 4%; Calcium 8%; Iron 15%   **exchanges:** 1 1/2 Starch, 1/2 Other Carbohydrate, 1 Very Lean Meat, 1/2 Fat   **carbohydrate choices:** 2

Black beans and rice are a natural pair, so try serving this hearty vegetarian chili over a mound of cooked rice, and sprinkle with chopped bell pepper and fresh cilantro for color and flavor. You can also have other chili fixings on hand—chopped onion, salsa, guacamole—whatever your favorites may be.

spicy black bean barbecue CHILI

prep time: 15 minutes   **start to finish:** 11 hours 45 minutes   6 servings

1 lb dried black beans (2 cups), sorted, rinsed
10 cups water
1 tablespoon olive or vegetable oil
1 large onion, chopped (1 cup)
6 cloves garlic, finely chopped
4 cups water
1 can (14.5 oz) diced tomatoes with green chilies, undrained
1 cup hickory barbecue sauce
1 chipotle chili in adobo sauce (from 7-oz can), finely chopped
1 teaspoon adobo sauce (from 7-oz can)
2 cups frozen soy-protein burger crumbles (from 12-oz package)

1. In 4-quart Dutch oven, heat beans and 10 cups water to boiling; reduce heat. Simmer uncovered 10 minutes; remove from heat. Cover and let stand 1 hour.

2. In 10-inch skillet, heat oil over medium-high heat. Cook onion and garlic in oil about 8 minutes, stirring occasionally, until onion is tender and light golden brown.

3. Drain beans. In 3 1/2- to 4-quart slow cooker, place beans. Add 4 cups water and onion mixture.

4. Cover; cook on Low heat setting 10 to 12 hours.

5. Stir in tomatoes, barbecue sauce, chili, adobo sauce and crumbles. Increase heat setting to High; cover and cook about 30 minutes longer or until hot.

1 serving: Calories 410 (Calories from Fat 35); Total Fat 3.5g (Saturated Fat 0.5g; Trans Fat 0g); Cholesterol 0mg; Sodium 810mg; Total Carbohydrate 68g (Dietary Fiber 20g; Sugars 20g); Protein 26g
% daily value: Vitamin A 8%; Vitamin C 8%; Calcium 15%; Iron 30%   **exchanges:** 3 1/2 Starch, 1 Other Carbohydrate, 2 Very Lean Meat   **carbohydrate choices:** 4 1/2

spicy black bean barbecue CHILI

Here's your new recipe for casual get-togethers or tailgating. Serve the sandwiches with chips and a tray of raw veggies and dip.

"cheeseburger" SANDWICHES (LOW fat)

prep time: 10 minutes   **start to finish:** 4 hours 10 minutes   9 sandwiches

3 cups frozen soy-protein burger crumbles (from 12-oz package)
1/2 teaspoon garlic-pepper blend
1 loaf (8 oz) prepared cheese product, diced (2 cups)
2 tablespoons milk
1 medium green bell pepper, chopped (1 cup)
1 small onion, chopped (1/4 cup)
2 cloves garlic, finely chopped
9 sandwich buns, split
Ketchup, if desired

1. Spray 3- to 3 1/2-quart slow cooker with cooking spray. Mix all ingredients except buns and ketchup in slow cooker.

2. Cover; cook on Low heat setting 4 to 5 hours. (If slow cooker has black liner, do not cook longer than 5 hours or mixture may burn around edge.)

3. Fill each bun with 1/3 cup mixture. Serve with ketchup if desired.

1 sandwich: Calories 260 (Calories from Fat 70); Total Fat 8g (Saturated Fat 4g; Trans Fat 0g); Cholesterol 20mg; Sodium 800mg; Total Carbohydrate 30g (Dietary Fiber 3g; Sugars 5g); Protein 17g
% daily value: Vitamin A 6%; Vitamin C 15%; Calcium 20%; Iron 15%   **exchanges:** 2 Starch, 1 1/2 Medium-Fat Meat
carbohydrate choices: 2

Mole sauce is a rich, spicy and slightly sweet Mexican sauce. Look for it with the other Mexican ingredients in your supermarket. If it's unavailable, enchilada sauce is a good substitute in these sophisticated tacos.

smoky chipotle SOFT TACOS (LOW fat)

prep time: 20 minutes   **start to finish:** 4 hours 20 minutes   18 tacos

1 large onion, chopped (1 cup)
1 Anaheim chili, chopped (1/3 cup)
6 cups frozen soy-protein burger crumbles (from two 12-oz packages)
3/4 cup chili sauce
1 1/2 cups water
1/2 cup mole sauce (from 8 1/4- to 9-oz container)
1 tablespoon chopped chipotle chilies in adobo sauce (from 7-oz can)
1 teaspoon ground cumin
3/4 teaspoon salt
18 flour tortillas (6 inch)
2 cups shredded Cheddar cheese (8 oz)
3 medium tomatoes, chopped (2 1/4 cups)

1. Generously spray 8-inch skillet with cooking spray. Add onion and Anaheim chili; spray onion and chili with cooking spray. Cook over medium heat 4 to 5 minutes, stirring occasionally, until onion is crisp-tender.

2. In 3- to 3 1/2-quart slow cooker, mix onion mixture and remaining ingredients except tortillas, cheese and tomatoes.

3. Cover; cook on Low heat setting 4 to 5 hours. (If slow cooker has black liner, do not cook longer than 5 hours or mixture may burn around edge.)

4. To serve, spoon 1/3 cup crumbles mixture onto each tortilla; top with 1 heaping tablespoon cheese and 2 tablespoons tomatoes. Roll up tortillas.

1 taco: Calories 250 (Calories from Fat 90); Total Fat 10g (Saturated Fat 3.5g; Trans Fat 0g); Cholesterol 15mg; Sodium 730mg; Total Carbohydrate 24g (Dietary Fiber 4g; Sugars 4g); Protein 15g
% daily value: Vitamin A 15%; Vitamin C 10%; Calcium 15%; Iron 15%   **exchanges:** 1 1/2 Starch, 1 1/2 Lean Meat, 1 Fat
carbohydrate choices: 1 1/2

BEAN AND VEGETABLE STEW with polenta *(page 225)*

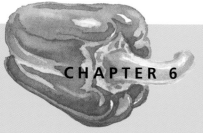

CHAPTER 6 soups, stews & chilies

Both dark and light red kidney beans are widely available, and either can be used in this recipe—make it easy and use whatever is on hand.

MINESTRONE

prep time: 40 minutes   **start to finish:** 40 minutes   4 servings

1 tablespoon olive or vegetable oil
1 large onion, coarsely chopped (1 cup)
1 medium green bell pepper, coarsely chopped (1 cup)
2 cans (14.5 oz each) Italian-style stewed tomatoes
    with basil, garlic and oregano, undrained
2 cans (14 oz each) vegetable broth
1 can (15 to 16 oz) dark red kidney beans, drained, rinsed
1 cup uncooked small pasta shells (4 oz)
1 medium yellow summer squash or zucchini, cut in half lengthwise,
    cut crosswise into slices (1 1/2 cups)
1/4 cup basil pesto
Shredded Parmesan cheese, if desired

1. In 3-quart saucepan, heat oil over medium-high heat. Add onion and bell pepper; cook 3 to 5 minutes, stirring occasionally, until crisp-tender.

2. Stir in tomatoes, broth and beans. Heat to boiling. Reduce heat to medium-low; simmer uncovered 5 minutes.

3. Stir in pasta and squash. Heat to boiling over medium-high heat. Boil 8 to 10 minutes, stirring occasionally, until pasta is tender. Top individual servings with pesto; swirl in slightly. Garnish with shredded Parmesan cheese if desired.

1 serving: Calories 460 (Calories from Fat 120); Total Fat 13g (Saturated Fat 2.5g; Trans Fat 0g); Cholesterol 0mg; Sodium 1580mg; Total Carbohydrate 69g (Dietary Fiber 12g; Sugars 17g); Protein 16g
% daily value: Vitamin A 30%; Vitamin C 60%; Calcium 15%; Iron 30%   **exchanges:** 3 Starch, 1 Other Carbohydrate, 2 Vegetable, 1/2 Very Lean Meat, 2 Fat   **carbohydrate choices:** 4 1/2

chicken MINESTRONE: **Add 1 cup cubed cooked chicken or turkey with the pasta in step 3.**

Lighten up this favorite chill-chasing soup by using low-fat sour cream and reduced-fat Cheddar cheese instead of the regular versions.

beer and cheese SOUP

prep time: 15 minutes   **start to finish:** 25 minutes   5 servings

2 tablespoons butter or margarine
2 medium carrots, finely chopped (1 cup)
1 large onion, chopped (1 cup)
1 medium stalk celery, finely chopped (1/2 cup)
1/4 cup all-purpose flour
1 can or bottle (12 oz) beer*
2 cups vegetable broth
1/2 teaspoon salt
1 cup sour cream
2 cups shredded sharp Cheddar cheese (8 oz)

1. In 3-quart saucepan, melt butter over medium heat. Add carrots, onion and celery; cook, stirring occasionally, until tender.

2. Stir in flour. Gradually stir in beer, broth and salt. Heat to boiling. Reduce heat to low; cover and simmer about 10 minutes or until vegetables are tender.

3. Remove saucepan from heat. Add sour cream and cheese; stir until cheese is melted.

To substitute for beer, use an additional 1 1/2 cups vegetable broth.

1 serving: Calories 380 (Calories from Fat 260); Total Fat 29g (Saturated Fat 17g; Trans Fat 1g); Cholesterol 90mg; Sodium 990mg; Total Carbohydrate 17g (Dietary Fiber 2g; Sugars 7g); Protein 14g
% daily value: Vitamin A 120%; Vitamin C 6%; Calcium 30%; Iron 6%   **exchanges:** 1/2 Starch, 1/2 Other Carbohydrate, 2 High-Fat Meat, 2 1/2 Fat   **carbohydrate choices:** 1

Brown rice isn't just for health fanatics—it has nutlike flavor and chewy texture because the bran and germ aren't removed. OK, it's good for you, but it also tastes good, so give it a try. And now its even faster to cook if you use instant brown rice!

brown rice and vegetable-cheese SOUP

prep time: 20 minutes   **start to finish:** 1 hour 10 minutes   4 servings

1/2 cup uncooked regular long grain brown rice
1 1/2 cups water
12 oz prepared cheese product (from 16-oz loaf), cubed (3 cups)
3 1/2 cups milk
1 teaspoon ground mustard
1 bag (1 lb) frozen broccoli, carrots and cauliflower, thawed, drained

1. Cook rice in water as directed on package.

2. In 3-quart saucepan, heat cheese and milk over medium heat, stirring occasionally, until cheese is melted. Stir in mustard until blended.

3. Stir in rice and thawed vegetables. Cook 4 to 5 minutes, stirring occasionally, until hot.

1 serving: Calories 510 (Calories from Fat 220); Total Fat 24g (Saturated Fat 14g; Trans Fat 0.5g); Cholesterol 85mg; Sodium 1690mg; Total Carbohydrate 47g (Dietary Fiber 7g; Sugars 21g); Protein 26g
% daily value: Vitamin A 90%; Vitamin C 30%; Calcium 70%; Iron 8%   **exchanges:** 1 Starch, 1 1/2 Other Carbohydrate, 2 Vegetable, 2 1/2 High-Fat Meat, 1 Fat   **carbohydrate choices:** 3

BROWN RICE AND VEGETABLE-CHEESE SOUP with ham: Add 2 cups chopped fully cooked turkey ham with the rice and vegetables in step 3.

legume COOKING CHART

Buying Legumes

Look for a wide variety of dried legumes in large supermarkets; whole food stores and food co-ops may carry heirloom or more unusual varieties. Fresh, high-quality legumes are bright in color with smooth, unbroken seed coats.

Storing Legumes

UNCOOKED: Most legumes will keep indefinitely but are best when used within one to two years. Store them in their original packaging or in airtight glass or plastic containers in a cool (60°F or less), dry place.

COOKED: Divide cooked legumes into portion sizes you will use in recipes or as a side dish. Tightly cover and refrigerate up to three days, or freeze in airtight containers up to six months.

Dried Legumes Cooking Chart

1. Place legumes into a shallow baking dish with sides so they spread out in a single layer. Sort through them with your fingers, throwing out stones and shriveled, small or damaged beans; rinse and drain.

2. With the exception *of black-eyed peas, lentils and split peas*, dried legumes need to be soaked before cooking to soften and plump them. Soaking also makes beans more digestible by dissolving some of the sugars that cause intestinal gas. There are two methods for soaking legumes:

   QUICK SOAK: Put dried legumes in a large saucepan; add enough water to cover them. Heat to boiling; boil 2 minutes. Remove from heat; cover and let stand at least 1 hour before cooking. Drain, then cook in clean cold water.

   LONG SOAK: Put dried legumes in large saucepan or bowl; add enough cold water to cover them. Let stand 8 to 24 hours. Drain, then cook in clean cold water.

3. After soaking, put 1 cup legumes in 3- to 4-quart saucepan. Add enough cold water (about 3 to 4 cups) to cover legumes.

4. Heat to boiling; boil uncovered 2 minutes.

5. Reduce heat to low. Cover and simmer (do not continue to boil or legumes will burst), stirring occasionally, for times given in the following chart or until tender.

Type (1 cup dried)	Approximate Simmer Time	Approximate Yield (in cups)
Adzuki beans Lentils	30 to 45 minutes	2 to 3
Mung beans Split peas	45 to 60 minutes	2 to 2 1/4
Black-eyed peas Butter beans Cannellini beans Great northern beans Lima beans Navy beans Pinto beans	1 to 1 1/2 hours	2 to 2 1/2
Anasazi beans Black beans Fava beans Kidney beans	1 to 2 hours	2
Garbanzo beans	2 to 2 1/2 hours	2
Soybeans	3 to 4 hours	2

Next to the ever-popular chicken and beef bouillon cubes, you will now find vegetable bouillon cubes. These cubes are a convenient way to add great flavor in a flash! They're also a must for people who don't want to use any animal products.

tortellini SOUP (LOW fat)

prep time: 40 minutes   **start to finish:** 40 minutes   5 servings

2 tablespoons butter or margarine
1 medium stalk celery, chopped (1/2 cup)
1 medium carrot, chopped (1/2 cup)
1 small onion, chopped (1/4 cup)
1 clove garlic, finely chopped
6 cups water
2 extra-large vegetarian vegetable bouillon cubes
2 1/2 cups dried cheese-filled tortellini (10 oz)
1 tablespoon chopped fresh parsley
1/2 teaspoon ground nutmeg
1/4 teaspoon pepper
Freshly grated Parmesan cheese, if desired

1. In 4-quart Dutch oven, melt butter over medium heat. Add celery, carrot, onion and garlic; cook, stirring frequently, until crisp-tender.

2. Stir in water and bouillon cubes. Heat to boiling. Reduce heat to low; stir in tortellini. Cover; simmer about 20 minutes, stirring occasionally, until tortellini are tender.

3. Stir in parsley, nutmeg and pepper. Sprinkle individual servings with cheese if desired.

1 serving: Calories 280 (Calories from Fat 90); Total Fat 10g (Saturated Fat 5g; Trans Fat 0g); Cholesterol 55mg; Sodium 1420mg; Total Carbohydrate 38g (Dietary Fiber 2g; Sugars 3g); Protein 11g
% daily value: Vitamin A 50%; Vitamin C 4%; Calcium 10%; Iron 8%   **exchanges:** 2 1/2 Starch, 1/2 High-Fat Meat, 1 Fat
carbohydrate choices: 2 1/2

tortellini SOUP

Lentils are low in calories, have very little fat and are a good source of fiber—protein doesn't get much better than that! Worldwide, hundreds of types of lentils are available in a variety of colors and have been an important food staple in the Middle East and India for centuries. The most common colors we see are grayish brown, yellow and red, but you can use whatever color you like.

tomato-lentil SOUP (LOW fat)

prep time: 15 minutes   **start to finish:** 50 minutes   6 servings

1 tablespoon olive or vegetable oil
1 large onion, finely chopped (1 cup)
1 medium stalk celery, cut into 1/2-inch pieces
2 cloves garlic, finely chopped
2 medium carrots, cut into 1/2-inch pieces (1 cup)
1 cup dried lentils (8 oz), sorted, rinsed
4 cups water
2 extra-large vegetarian vegetable bouillon cubes
1 teaspoon dried thyme leaves
1/4 teaspoon pepper
1 dried bay leaf
1 can (28 oz) diced tomatoes, undrained

1. In 3-quart saucepan, heat oil over medium-high heat. Add onion, celery and garlic; cook about 5 minutes, stirring occasionally, until softened.

2. Stir in remaining ingredients except tomatoes. Heat to boiling. Reduce heat; cover and simmer 15 to 20 minutes or until lentils and vegetables are tender.

3. Stir in tomatoes. Simmer uncovered about 15 minutes or until heated through. Remove bay leaf before serving.

1 serving: Calories 200 (Calories from Fat 30); Total Fat 3g (Saturated Fat 0g; Trans Fat 0g); Cholesterol 0mg; Sodium 930mg; Total Carbohydrate 33g (Dietary Fiber 9g; Sugars 6g); Protein 12g
% daily value: Vitamin A 90%; Vitamin C 20%; Calcium 8%; Iron 25%   **exchanges:** 2 Starch, 1 Vegetable, 1/2 Very Lean Meat, 1/2 Fat
carbohydrate choices: 2

Give this soup a dash of restaurant pizzazz by topping each bowl with chopped fresh basil leaves and curls of Parmesan cheese, or top with a dollop of guacamole. Pair with grilled cheese sandwiches for a casual supper.

chunky tomato SOUP (LOW fat)

prep time: 15 minutes   **start to finish:** 1 hour 35 minutes   8 servings

2 tablespoons olive or vegetable oil
2 medium stalks celery, coarsely chopped (1 cup)
2 medium carrots, coarsely chopped (1 cup)
2 cloves garlic, finely chopped
2 cans (28 oz each) roma (plum) tomatoes, undrained
2 cups water
1 teaspoon dried basil leaves
1/2 teaspoon pepper
2 cans (14 oz each) vegetable broth

1. In 5- to 6-quart Dutch oven, heat oil over medium-high heat. Add celery, carrots and garlic; cook 5 to 7 minutes, stirring frequently, until carrots are crisp-tender.

2. Stir in tomatoes, breaking up tomatoes coarsely. Stir in water, basil, pepper and broth. Heat to boiling. Reduce heat to low. Cover; simmer 1 hour, stirring occasionally.

1 serving: Calories 90 (Calories from Fat 35); Total Fat 3.5g (Saturated Fat 0.5g; Trans Fat 0g); Cholesterol 0mg; Sodium 750mg; Total Carbohydrate 13g (Dietary Fiber 3g; Sugars 6g); Protein 2g
% daily value: Vitamin A 80%; Vitamin C 25%; Calcium 8%; Iron 8%   **exchanges:** 1/2 Other Carbohydrate, 1 Vegetable, 1/2 Fat
carbohydrate choices: 1

This light soup is bursting with flavor! Complete the meal by serving it with a variety of rice crackers and cooked shelled edamame—it's often found in the supermarket with the fresh sushi.

oriental wild rice SOUP (LOW fat)

prep time: 5 minutes   **start to finish:** 1 hour 5 minutes   4 servings

1/2 cup uncooked wild rice
3 cups water
1 small red bell pepper, chopped (1/2 cup)
1 can (14 oz) vegetable broth
1 1/2 cups sliced fresh mushrooms (4 oz)
1 1/2 cups pieces (1/2 inch) fresh snow pea pods
3 tablespoons soy sauce
1/4 teaspoon garlic powder
1/4 teaspoon ground ginger
Chopped fresh cilantro, if desired

1. In 3-quart saucepan, heat wild rice and water to boiling over high heat. Reduce heat to low; cover and simmer 45 minutes, stirring occasionally.

2. Stir in bell pepper and broth. Cook uncovered over medium heat 5 minutes, stirring occasionally.

3. Stir in remaining ingredients except cilantro. Cook uncovered over medium heat 5 to 8 minutes, stirring occasionally, until vegetables are crisp-tender. Sprinkle each serving with cilantro if desired.

1 serving: Calories 130 (Calories from Fat 0); Total Fat 0.5g (Saturated Fat 0g; Trans Fat 0g); Cholesterol 0mg; Sodium 1130mg; Total Carbohydrate 24g (Dietary Fiber 3g; Sugars 4g); Protein 6g
% daily value: Vitamin A 30%; Vitamin C 45%; Calcium 2%; Iron 10%   **exchanges:** 1 1/2 Starch, 1 Vegetable   **carbohydrate choices:** 1 1/2

oriental chicken and wild rice SOUP: **Add 1 cup diced cooked chicken or turkey with the remaining ingredients in step 3.**

Wild rice isn't rice? No, it's an aquatic grass native to North America. The chewy texture of wild rice makes it a perfect meat substitute, but cooked white or brown rice can be used instead.

creamy wild rice SOUP

prep time: 40 minutes   **start to finish:** 40 minutes   5 servings

1/2 cup uncooked wild rice
1 3/4 cups water
2 tablespoons butter or margarine
2 medium stalks celery, sliced (1 cup)
1 medium carrot, coarsely shredded (1/2 cup)
1 medium onion, chopped (1/2 cup)
1 small green bell pepper, chopped (1/2 cup)
3 tablespoons all-purpose flour
1/2 teaspoon salt
1/4 teaspoon pepper
1 can (14 oz) vegetable broth
1 cup half-and-half
1/3 cup slivered almonds, toasted*
1/4 cup chopped fresh parsley

1. Cook wild rice in 1 1/4 cups water as directed on package.

2. In 3-quart saucepan, melt butter over medium heat. Add celery, carrot, onion and bell pepper; cook, stirring occasionally, until celery is tender.

3. Stir in flour, salt and pepper. Stir in wild rice, remaining 1/2 cup water and the broth. Heat to boiling. Reduce heat to low; cover and simmer 15 minutes, stirring occasionally.

4. Stir in remaining ingredients. Heat just until hot (do not boil).

*To toast the almonds in the microwave, place 1/2 teaspoon vegetable oil and the almonds in a 1- or 2-cup glass measuring cup. Microwave uncovered on High 2 minutes 30 seconds to 3 minutes 30 seconds, stirring every 30 seconds, until light brown.

1 serving: Calories 250 (Calories from Fat 130); Total Fat 15g (Saturated Fat 6g; Trans Fat 0g); Cholesterol 30mg; Sodium 660mg; Total Carbohydrate 23g (Dietary Fiber 3g; Sugars 6g); Protein 6g
% daily value: Vitamin A 60%; Vitamin C 20%; Calcium 10%; Iron 8%   **exchanges:** 1 1/2 Starch, 3 Fat   **carbohydrate choices:** 1 1/2

creamy chicken wild rice SOUP: Add 2 cups chopped cooked chicken with the remaining ingredients in step 4.

Stale tortillas are never wasted by Mexican cooks and are used in many ways. Feel free to use your stale, or fresh, tortillas. Sliced and fried, they add a distinctive flavor to this tomato soup.

tortilla SOUP

prep time: 15 minutes   **start to finish:** 35 minutes   4 servings

3 teaspoons vegetable oil
4 corn tortillas (5 or 6 inch), cut into 2 × 1/2-inch strips
1 medium onion, chopped (1/2 cup)
2 cans (14 oz each) vegetable broth
1 can (10 oz) chopped tomatoes and green chilies, undrained
1 tablespoon lime juice
1 tablespoon chopped fresh cilantro or parsley

1. In 2-quart nonstick saucepan, heat 2 teaspoons oil over medium–high heat. Add tortilla strips; cook 30 to 60 seconds, stirring occasionally, until crisp and light golden brown. Remove from saucepan; drain on paper towels.

2. In same saucepan, cook remaining 1 teaspoon oil and the onion over medium–high heat, stirring occasionally, until onion is tender.

3. Stir in broth and tomatoes. Heat to boiling. Reduce heat to low; simmer uncovered 20 minutes.

4. Stir in lime juice. Serve soup over tortilla strips; garnish with cilantro.

1 serving: Calories 110 (Calories from Fat 35); Total Fat 4g (Saturated Fat 0.5g; Trans Fat 0g); Cholesterol 0mg; Sodium 1100mg; Total Carbohydrate 17g (Dietary Fiber 2g; Sugars 7g); Protein 2g
% daily value: Vitamin A 15%; Vitamin C 10%; Calcium 6%; Iron 4%   **exchanges:** 1/2 Starch, 1/2 Other Carbohydrate, 1 Fat
carbohydrate choices: 1

chicken tortilla SOUP: Cut 2 boneless skinless chicken breasts (about 1/2 lb) into 3/4-inch pieces. Cook with the onion in step 2 for about 5 minutes or until chicken is no longer pink in center.

tortilla SOUP

Navy beans fed many a sailor in the early 1800s, thus their name. Although larger in size, cannellini or great northern beans can be substituted—don't worry, the Navy won't mind.

navy bean SOUP

prep time: 1 hour 15 minutes   **start to finish:** 2 hours 15 minutes   6 servings

1 bag (16 oz) dried navy beans, sorted, rinsed
8 cups water
1/2 cup chili sauce
1/2 teaspoon dried marjoram leaves
2 medium carrots, chopped (1 cup)
1 large onion, chopped (1 cup)
1 medium stalk celery, chopped (1/2 cup)
1 can (14 oz) vegetable broth
2 tablespoons chopped fresh parsley

1. In 8-quart Dutch oven, heat beans and water to boiling. Boil uncovered 2 minutes. Remove from heat; cover and let stand 1 hour.

2. Stir in remaining ingredients except parsley. Heat to boiling. Reduce heat to low; cover and simmer about 1 hour, stirring occasionally, until beans are tender.

3. Stir in parsley. Cook 2 to 3 minutes.

1 serving: Calories 300 (Calories from Fat 10); Total Fat 1g (Saturated Fat 0g; Trans Fat 0g); Cholesterol 0mg; Sodium 610mg; Total Carbohydrate 56g (Dietary Fiber 14g; Sugars 11g); Protein 16g
% daily value: Vitamin A 90%; Vitamin C 10%; Calcium 15%; Iron 25%   **exchanges:** 2 1/2 Starch, 1 Other Carbohydrate, 1 Very Lean Meat
carbohydrate choices: 4

NAVY BEAN SOUP with ham: Add 1 cup diced fully cooked turkey ham with the remaining ingredients in step 2.

Offer warm wedges of a cheesy focaccia on the side—they're great for dipping into the chowder!

chunky vegetable CHOWDER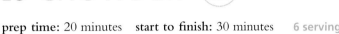

prep time: 20 minutes   **start to finish:** 30 minutes   6 servings

1 tablespoon butter or margarine
1 medium green bell pepper, coarsely chopped (1 cup)
1 medium red bell pepper, coarsely chopped (1 cup)
8 medium green onions, sliced (1/2 cup)
3 cups water
3/4 lb small red potatoes, cut into 1-inch pieces (2 1/2 cups)
1 tablespoon chopped fresh or 1 teaspoon dried thyme leaves
1/2 teaspoon salt
1 cup half-and-half
1/8 teaspoon pepper
2 cans (14.75 oz each) cream-style corn

1. In 4-quart Dutch oven, melt butter over medium heat. Add bell peppers and onions; cook 3 minutes, stirring occasionally.

2. Stir in water, potatoes, thyme and salt. Heat to boiling. Reduce heat to low; cover and simmer about 10 minutes or until potatoes are tender.

3. Stir in remaining ingredients. Cook until hot (do not boil).

1 serving: Calories 260 (Calories from Fat 70); Total Fat 8g (Saturated Fat 4g; Trans Fat 0g); Cholesterol 20mg; Sodium 530mg; Total Carbohydrate 41g (Dietary Fiber 5g; Sugars 9g); Protein 7g
% daily value: Vitamin A 40%; Vitamin C 70%; Calcium 6%; Iron 10%   **exchanges:** 2 Starch, 1/2 Other Carbohydrate, 1 1/2 Fat
carbohydrate choices: 3

Jalapeño chilies add spunky flavor to this potato chowder, one that will satisfy even the heartiest appetites. However, if your family likes to take a walk on the mild side, just leave it out. This is great served with warm corn bread and cold milk.

jalapeño-potato CHOWDER

prep time: 35 minutes   **start to finish:** 35 minutes   4 servings

3 tablespoons butter or margarine
1 medium onion, chopped (1/2 cup)
1 small green bell pepper, chopped (1/2 cup)
3 tablespoons all-purpose flour
2 1/2 cups milk
3 cups diced cooked potatoes
1 cup frozen whole kernel corn (from 1-lb bag)
1 to 2 tablespoons fresh or canned chopped jalapeño chilies
3/4 teaspoon salt
1 teaspoon fresh or 1/4 teaspoon dried thyme leaves
1/2 cup shredded Swiss cheese (2 oz), if desired

1. In 2-quart saucepan, melt butter over medium heat. Add onion and bell pepper; cook 3 to 5 minutes, stirring occasionally, until crisp-tender.

2. Stir in flour. Gradually add milk, stirring constantly, until mixture is boiling.

3. Stir in remaining ingredients. Cook 5 to 10 minutes, stirring occasionally, until corn is tender. Serve soup topped with cheese if desired.

1 serving: Calories 320 (Calories from Fat 110); Total Fat 12g (Saturated Fat 6g; Trans Fat 0.5g); Cholesterol 35mg; Sodium 580mg; Total Carbohydrate 43g (Dietary Fiber 3g; Sugars 11g); Protein 9g
% daily value: Vitamin A 15%; Vitamin C 25%; Calcium 20%; Iron 6%   **exchanges:** 2 1/2 Starch, 1/2 Other Carbohydrate, 2 Fat
carbohydrate choices: 3

jalapeño-tuna-potato CHOWDER: Omit whole kernel corn. Add 1 can (6 oz) white tuna in water, drained, with the remaining ingredients in step 3.

Quick-cooking barley is a super time-saver—it cooks in less than half the time of regular barley. If Cajun or Creole seasoning isn't handy, use 2 teaspoons chili powder, 1/2 teaspoon salt and 1/4 teaspoon pepper.

cajun barley STEW (LOW fat)

prep time: 15 minutes   **start to finish:** 35 minutes   4 servings

2 teaspoons vegetable oil
1 large onion, chopped (1 cup)
1 medium stalk celery, chopped (1/2 cup)
1/2 cup uncooked quick-cooking barley
5 cups tomato juice
1 to 2 teaspoons Cajun or Creole seasoning
2 cans (15 to 16 oz each) great northern or navy beans, drained, rinsed
1/4 cup chopped fresh parsley

1. In 12-inch skillet, heat oil over medium-high heat. Add onion and celery; cook, stirring occasionally, until crisp-tender.

2. Stir in remaining ingredients except parsley. Heat to boiling. Reduce heat to low; cover and simmer about 20 minutes or until barley is tender. Stir in parsley.

1 serving: Calories 460 (Calories from Fat 30); Total Fat 3.5g (Saturated Fat 0.5g; Trans Fat 0g); Cholesterol 0mg; Sodium 1260mg; Total Carbohydrate 83g (Dietary Fiber 18g; Sugars 14g); Protein 23g
% daily value: Vitamin A 50%; Vitamin C 50%; Calcium 20%; Iron 50%   **exchanges:** 3 1/2 Starch, 1 Other Carbohydrate, 3 Vegetable, 1 Very Lean Meat, 1/2 Fat   **carbohydrate choices:** 5 1/2

Dill weed and hard-cooked egg add a Scandinavian touch to this soup brimming with fresh garden flavor. Always add dill weed close to the end of cooking because it loses flavor quickly when heated.

scandinavian vegetable STEW

prep time: 20 minutes   **start to finish:** 30 minutes   4 servings

8 to 10 small red potatoes, cut into quarters (3 cups)
2 cups ready-to-eat baby-cut carrots
3 tablespoons butter or margarine
3 medium green onions, sliced (1/3 cup)
3 tablespoons all-purpose flour
2 cups milk
1/2 cup frozen sweet peas
3/4 teaspoon salt
1/8 teaspoon pepper
2 tablespoons chopped fresh or 1/2 teaspoon dried dill weed
1 hard-cooked egg, chopped

1. In 3-quart saucepan, place potatoes and carrots; add enough water to cover. Heat to boiling. Reduce heat to medium; cover and cook 8 to 10 minutes or until tender. Drain in colander. Wipe out saucepan with paper towel.

2. In same saucepan, melt butter over medium heat. Add onions; cook 2 minutes, stirring occasionally. Stir in flour. Gradually add milk, stirring constantly, until mixture thickens and boils.

3. Stir in potatoes and carrots, peas, salt and pepper. Cook 5 to 6 minutes, stirring occasionally, until peas are tender.

4. Stir in dill weed. Cook 2 minutes, stirring constantly. Top individual servings with chopped egg and, if desired, additional dill weed.

1 serving: Calories 310 (Calories from Fat 110); Total Fat 13g (Saturated Fat 6g; Trans Fat 0.5g); Cholesterol 85mg; Sodium 610mg; Total Carbohydrate 39g (Dietary Fiber 5g; Sugars 12g); Protein 10g
% daily value: Vitamin A 240%; Vitamin C 20%; Calcium 20%; Iron 15%   **exchanges:** 2 Starch, 1/2 Other Carbohydrate, 1 Vegetable, 2 1/2 Fat   **carbohydrate choices:** 2 1/2

SCANDINAVIAN VEGETABLE STEW with ham: **Add 1 cup diced fully cooked turkey ham with the peas in step 3.**

scandinavian vegetable STEW

Curry powder is made of many flavors, most often including cardamom, chilies, cinnamon, fennel seed, fenugreek, cumin, turmeric, nutmeg, coriander and cloves. Different brands use different recipes, so experiment to find the one that "curries" favor with you! The apple juice added to this easy stew adds just a touch of sweetness and enhances the curry.

indian lentil STEW

prep time: 55 minutes   **start to finish:** 55 minutes   4 servings

2 tablespoons butter or margarine
1 large onion, chopped (1 cup)
1 tablespoon curry powder
2 tablespoons all-purpose flour
1 can (14 oz) vegetable broth
3/4 cup dried lentils (6 oz), sorted, rinsed
1/2 teaspoon salt
1/2 cup apple juice
3 cups pieces (1 inch) peeled dark-orange sweet potatoes
1 cup frozen sweet peas (from 1-lb bag)
Sour cream or plain yogurt, if desired
Chutney, if desired

1. In 3-quart saucepan, melt butter over medium-high heat. Add onion and curry powder; cook 2 minutes, stirring occasionally. Stir in flour. Gradually add broth, stirring constantly, until thickened.

2. Stir in lentils and salt. Reduce heat to low; cover and simmer 20 minutes, stirring occasionally.

3. Stir in apple juice, sweet potatoes and peas. Heat to boiling. Reduce heat to low; cover and simmer 15 to 20 minutes, stirring occasionally, until vegetables are tender. Top individual servings with sour cream and chutney if desired.

1 serving: Calories 360 (Calories from Fat 60); Total Fat 7g (Saturated Fat 3g; Trans Fat 0g); Cholesterol 15mg; Sodium 790mg; Total Carbohydrate 62g (Dietary Fiber 12g; Sugars 22g); Protein 14g
% daily value: Vitamin A 320%; Vitamin C 25%; Calcium 8%; Iron 30%   **exchanges:** 2 1/2 Starch, 1 1/2 Other Carbohydrate, 1 Very Lean Meat, 1 Fat   **carbohydrate choices:** 4

Call your friends, and treat them to this Italian-style stew. Toss together a Caesar salad, pick up some rolls and cannoli from your favorite bakery and share great conversation over a glass of red wine.

BEAN AND VEGETABLE STEW
with polenta (LOW fat)

prep time: 1 hour 15 minutes   **start to finish:** 1 hour 15 minutes   4 servings

1 tablespoon olive or vegetable oil
1 medium yellow or green bell pepper, coarsely chopped (1 cup)
1 medium onion, coarsely chopped (1/2 cup)
2 teaspoons finely chopped garlic
2 medium carrots, cut into 1/4-inch slices (1 cup)
2 cans (14.5 oz each) diced tomatoes with basil, garlic and oregano, undrained
1 can (15 to 16 oz) black-eyed peas, drained, rinsed
1 can (19 oz) cannellini beans (white kidney beans), drained, rinsed
1 cup water
1 teaspoon Italian seasoning
1/2 teaspoon salt
1/4 teaspoon pepper
1 tube (16 oz) refrigerated polenta
1 cup frozen cut green beans (from 1-lb bag)

1. In 4 1/2- to 5-quart Dutch oven, heat oil over medium heat. Add bell pepper, onion and garlic; cook 5 to 6 minutes, stirring frequently, until onion is softened.

2. Stir in remaining ingredients except polenta and green beans. Heat to boiling. Reduce heat to medium-low; cover and cook 35 to 40 minutes, stirring occasionally, until carrots are tender and stew is hot.

3. Meanwhile, cook polenta as directed on package; keep warm.

4. Stir green beans into stew. Cover; cook 5 to 6 minutes, stirring occasionally, until beans are hot. Serve stew over polenta.

1 serving: Calories 480 (Calories from Fat 45); Total Fat 5g (Saturated Fat 0.5g; Trans Fat 0g); Cholesterol 0mg; Sodium 1560mg; Total Carbohydrate 87g (Dietary Fiber 15g; Sugars 19g); Protein 22g
% daily value: Vitamin A 120%; Vitamin C 80%; Calcium 20%; Iron 50%   **exchanges:** 4 Starch, 1 Other Carbohydrate, 2 Vegetable, 1 Very Lean Meat, 1/2 Fat   **carbohydrate choices:** 6

A serving of this power-packed meatless stew will give you 100% RDA of vitamin A, nearly 50% of vitamin C and 30% of iron. An added bonus is that it's an excellent source of fiber.

SOUTHWESTERN STEW
with corn dumplings

prep time: 15 minutes   **start to finish:** 40 minutes   4 servings

1 tablespoon vegetable oil
1 large onion, chopped (1 cup)
2 cups cubed peeled dark-orange sweet potatoes or butternut squash
1 cup frozen whole kernel corn (from 1-lb bag)
1 can (15 to 16 oz) garbanzo beans, drained, rinsed
1 jar (16 oz) chunky-style salsa (2 cups)
1 cup water
1/4 teaspoon ground cinnamon
1 pouch (6.5 oz) golden corn muffin and bread mix
1/2 cup fat free (skim) milk
1 tablespoon vegetable oil
1 tablespoon roasted sunflower nuts, if desired

1. Heat oven to 425°F. In ovenproof 4-quart Dutch oven, heat 1 tablespoon oil over medium-high heat. Add onion; cook about 5 minutes, stirring occasionally, until crisp-tender. Stir in sweet potatoes, corn, beans, salsa, water and cinnamon. Heat to boiling, stirring occasionally.

2. In small bowl, mix corn muffin mix, milk and 1 tablespoon oil. Stir in nuts if desired. Drop dough by 8 spoonfuls onto vegetable mixture.

3. Bake uncovered 20 to 25 minutes or until toothpick inserted in center of dumplings comes out clean.

1 serving: Calories 560 (Calories from Fat 140); Total Fat 15g (Saturated Fat 3g; Trans Fat 0.5g); Cholesterol 0mg; Sodium 1030mg; Total Carbohydrate 90g (Dietary Fiber 15g; Sugars 26g); Protein 16g
% daily value: Vitamin A 170%; Vitamin C 30%; Calcium 15%; Iron 30%   **exchanges:** 4 Starch, 2 Other Carbohydrate, 1/2 Very Lean Meat, 2 1/2 Fat   **carbohydrate choices:** 6

Resist the urge to stir too much! Dumplings require very little mixing when the milk is added to the dry ingredients. If the dough is overmixed, the dumplings can be heavy and tough, so mix just until the dry ingredients are moistened.

TOMATO-VEGETABLE STEW
with cheddar cheese dumplings

prep time: 20 minutes   **start to finish:** 1 hour 5 minutes   5 servings

STEW
2 tablespoons vegetable oil
2 large onions, coarsely chopped (2 cups)
2 medium stalks celery, coarsely chopped (3/4 cup)
2 cups frozen Italian green beans
1 can (28 oz) diced tomatoes, undrained
1 can (14 oz) vegetable broth
1 teaspoon dried basil leaves
1/4 teaspoon pepper

DUMPLINGS
1 1/2 cups all-purpose flour
2 1/4 teaspoons baking powder
1/4 teaspoon salt
1/2 teaspoon ground mustard
1/4 cup shortening
1/2 cup shredded sharp Cheddar cheese (2 oz)
2/3 cup milk

1. In 4 1/2- to 5-quart Dutch oven, heat oil over medium-high heat. Add onions and celery; cook, stirring frequently, until tender.

2. Stir in remaining stew ingredients. Heat to boiling. Reduce heat to low; simmer uncovered 15 to 20 minutes or until beans are tender.

3. Meanwhile, in medium bowl, stir together flour, baking powder, salt and mustard. With pastry blender or fork, cut in shortening until mixture looks like coarse crumbs. Stir in cheese. Add milk; stir just until dry ingredients are moistened.

4. Drop dough by rounded tablespoonfuls onto simmering stew. Cover; cook over medium-low heat 20 to 25 minutes or until dumplings are firm when pressed.

1 serving: Calories 420 (Calories from Fat 190); Total Fat 21g (Saturated Fat 6g; Trans Fat 2g); Cholesterol 15mg; Sodium 1510mg; Total Carbohydrate 47g (Dietary Fiber 6g; Sugars 11g); Protein 11g
% daily value: Vitamin A 25%; Vitamin C 25%; Calcium 45%; Iron 20%   **exchanges:** 2 Starch, 1/2 Other Carbohydrate, 2 Vegetable, 4 Fat   **carbohydrate choices:** 3

Chilies are not all the same—differing flavors add wonderful depth to recipes. Pasilla chilies, six to eight inches long, are medium-hot in flavor. When fresh, they are sometimes referred to as chilaca chilies. Canned green chiles can be substituted, but the flavor may be slightly milder.

home-style vegetable CHILI (LOW fat)

prep time: 40 minutes   **start to finish:** 40 minutes   6 servings

2 tablespoons vegetable oil
1 large onion, chopped (1 cup)
1 medium green bell pepper, chopped (1 cup)
2 medium carrots, chopped (1 cup)
1 pasilla chili, seeded, chopped (3/4 cup), or 1 can (4.5 oz) chopped green chiles
1 cup water
1 tablespoon chili powder
1 teaspoon ground cumin
3/4 teaspoon salt
2 cans (15 to 16 oz each) red kidney beans, drained, rinsed
2 cans (14.5 oz each) diced tomatoes, undrained
Shredded Cheddar cheese, if desired

1. In 3-quart saucepan, heat oil over medium-high heat. Add onion, bell pepper, carrots and chili; cook 3 to 5 minutes, stirring occasionally until crisp-tender.

2. Stir in remaining ingredients except cheese. Heat to boiling. Reduce heat to medium-low; simmer uncovered 10 to 15 minutes, stirring occasionally, until vegetables are tender. Sprinkle individual servings with cheese if desired.

1 serving: Calories 280 (Calories from Fat 50); Total Fat 6g (Saturated Fat 1g; Trans Fat 0g); Cholesterol 0mg; Sodium 520mg; Total Carbohydrate 43g (Dietary Fiber 11g; Sugars 7g); Protein 13g
% daily value: Vitamin A 100%; Vitamin C 80%; Calcium 10%; Iron 30%   **exchanges:** 2 Starch, 1/2 Other Carbohydrate, 1 Vegetable, 1/2 Very Lean Meat, 1 Fat   **carbohydrate choices:** 3

home-style turkey vegetable CHILI: **Before cooking vegetables and chili in step 1, cook 1/2 lb ground turkey in the oil until light brown; drain if desired. Add vegetables and chili. Continue as directed.**

Break out of the box—any combination of your favorite vegetables or canned beans will work well in this recipe.

vegetable and bean CHILI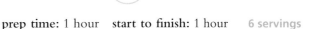

prep time: 1 hour   **start to finish:** 1 hour   6 servings

1 tablespoon olive or vegetable oil
1 large onion, coarsely chopped (1 cup)
2 teaspoons finely chopped garlic
1 bag (1 lb) frozen broccoli, carrots and cauliflower
1 can (15 to 16 oz) red beans, drained, rinsed
1 can (15 to 16 oz) garbanzo beans, drained, rinsed
2 cans (14.5 oz each) diced tomatoes with green chilies, undrained
1 can (8 oz) tomato sauce
2 cups frozen whole kernel corn (from 1-lb bag)
2 tablespoons chili powder
1 tablespoon ground cumin
3/4 teaspoon salt
1/8 teaspoon ground red pepper (cayenne)

1. In 4 1/2- to 5-quart Dutch oven, heat oil over medium-high heat. Add onion and garlic; cook 4 to 5 minutes, stirring frequently, until onions are softened.

2. Stir in remaining ingredients. Heat to boiling. Reduce heat to medium-low; cover and cook 15 to 20 minutes, stirring occasionally, until chili is hot and vegetables are crisp-tender.

1 serving: Calories 360 (Calories from Fat 50); Total Fat 5g (Saturated Fat 0.5g; Trans Fat 0g); Cholesterol 0mg; Sodium 950mg; Total Carbohydrate 62g (Dietary Fiber 15g; Sugars 14g); Protein 16g
% daily value: Vitamin A 70%; Vitamin C 45%; Calcium 15%; Iron 35%   **exchanges:** 2 1/2 Starch, 1 Other Carbohydrate, 2 Vegetable, 1/2 Very Lean Meat, 1/2 Fat   **carbohydrate choices:** 4

Turn up the heat—don't worry, three fire trucks won't appear at your door! This chili recipe is based on the well-known Cincinnati chili, which is traditionally served over spaghetti. In this streamlined version, the spaghetti is cooked right along with the spicy chili.

three-alarm spaghetti and pinto bean CHILI

(LOW fat)

prep time: 35 minutes   **start to finish:** 35 minutes   4 servings

1 tablespoon vegetable oil
1 large onion, chopped (1 cup)
1 medium green bell pepper, chopped (1 cup)
3 cups water
1/2 cup taco sauce
2 teaspoons chili powder
1/2 teaspoon salt
1/4 teaspoon ground cinnamon
2 cans (10 oz each) diced tomatoes and green chilies, undrained
4 oz uncooked spaghetti, broken into thirds (1 1/2 cups)
1 can (15 to 16 oz) pinto beans, drained, rinsed
Sour cream, if desired
Jalapeño chilies, if desired

1. In 4-quart Dutch oven, heat oil over medium-high heat. Add onion and bell pepper; cook 3 to 5 minutes, stirring occasionally, until crisp-tender.

2. Stir in remaining ingredients except spaghetti, beans, sour cream and jalapeño chilies. Heat to boiling. Reduce heat to medium-low; simmer uncovered 5 minutes, stirring occasionally.

3. Stir in uncooked spaghetti and beans. Heat to boiling. Reduce heat to medium; cook uncovered 8 to 10 minutes, stirring occasionally, until spaghetti is tender. Top individual servings with sour cream and jalapeño chilies if desired.

1 serving: Calories 360 (Calories from Fat 45); Total Fat 5g (Saturated Fat 1g; Trans Fat 0g); Cholesterol 0mg; Sodium 840mg; Total Carbohydrate 65g (Dietary Fiber 13g; Sugars 12g); Protein 14g
% daily value: Vitamin A 25%; Vitamin C 50%; Calcium 10%; Iron 25%   **exchanges:** 2 1/2 Starch, 1 Other Carbohydrate, 2 Vegetable, 1/2 Very Lean Meat, 1/2 Fat   **carbohydrate choices:** 4

Go blonde! White chili is a twist on traditional tomato-based chili, using vegetable or chicken broth as its base instead. White chilies are usually more broth-like in contrast to the usually thicker red chilies.

white bean CHILI (LOW fat)

prep time: 1 hour 10 minutes   **start to finish:** 1 hour 10 minutes   6 servings

1/4 cup butter or margarine
1 large onion, chopped (1 cup)
1 clove garlic, finely chopped
1/4 cup chopped fresh or 1 teaspoon dried basil leaves
3 cups vegetable broth
2 tablespoons chopped fresh cilantro or parsley
2 teaspoons chili powder
1/4 teaspoon ground cloves
2 cans (15 to 16 oz each) great northern beans, undrained
1 medium tomato, chopped (3/4 cup)
Corn tortilla chips, if desired

1. In 4-quart Dutch oven, melt butter over medium-high heat. Add onion and garlic; cook, stirring occasionally, until onion is tender.

2. Stir in remaining ingredients except tomato and tortilla chips. Heat to boiling. Reduce heat to low; cover and simmer 1 hour, stirring occasionally. Top individual servings with tomato and tortilla chips if desired.

1 serving: Calories 270 (Calories from Fat 80); Total Fat 8g (Saturated Fat 4g; Trans Fat 0g); Cholesterol 20mg; Sodium 570mg; Total Carbohydrate 36g (Dietary Fiber 9g; Sugars 4g); Protein 13g
% daily value: Vitamin A 25%; Vitamin C 6%; Calcium 15%; Iron 30%   **exchanges:** 2 1/2 Starch, 1 Very Lean Meat, 1 Fat
carbohydrate choices: 2 1/2

chicken and white bean CHILI: Omit 1 can of great northern beans. Increase vegetable broth to 3 1/2 cups. Stir in 3 cups cut-up cooked chicken with the remaining ingredients in step 2.

Ever wondered about pinto beans? They are two-tone kidney-shaped beans widely used in Central and South American cooking. They turn pink when cooked and are the most widely used bean in refried beans.

three-bean enchilada CHILI

prep time: 35 minutes   **start to finish:** 35 minutes   5 servings

1 tablespoon vegetable oil
1 large onion, chopped (1 cup)
1 medium green bell pepper, chopped (1 cup)
1 can (28 oz) crushed tomatoes, undrained
1 can (15 to 16 oz) pinto beans, drained, rinsed
1 can (15 to 16 oz) dark red kidney beans, drained, rinsed
1 can (15 oz) black beans, drained, rinsed
1 can (10 oz) enchilada sauce (1 1/4 cups)
1 teaspoon dried oregano leaves
Tortilla chips, broken, if desired
Shredded Cheddar cheese, if desired

1. In 3-quart saucepan, heat oil over medium-high heat. Add onion and bell pepper; cook 5 minutes, stirring occasionally, until crisp-tender.

2. Stir in remaining ingredients except tortilla chips and cheese. Heat to boiling. Reduce heat to medium-low; simmer uncovered 10 to 15 minutes, stirring occasionally. Sprinkle individual servings with chips and cheese if desired.

1 serving: Calories 410 (Calories from Fat 40); Total Fat 4.5g (Saturated Fat 0.5g; Trans Fat 0g); Cholesterol 0mg; Sodium 490mg; Total Carbohydrate 70g (Dietary Fiber 19g; Sugars 11g); Protein 22g
% daily value: Vitamin A 20%; Vitamin C 50%; Calcium 20%; Iron 40%   **exchanges:** 3 1/2 Starch, 1/2 Other Carbohydrate, 1 Vegetable, 1 1/2 Very Lean Meat, 1/2 Fat   **carbohydrate choices:** 4 1/2

turkey-bean enchilada CHILI: **Before cooking onion and bell pepper in step 1, cook 1/2 lb ground turkey in the oil until light brown; drain if desired. Add onion and bell pepper. Continue as directed.**

From the Provence region of France, the popular dish of ratatouille is often served as a side dish or appetizer. The flavors typical of this dish include eggplant, zucchini, tomatoes, olive oil and garlic, all of which are found in this savory France meets Mexico version of chili.

ratatouille CHILI (LOW fat)

prep time: 25 minutes   **start to finish:** 25 minutes   4 servings

2 tablespoons olive or vegetable oil
1 large eggplant (1 lb), cut into 1/2-inch cubes (4 cups)
1 large onion, chopped (1 cup)
1 medium green bell pepper, chopped (1 cup)
1 clove garlic, finely chopped
1/2 cup sliced zucchini
3 teaspoons chili powder
1 teaspoon chopped fresh or 1/4 teaspoon dried basil leaves
1/4 teaspoon salt
1 can (15 to 16 oz) great northern beans, drained, rinsed
1 can (14.5 oz) whole tomatoes, undrained
1 can (8 oz) tomato sauce

1. In 4-quart Dutch oven, heat oil over medium–high heat. Add eggplant, onion, bell pepper and garlic; cook, stirring occasionally, until vegetables are crisp-tender.

2. Stir in remaining ingredients, breaking up tomatoes. Cook about 10 minutes, stirring occasionally, until zucchini is tender.

1 serving: Calories 300 (Calories from Fat 70); Total Fat 8g (Saturated Fat 1g; Trans Fat 0g); Cholesterol 0mg; Sodium 670mg; Total Carbohydrate 45g (Dietary Fiber 12g; Sugars 11g); Protein 13g
% daily value: Vitamin A 35%; Vitamin C 50%; Calcium 15%; Iron 30%   **exchanges:** 1 Starch, 1 Other Carbohydrate, 3 Vegetable, 1/2 Very Lean Meat, 1 1/2 Fat   **carbohydrate choices:** 3

turkey ratatouille CHILI: **Before cooking vegetables in step 1, cook 1/2 lb ground turkey in the oil until light brown; drain if desired. Add vegetables. Continue as directed.**

Butter beans are really large, cream-colored lima beans, but that's where the similarity ends. Butter beans don't taste like limas; they are very mild and rich.

PEPPER AND BEAN CHILI
with salsa cream (LOW fat)

prep time: 30 minutes   **start to finish:** 35 minutes   6 servings

1 can (28 oz) whole tomatoes, undrained
1 can (15 to 16 oz) garbanzo beans, drained, rinsed
1 can (15 to 16 oz) kidney beans, drained, rinsed
1 can (15 to 16 oz) butter beans, drained, rinsed
1 can (15 oz) tomato sauce
3 small bell peppers (any color), cut into 1-inch pieces
1 Anaheim or jalapeño chili, seeded, chopped
1 to 2 tablespoons chili powder
1/4 teaspoon pepper
1/2 cup sour cream
3 tablespoons chunky-style salsa

1. In 4-quart Dutch oven, mix all ingredients except sour cream and salsa. Heat to boiling, breaking up tomatoes. Reduce heat to low; cover and simmer 15 to 20 minutes, stirring occasionally, until bell peppers are tender.

2. In small bowl, mix sour cream and salsa. Top individual servings with salsa cream.

1 serving: Calories 370 (Calories from Fat 60); Total Fat 6g (Saturated Fat 2.5g; Trans Fat 0g); Cholesterol 15mg; Sodium 690mg; Total Carbohydrate 59g (Dietary Fiber 16g; Sugars 10g); Protein 19g
% daily value: Vitamin A 45%; Vitamin C 70%; Calcium 15%; Iron 40%   **exchanges:** 3 Starch, 1/2 Other Carbohydrate, 2 Vegetable, 1 Very Lean Meat, 1/2 Fat   **carbohydrate choices:** 4

This recipe was developed using salsa verde, meaning "green salsa" that's made with tomatillos and green chilies, versus those made strictly with jalapeños.

CHILI verde

prep time: 45 minutes **start to finish:** 45 minutes 4 servings

2 small zucchini, cut into 1/2-inch pieces (2 cups)
1 large green bell pepper, cut into 1/2-inch pieces (1 1/2 cups)
1/2 lb small red potatoes, cut into 1/2-inch pieces (1 1/2 cups)
2 1/2 cups water
1/2 cup salsa verde (from 12- to 16-oz jar)
1 can (15.5 oz) white or yellow hominy, drained, rinsed
1 extra-large vegetarian vegetable bouillon cube
2 teaspoons chili powder
1/4 cup sour cream

1. In 3-quart saucepan, mix ingredients except sour cream. Heat to boiling over high heat. Reduce heat to low; cover and simmer 15 to 18 minutes, stirring occasionally, until potatoes are tender.

2. Top individual servings with 1 tablespoon sour cream.

1 serving: Calories 200 (Calories from Fat 40); Total Fat 4.5g (Saturated Fat 2g; Trans Fat 0g); Cholesterol 10mg; Sodium 940mg; Total Carbohydrate 35g (Dietary Fiber 7g; Sugars 5g); Protein 5g
% daily value: Vitamin A 30%; Vitamin C 60%; Calcium 6%; Iron 15% **exchanges:** 1 1/2 Starch, 1/2 Other Carbohydrate, 1 Vegetable, 1/2 Fat **carbohydrate choices:** 2

If you crave a hot bite, use Monterey Jack cheese with jalapeño peppers! For fun, top with crushed colored tortilla chips.

CHILI blanco

prep time: 30 minutes   **start to finish:** 30 minutes   4 servings

1 cup chopped onions (2 medium)
2 cloves garlic, finely chopped
2 cans (15.5 oz each) great northern beans, drained, rinsed
1 can (11 oz) vacuum-packed white shoepeg corn, undrained
1 can (4.5 oz) chopped green chiles, undrained
1 extra-large vegetarian vegetable bouillon cube
2 teaspoons ground cumin
1/4 teaspoon salt
1/4 teaspoon pepper
2 1/2 cups water
1/4 cup chopped cilantro
1/2 cup shredded Monterey Jack cheese (2 oz), if desired
1/2 cup broken tortilla chips, if desired

1. Spray 3-quart saucepan with cooking spray; heat over medium-high heat. Add onions and garlic; cook and stir 1 minute.

2. Stir in beans, corn, green chiles, bouillon cube, cumin, salt, pepper and water. Heat to boiling. Reduce heat to low; cover and simmer about 15 minutes to blend flavors, stirring occasionally.

3. Remove from heat. Stir in cilantro. To serve, place 2 tablespoons cheese in each individual soup bowl if desired. Spoon chili over cheese. Top with tortilla chips if desired.

1 serving: Calories 370 (Calories from Fat 15); Total Fat 2g (Saturated Fat 0g; Trans Fat 0g); Cholesterol 0mg; Sodium 970mg; Total Carbohydrate 67g (Dietary Fiber 15g; Sugars 6g); Protein 21g
% daily value: Vitamin A 6%; Vitamin C 15%; Calcium 20%; Iron 50%   **exchanges:** 4 1/2 Starch, 1 Very Lean Meat
carbohydrate choices: 4 1/2

CHILI blanco

mexican tofu–rice SKILLET *(page 256)*

CHAPTER 7 unbelievable! it's soy

The burgers in this recipe are microwaved for a brief flash to thaw them before the dish is assembled and baked. This step ensures they will heat through during baking.

italian "veggie burger" BAKE

prep time: 25 minutes   **start to finish:** 1 hour 15 minutes   4 servings

1 cup uncooked orzo or rosamarina pasta (6 oz)
4 frozen soy-protein burgers
3 cups frozen bell pepper and onion stir-fry (from 1-lb bag)
1 can (14.5 oz) diced tomatoes with basil, garlic and oregano, undrained
1 container (7 or 8 oz) plain hummus (3/4 cup)
1 cup crumbled tomato-basil feta cheese (4 oz)
1/3 cup pitted Kalamata olives, coarsely chopped

1. Heat oven to 350°F. Spray 8-inch square (2-quart) glass baking dish with cooking spray. Cook and drain pasta as directed on package.

2. Meanwhile, on large microwavable plate, microwave burgers uncovered on High 2 to 3 minutes, turning once, until thawed.

3. Spray 12-inch skillet with cooking spray; heat over medium-high heat until hot. Add pepper and onion stir-fry; cook 2 to 3 minutes, stirring frequently, until crisp-tender. Stir in diced tomatoes. Cook 4 to 6 minutes, stirring frequently, until slightly thickened. Remove from heat.

4. In medium bowl, stir pasta and hummus until coated. In baking dish, layer half each of the pasta mixture, vegetable mixture and cheese; top with burgers. Repeat with remaining pasta mixture, vegetable mixture and cheese. Sprinkle olives evenly over top.

5. Cover tightly with foil; bake 35 minutes. Uncover; bake 5 to 10 minutes longer or until heated through. Let stand 5 minutes before serving.

1 serving: Calories 510 (Calories from Fat 140); Total Fat 15g (Saturated Fat 5g; Trans Fat 0g); Cholesterol 25mg; Sodium 1330mg; Total Carbohydrate 66g (Dietary Fiber 7g; Sugars 10g); Protein 27g
% daily value: Vitamin A 10%; Vitamin C 50%; Calcium 30%; Iron 35%   **exchanges:** 3 1/2 Starch, 1/2 Other Carbohydrate, 1 Vegetable, 2 Lean Meat, 1 1/2 Fat   **carbohydrate choices:** 4 1/2

If you can't find Caribbean jerk seasoning, you can substitute any type of seasoning labeled "jerk," or try Cajun or Creole seasoning.

caribbean soybean and rice BAKE

prep time: 15 minutes   **start to finish:** 50 minutes   4 servings

1 1/2 cups uncooked instant brown rice
1 cup frozen shelled edamame (green) soybeans (from 12-oz bag)
1/2 medium green bell pepper, coarsely chopped (1/2 cup)
4 medium sliced green onions (1/4 cup)
1 tablespoon Caribbean jerk seasoning
1 cup water
1 can (15 oz) soybeans, drained, rinsed
1 can (14 1/2 oz) stewed tomatoes with Italian herbs, undrained, cut up
1 cup shredded Cheddar cheese (4 oz)

1. Heat oven to 375°F. Spray 11 × 7-inch (2-quart) glass baking dish with cooking spray. In dish, mix all ingredients except cheese.

2. Cover tightly with foil; bake 25 to 30 minutes or until liquid is absorbed and rice is tender. Uncover; stir in 1/2 cup cheese. Sprinkle remaining cheese over top. Bake uncovered 5 minutes longer or until cheese is melted.

1 serving: Calories 560 (Calories from Fat 200); Total Fat 22g (Saturated Fat 8g; Trans Fat 0g); Cholesterol 30mg; Sodium 810mg; Total Carbohydrate 58g (Dietary Fiber 11g; Sugars 8g); Protein 32g
% daily value: Vitamin A 15%; Vitamin C 35%; Calcium 35%; Iron 40%   **exchanges:** 3 Starch, 1/2 Other Carbohydrate, 1 Vegetable, 3 Lean Meat, 2 Fat   **carbohydrate choices:** 4

Lightly salted soy nuts add lots of crunch to this "soy-ful" warm salad. Look for them alongside other salty snacks in the self-serve bins or health food section of the store.

edamame stir-fry SALAD (LOW fat)

prep time: 20 minutes   **start to finish:** 20 minutes   6 servings

1 bag (1 lb 5 oz) frozen stir-fry sesame meal starter
1 bag (12 oz) frozen shelled edamame (green) soybeans
2 tablespoons rice vinegar
4 cups thinly sliced Chinese (napa) cabbage
2 tablespoons chopped fresh cilantro
1/4 cup salted roasted soy nuts

1. Cut large slit in frozen sesame sauce packet from meal starter. Microwave on High 30 to 60 seconds. In large bowl, reserve 1/4 cup sesame sauce.

2. Spray 12-inch skillet with cooking spray; heat over medium-high heat. Add soybeans, remaining sesame sauce and frozen vegetables from meal starter. Cover; cook 5 to 7 minutes, stirring frequently, just until vegetables are crisp-tender. Remove from heat.

3. To sesame sauce in bowl, stir in vinegar. Add cabbage, cilantro and cooked vegetable mixture; toss to mix. Top with soy nuts. Serve immediately.

1 serving: Calories 170 (Calories from Fat 60); Total Fat 7g (Saturated Fat 1g; Trans Fat 0g); Cholesterol 0mg; Sodium 570mg; Total Carbohydrate 15g (Dietary Fiber 6g; Sugars 3g); Protein 11g

% daily value: Vitamin A 60%; Vitamin C 45%; Calcium 15%; Iron 15%   **exchanges:** 1/2 Starch, 1 Vegetable, 1 Very Lean Meat, 1 1/2 Fat
carbohydrate choices: 1

edamame stir-fry SALAD

Is company coming? Serve the patties over steaming-hot spaghetti and top with the pasta sauce and cheese. Add a bagged salad with Italian dressing and some sorbet for dessert and you're all set.

skillet "CHICKEN" PARMIGIANA

prep time: 15 minutes   **start to finish:** 25 minutes   4 servings

1 tablespoon olive or vegetable oil
1 package (10 oz) frozen chicken-style breaded soy-protein patties
2 cups tomato pasta sauce
1/2 cup shredded mozzarella cheese (2 oz)

1. In 10-inch skillet, heat oil over medium heat. Add patties; cook 5 to 7 minutes, turning once, until heated through.

2. Pour pasta sauce over patties in skillet; sprinkle with cheese. Reduce heat to low; cover and cook 5 to 7 minutes or until sauce is hot and cheese is melted.

1 serving: Calories 360 (Calories from Fat 150); Total Fat 17g (Saturated Fat 4g; Trans Fat 1g); Cholesterol 10mg; Sodium 1120mg; Total Carbohydrate 35g (Dietary Fiber 3g; Sugars 10g); Protein 17g
% daily value: Vitamin A 15%; Vitamin C 15%; Calcium 15%; Iron 15%   **exchanges:** 1 1/2 Starch, 1 Other Carbohydrate, 2 Medium-Fat Meat, 1 Fat   **carbohydrate choices:** 2

This is great served over hot cooked rice or Japanese curly noodles; try sprinkling toasted regular sesame seed or untoasted black sesame seed over the top for extra Asian taste.

sweet-and-sour "CHICKEN" (LOW fat)

prep time: 20 minutes   **start to finish:** 20 minutes   4 servings

1 package (10 to 10.5 oz) frozen chicken-style
**   breaded soy-protein nuggets**
1 bag (1 lb) frozen broccoli, carrots and water chestnuts
1 can (20 oz) pineapple chunks, drained
1 jar (10 oz) sweet-and-sour sauce (1 1/3 cups)

1. Bake nuggets as directed on package.

2. Meanwhile, in 3-quart saucepan, heat 1/4 cup water to boiling. Add frozen vegetables; reduce heat to medium. Cover; cook 7 to 8 minutes, stirring occasionally and breaking apart large pieces, until hot. Drain; return vegetables to saucepan.

3. Stir in nuggets, pineapple and sweet-and-sour sauce. Cook over medium heat 3 to 4 minutes, stirring occasionally, until hot.

1 serving: Calories 320 (Calories from Fat 60); Total Fat 7g (Saturated Fat 1g; Trans Fat 0g); Cholesterol 0mg; Sodium 840mg; Total Carbohydrate 52g (Dietary Fiber 6g; Sugars 28g); Protein 14g
% daily value: Vitamin A 35%; Vitamin C 35%; Calcium 10%; Iron 15%   **exchanges:** 1 Starch, 2 Other Carbohydrate, 1 Vegetable, 1 1/2 Medium-Fat Meat   **carbohydrate choices:** 3 1/2

Chicken-style breaded soy-protein patties cook up crispy on the outside just like their real chicken counterparts, but the patty itself has a slightly softer texture. Look for regular and spicy varieties.

hot "chicken" SUB

prep time: 30 minutes   **start to finish:** 30 minutes   6 servings

6 frozen chicken-style breaded soy-protein patties
   (from two 10-oz packages)
1 loaf (1 lb) French bread, cut in half horizontally
1/2 cup creamy Italian dressing
Lettuce
1 large tomato, thinly sliced

1. Heat patties as directed on package.

2. Spread cut sides of bread with dressing. Layer lettuce, patties and tomato on bottom half of bread. Cover with top half of bread. Cut into slices to serve.

1 serving: Calories 440 (Calories from Fat 150); Total Fat 17g (Saturated Fat 2g; Trans Fat 1.5g); Cholesterol 0mg; Sodium 1050mg; Total Carbohydrate 52g (Dietary Fiber 3g; Sugars 4g); Protein 19g
% daily value: Vitamin A 6%; Vitamin C 6%; Calcium 15%; Iron 25%   **exchanges:** 3 1/2 Starch, 1 Medium-Fat Meat, 2 Fat
carbohydrate choices: 3 1/2

Be sure you're on the right page—coconut milk is made from the flesh of coconut, not the thin liquid found inside the ripe fruit. It gives the sauce subtle coconut flavor and a creamy texture. Look for regular and reduced-fat (lite) coconut milk in the Asian foods aisle.

pepper and soybean STIR-FRY

prep time: 20 minutes   **start to finish:** 20 minutes   4 servings

2/3 cup uncooked jasmine rice
1 cup water
1 tablespoon vegetable oil
1 tablespoon curry powder
1 bag (1 lb) frozen bell pepper and onion stir-fry
1 bag (12 oz) frozen shelled edamame (green) soybeans
4 cloves garlic, finely chopped
1 cup unsweetened coconut milk (not cream of coconut)
1/2 cup salted roasted cashews
Chopped fresh cilantro or parsley, if desired

1. Cook rice in water as directed on package.

2. Meanwhile, in 12-inch nonstick skillet, heat oil over medium-high heat. Add curry powder; cook 1 minute, stirring frequently. Stir in bell pepper and onion stir-fry, soybeans and garlic. Cook 2 minutes, stirring frequently. Cover; cook about 3 minutes longer or until vegetables are tender.

3. Stir in coconut milk. Reduce heat to medium-low; simmer uncovered 2 minutes, stirring occasionally.

4. Serve mixture over rice. Sprinkle with cashews and cilantro if desired.

1 serving: Calories 540 (Calories from Fat 250); Total Fat 28g (Saturated Fat 12g; Trans Fat 0g); Cholesterol 0mg; Sodium 370mg; Total Carbohydrate 53g (Dietary Fiber 11g; Sugars 8g); Protein 19g
% daily value: Vitamin A 8%; Vitamin C 50%; Calcium 15%; Iron 25%   **exchanges:** 2 1/2 Starch, 1/2 Other Carbohydrate, 1 Vegetable, 1 1/2 Very Lean Meat, 5 Fat   **carbohydrate choices:** 3 1/2

The produce department is loaded with convenience items; look for preshredded carrots to save time. Toasted sliced almonds would add another layer of flavor to this salad. To toast them, place 1/4 cup in an ungreased heavy skillet and cook over medium-low heat about 5 minutes, stirring frequently until they begin to brown, then stirring constantly until golden brown.

crunchy oriental "chicken" SALAD

prep time: 25 minutes   **start to finish:** 25 minutes   4 servings

DRESSING
1/3 cup mayonnaise or salad dressing
1/4 cup Asian sesame dressing and marinade

SALAD
1 package (10 or 10.5 oz) frozen chicken-style breaded soy-protein nuggets
8 cups torn mixed salad greens
1 cup shredded red cabbage
1 cup shredded carrots (1 1/2 medium)
2 medium green onions, sliced (2 tablespoons)
1 cup wide chow mein noodles

1. In small bowl, mix dressing ingredients with wire whisk until creamy.

2. Heat nuggets as directed on package.

3. Divide salad greens, cabbage, carrots and onions unto 4 plates or into 4 shallow bowls. Top with nuggets; sprinkle with noodles. Drizzle with dressing.

1 serving: Calories 410 (Calories from Fat 210); Total Fat 24g (Saturated Fat 3.5g; Trans Fat 0g); Cholesterol 10mg; Sodium 1010mg; Total Carbohydrate 33g (Dietary Fiber 6g; Sugars 9g); Protein 15g
% daily value: Vitamin A 170%; Vitamin C 35%; Calcium 10%; Iron 20%   **exchanges:** 1 Starch, 1/2 Other Carbohydrate, 2 Vegetable, 1 Medium-Fat Meat, 4 Fat   **carbohydrate choices:** 2

crunchy oriental "chicken" SALAD

Pureed soft silken tofu gives dips and sauces—like the one in this recipe—the creamy, smooth texture of sour cream without the fat—and it adds protein!

PASTA with sweet beans and basil "cream" (LOW fat)

prep time: 20 minutes   **start to finish:** 20 minutes   6 servings

6 cups uncooked farfalle (bow-tie) pasta (12 oz)
1 1/2 cups frozen shelled edamame (green) soybeans (from 12-oz bag)
1 cup original-flavored soy milk
1/4 cup chopped fresh or 1 tablespoon dried basil leaves
1 tablespoon olive or vegetable oil
1 teaspoon salt
1 package (12 oz) soft silken tofu
1/4 cup grated Parmesan cheese

1. In 5-quart Dutch oven, heat 4 quarts (16 cups) salted water to boiling. Add pasta; boil uncovered 6 minutes, stirring occasionally. Add soybeans; return to boiling. Cook uncovered about 6 minutes longer, stirring occasionally, until pasta is tender. Drain; return to saucepan.

2. Meanwhile, in blender or food processor, place remaining ingredients except cheese. Cover; blend on high speed until smooth, stopping to scrape down sides as needed.

3. Stir tofu mixture into pasta in saucepan. Reduce heat to low; cook about 3 minutes, stirring constantly, until warm. Just before serving, sprinkle with cheese; toss.

1 serving: Calories 380 (Calories from Fat 90); Total Fat 10g (Saturated Fat 2g; Trans Fat 0g); Cholesterol 0mg; Sodium 840mg; Total Carbohydrate 54g (Dietary Fiber 6g; Sugars 3g); Protein 20g
% daily value: Vitamin A 6%; Vitamin C 6%; Calcium 20%; Iron 25%   **exchanges:** 3 1/2 Starch, 1 1/2 Lean Meat, 1/2 Fat
carbohydrate choices: 3 1/2

Edamame is the Japanese name for fresh green soybeans, tasty little, bright green gems that are high in protein and easily digested. Try eating them as a snack or appetizer—you may become addicted!

hearty soybean and cheddar–pasta
SALAD

prep time: 30 minutes   **start to finish:** 1 hour 30 minutes   4 servings

1 cup uncooked penne pasta (3 oz)
2 cups frozen shelled edamame (green) soybeans (from 12-oz bag)
6 oz Cheddar cheese, cut into 1/2-inch cubes (1 1/2 cups)
1 large tomato, coarsely chopped (1 cup)
1/2 medium cucumber, coarsely chopped (1/2 cup)
1 small yellow bell pepper, coarsely chopped (1/2 cup)
2/3 cup Italian dressing

1. Cook and drain pasta as directed on package. Rinse with cold water; drain.

2. Meanwhile, cook soybeans as directed on package. Rinse with cold water; drain.

3. In large bowl, toss pasta, soybeans and remaining ingredients. Cover; refrigerate at least 1 hour before serving.

1 serving: Calories 570 (Calories from Fat 330); Total Fat 37g (Saturated Fat 11g; Trans Fat 0g); Cholesterol 50mg; Sodium 910mg; Total Carbohydrate 35g (Dietary Fiber 6g; Sugars 8g); Protein 26g
% daily value: Vitamin A 20%; Vitamin C 50%; Calcium 40%; Iron 20%   **exchanges:** 2 Starch, 1/2 Other Carbohydrate, 3 High-Fat Meat, 2 Fat   **carbohydrate choices:** 2

Here's a light, golden, flavor-rich egg dish for your next weekend brunch! Vary the flavor by using broccoli or mushrooms instead of bell pepper and different varieties of cheese or seasoned stuffing mix.

italian "sausage" egg BAKE   (LOW fat)

prep time: 10 minutes   **start to finish:** 1 hour 5 minutes   12 servings

1 package (6 oz) seasoned stuffing mix
1 package (12 oz) frozen sausage-style soy-protein crumbles
1 medium red bell pepper, cut into 1/2-inch pieces
2 medium green onions, sliced (2 tablespoons)
1 cup shredded Swiss cheese (4 oz)
2 cups original-flavored soy milk
1/2 teaspoon Italian seasoning
1/2 teaspoon salt
1 can (10 3/4 oz) condensed cream of mushroom soup
6 eggs

1. Heat oven to 350°F. Spray 13 × 9-inch (3-quart) glass baking dish with cooking spray. In dish, layer stuffing mix, crumbles, bell pepper, green onions and cheese.

2. In small bowl, mix remaining ingredients with wire whisk until blended; pour over ingredients in dish.

3. Bake uncovered 45 to 55 minutes or until knife inserted in center comes out clean and top is set and lightly browned. Let stand 5 minutes before serving.

1 serving: Calories 220 (Calories from Fat 80); Total Fat 9g (Saturated Fat 3.5g; Trans Fat 0g); Cholesterol 115mg; Sodium 810mg; Total Carbohydrate 19g (Dietary Fiber 2g; Sugars 3g); Protein 15g
% daily value: Vitamin A 20%; Vitamin C 15%; Calcium 20%; Iron 10%   **exchanges:** 1 Starch, 1 1/2 Medium-Fat Meat, 1/2 Fat
carbohydrate choices: 1

Frittata is Italian for "omelet," although frittatas are different from traditional omelets. Frittatas aren't filled and folded; instead, the filling becomes part of the egg mixture and ingredients may be sprinkled on top. Frittatas are cut into wedges for serving.

denver eggs FRITTATA

prep time: 15 minutes   **start to finish:** 30 minutes   4 servings

2 tablespoons vegetable oil
4 frozen soy-protein breakfast sausage links, thawed and cut into 1/4-inch pieces
1/2 medium green bell pepper, cut into bite-size strips
1/2 medium red bell pepper, cut into bite-size strips
1 medium onion, sliced
8 eggs
1/2 teaspoon salt
1/2 cup shredded Cheddar cheese (2 oz)

1. In 12-inch nonstick skillet, heat oil over medium-high heat. Add sausage pieces, bell peppers and onion; cook about 5 minutes, stirring occasionally, until tender. Spread vegetables evenly in skillet.

2. In medium bowl, beat eggs and salt with wire whisk. Pour eggs over vegetables. Reduce heat to medium-low; cover and cook 9 to 11 minutes or until eggs are set. Remove from heat.

3. Sprinkle with cheese. Cover; let stand about 2 minutes or until cheese is melted. Cut into wedges to serve.

1 serving: Calories 290 (Calories from Fat 200); Total Fat 22g (Saturated Fat 7g; Trans Fat 0g); Cholesterol 440mg; Sodium 510mg; Total Carbohydrate 6g (Dietary Fiber 1g; Sugars 4g); Protein 17g
% daily value: Vitamin A 35%; Vitamin C 35%; Calcium 15%; Iron 8%   **exchanges:** 2 1/2 Medium-Fat Meat, 2 Fat
carbohydrate choices: 1/2

If turnips and rutabagas aren't your favorites, just increase the amount of potatoes in the recipe to 3 cups and add 3 cups sliced fresh mushrooms (8 ounces). This satisfying stew will be welcome by carnivores as well as vegetarians—it will fight winter chills and keep the whole family warm and happy.

baked "veggie burger" STEW (LOW fat)

prep time: 15 minutes   **start to finish:** 1 hour 15 minutes   4 servings

4 frozen soy-protein burgers
2 medium potatoes, cubed (2 cups)
2 small turnips, peeled, cubed (2 cups)
1/2 medium rutabaga, peeled, cubed (2 cups)
2 medium stalks celery, sliced (1 cup)
2 medium carrots, sliced (1 cup)
3 small onions, cut into quarters
1/2 cup all-purpose flour
2 cups vegetable broth
1 can (14.5 oz) whole tomatoes, undrained
2 tablespoons chopped fresh or 3/4 teaspoon dried thyme leaves
2 tablespoons chopped fresh or 3/4 teaspoon dried marjoram leaves
1/4 teaspoon salt
1/4 teaspoon pepper
1 dried bay leaf

1. Heat oven to 350°F. On large microwavable plate, microwave burgers uncovered on High 2 to 3 minutes, turning once, until thawed. Cut into 1-inch pieces; set aside.

2. In ovenproof 4-quart Dutch oven, mix potatoes, turnips, rutabaga, celery, carrots and onions.

3. In small bowl, mix flour and broth until smooth. Stir broth mixture and remaining ingredients except burger pieces into vegetable mixture, breaking up tomatoes. Heat to boiling over medium-high heat. Stir in burger pieces.

4. Cover; bake 50 to 60 minutes, stirring occasionally, until vegetables are tender. Remove bay leaf before serving.

1 serving: Calories 310 (Calories from Fat 30); Total Fat 3.5g (Saturated Fat 0.5g; Trans Fat 0g); Cholesterol 0mg; Sodium 1230mg; Total Carbohydrate 53g (Dietary Fiber 8g; Sugars 11g); Protein 18g
% daily value: Vitamin A 130%; Vitamin C 40%; Calcium 15%; Iron 25%   **exchanges:** 2 Starch, 1 Other Carbohydrate, 2 Vegetable, 1 Lean Meat   **carbohydrate choices:** 3 1/2

For a more intense Cheddar flavor, use sharp Cheddar. Want a fun garnish for this creamy soup? Throw on a handful of popcorn, but keep the bowl handy—folks will sneak on more!

broccoli–cheese SOUP

prep time: 25 minutes   **start to finish:** 25 minutes   5 servings

1 tablespoon butter or margarine
1 medium onion, chopped (1/2 cup)
1 tablespoon all-purpose flour
1 teaspoon salt
3 cups original-flavored soy milk
2 teaspoons cornstarch
3 cups bite-size fresh or frozen (thawed) broccoli florets
1 1/2 cups shredded Cheddar cheese (6 oz)

1. In 3-quart saucepan, melt butter over medium heat. Stir in onion, flour and salt. Cook 2 to 3 minutes, stirring constantly, until onion is soft.

2. In small bowl, mix soy milk and cornstarch with wire whisk until smooth. Gradually stir into onion mixture. Heat to boiling; boil 1 minute, stirring constantly, until bubbly and thickened.

3. Stir in broccoli. Cook 4 to 5 minutes, stirring frequently. Stir in cheese. Cook 2 to 4 minutes, stirring frequently, until cheese is melted.

1 serving: Calories 270 (Calories from Fat 150); Total Fat 16g (Saturated Fat 9g; Trans Fat 0g); Cholesterol 40mg; Sodium 790mg; Total Carbohydrate 16g (Dietary Fiber 3g; Sugars 6g); Protein 15g
% daily value: Vitamin A 25%; Vitamin C 35%; Calcium 40%; Iron 10%   **exchanges:** 1/2 Starch, 1 Vegetable, 1 1/2 High-Fat Meat, 1 Fat
carbohydrate choices: 1

cauliflower–cheese SOUP: Use bite-size cauliflower pieces instead of the broccoli.

Looking for an icebreaker for introducing tofu into your eating plan? This recipe is it! Why? The dish starts with familiar Mexican flavors and lets tofu do its chameleon act of absorbing all the wonderful flavors in the dish.

mexican tofu–rice SKILLET

prep time: 30 minutes   **start to finish:** 35 minutes   4 servings

1 package (12 oz) extra-firm tofu packed in water, drained
1 cup frozen whole kernel corn (from 1-lb bag)
1 can (14.5 oz) diced tomatoes with green chilies, undrained
1 package (5.6 oz) Spanish rice–flavor rice and
    pasta blend mix in tomato sauce
1 1/4 cups water
1 cup shredded Mexican cheese blend (4 oz)
1 1/2 cups shredded lettuce
1 large tomato, seeded, chopped (1 cup)
4 medium green onions, sliced (1/4 cup)

1. Place drained tofu between 2 layers of paper towels; press gently to remove as much water as possible. Cut into 1/2-inch cubes; set aside.

2. In 12-inch nonstick skillet, mix corn, diced tomatoes with chilies, contents of rice mix package and water. Gently stir in tofu. Heat to boiling. Reduce heat to low; cover and simmer 12 to 14 minutes, stirring occasionally, until rice is tender.

3. Remove skillet from heat. Sprinkle cheese over rice mixture. Cover; let stand 4 to 5 minutes or until liquid is absorbed and cheese is melted. Top with lettuce, chopped tomato and onions.

1 serving: Calories 420 (Calories from Fat 140); Total Fat 16g (Saturated Fat 6g; Trans Fat 0g); Cholesterol 25mg; Sodium 1060mg; Total Carbohydrate 48g (Dietary Fiber 5g; Sugars 9g); Protein 23g
% daily value: Vitamin A 35%; Vitamin C 20%; Calcium 35%; Iron 20%   **exchanges:** 3 Starch, 1 Vegetable, 1 1/2 High-Fat Meat, 1/2 Fat
carbohydrate choices: 3

STIR-FRIED TOFU with almonds

prep time: 30 minutes   **start to finish:** 30 minutes   4 servings

4 oz uncooked spinach fettuccine or fettuccine,
    broken into 3-inch pieces
1/2 cup vegetable broth
1/3 cup dry white wine or vegetable broth
1 tablespoon cornstarch
3 tablespoons hoisin sauce
1/8 teaspoon pepper
1 package (14 oz) firm tofu packed in water, drained
2 tablespoons vegetable oil
1 1/2 cups bite-size fresh cauliflower florets
1 large red or green bell pepper, cut into bite-size strips
2 cloves garlic, finely chopped
1/3 cup sliced almonds, toasted

1. Cook and drain fettuccine as directed on package.

2. Meanwhile, in small bowl, mix broth, wine, cornstarch, hoisin sauce and pepper; set aside. Place drained tofu between 2 layers of paper towels; press gently to remove as much water as possible. Cut into 3/4-inch cubes; set aside.

3. Heat wok or 12-inch skillet over high heat. Add 1 tablespoon of the oil; rotate wok to coat side. Add cauliflower and bell pepper; cook and stir about 4 minutes or until vegetables are crisp-tender. Remove vegetables from wok.

4. Add remaining tablespoon oil to wok; rotate wok to coat side. Add tofu and garlic; cook and stir gently over high heat 5 minutes. Stir in broth mixture. Cook and stir about 1 minute or until thickened. Stir in vegetables and fettuccine; heat through. Sprinkle with almonds.

1 serving: Calories 380 (Calories from Fat 170); Total Fat 19g (Saturated Fat 2.5g; Trans Fat 0g); Cholesterol 25mg; Sodium 470mg; Total Carbohydrate 35g (Dietary Fiber 4g; Sugars 6g); Protein 17g
% daily value: Vitamin A 10%; Vitamin C 45%; Calcium 20%; Iron 20%   **exchanges:** 2 Starch, 1 1/2 Medium-Fat Meat, 2 Fat
carbohydrate choices: 2

all about SOY

Soy is now on our radar screens—and what an impressive emergence it has made. A staple of the Asian diet for thousands of years, soy has made inroads into the American diet, from receiving mild curiosity a few decades ago to now being firmly rooted and here to stay! Now one of our nation's largest crops, soybeans are being used in a myriad of ways with great enthusiasm. Read on for information on the health benefits of soy and the variety of soy products.

Healthy Soy

Soy is a healthy food; it has no cholesterol, and unlike most plant foods, it is a good source of high-quality protein, making it a great substitute for animal protein. Most soy foods, like soy milk and tofu, are also cholesterol-free and are fortified with calcium as well. Heart health continues to be the most promising benefit for soy, with major studies underway. Soy has been shown to reduce LDL, or "bad" cholesterol, although this needs further study, and it may modestly increase HDL, or "good" cholesterol. At this time, data is inconsistent for the effects of soy on bone density, but studies continue. Data on soy relieving menopausal symptoms like hot flashes is weak, and scientific evidence for soy reducing breast and prostate cancers is limited.

Dried Soybeans can be used like any dried legume. Dried soybeans take 3 to 4 hours to cook, which is two to three times longer than other dried legumes. Canned cooked soybeans are also available.

Edamame is the Japanese name for fresh green soybeans—tasty little, bright green gems that are high in protein and easily digested. The soybeans are picked before they are completely mature and are often sold in their fuzzy green pods. Fresh edamame is available spring through fall in raw and ready-to-eat forms at co-ops, natural-foods stores or large supermarkets. Raw beans should be steamed 20 minutes before eating and are usually served chilled. They're also available frozen in boxes or bags. Once cooked, edamame can be served right in the pods as a fun appetizer or snack, and it can be shelled and used in salads or other cold or hot side dishes.

Frozen Desserts often use soy milk to replace dairy products for products similar to ice cream.

Meat Analogs (Meat Substitutes) or soy-protein products have come a long way in taste, texture and variety since the first soy burgers hit the freezer case, as vegetarian appetites for premium-quality products has increased. Look for products in these categories: breakfast, burgers, chicken, ground, hot dogs, pepperoni, sausages and entrées. Some soy-protein products may contain small amounts of cheese, dairy or egg products.

Soy Cheese is made from tofu or soy milk and tastes similar to cheese made with cow's milk. Although soy cheeses do contain fat, there are reduced-fat brands available, and all soy cheese is cholesterol-free. Some may contain milk/dairy, so we can't say this is vegan.

Soy Margarine is made with liquid soybean oil and partially hydrogenated soybean oil along with other ingredients like salt, coloring and vitamin A.

Soy Milk is made by pressing ground cooked soybeans. It is higher in protein than cow's milk. Because it's a nondairy product, it's a common substitute used by those with milk allergies and is also used by vegans. Flavored varieties, like vanilla, are available.

Soy Yogurt is made from cultured soy milk and is available in many flavors. Soy yogurt is lactose-free and cholesterol-free.

Tempeh, Indonesian in origin, is made from fermented whole soybeans in a process similar to making cheese or wine. The soybeans are formed into chunky cakes that sometimes include grains. Tempeh has a firm, chewy texture and a mild flavor similar to nutty cheese or fresh mushrooms. Look for golden brown soybeans held together in a white or cream-colored cake with a few brown or gray spots. As tempeh ages, the flavor becomes stronger and more spots appear, including some black spots. If it's full of gray-black or black spots or smells like ammonia, it's spoiled and should not be used. It is sold raw, either flavored or unflavored, and ready to cook in the refrigerated or freezer case. Most unflavored tempeh is first marinated before cooking; try it sautéed or grilled, or add it to soups, stews, casseroles and chili.

Texturized Soy Protein (also known as TSP) is made from fat-free soy flour that has been compressed and processed into chunks, flakes or granules that require rehydration. It has a texture similar to ground beef. It can be used to replace part or all of the ground meat in some recipes. Chunk-size pieces also are available to replace stew meat.

Toasted Soy Nuts are a crunchy snack sold either salted or unsalted.

Tofu, also known as soybean curd or bean curd, is made from soybeans. The soybeans are soaked, cooked, ground and then mixed with a curdling ingredient. The resulting curds are drained and pressed into cakes, which are tofu. It is very mildly flavored with a taste similar to a very mild cheese. Because it is so mild, it easily absorbs the flavors of the herbs, spices and foods it is cooked with. Look for tofu in the produce, dairy, deli or natural-foods section of the supermarket.

There are two forms of tofu:

1. Japanese-style, or silken, tofu is packaged in aseptic shelf-stable packages.
2. Chinese-style tofu is packed in water and must be kept refrigerated at all times.

Japanese- and Chinese-style tofus come in these varieties:

EXTRA-FIRM AND FIRM tofu is solid and dense and works well for stir-frying, grilling, casseroles, deep-frying or any dish where you want to keep the shape of the tofu. This type of tofu is higher in protein, fat and calcium than other types of tofu.

SOFT TOFU can be used in recipes like soup, chili and meat loaf, and in cream pie fillings and puddings.

SILKEN TOFU has a creamy, custardlike texture that can be used in sauces, dips, beverages and desserts, and in any blended or pureed dishes.

FLAVORED TOFU is packaged in a marinade to give it a specific flavor, and often the tofu is baked or broiled.

REDUCED-FAT OR LITE TOFU, having a texture similar to soft tofu, is available for those watching fat grams. Use it in the same type of recipes as soft tofu.

In the mood for a tasty side dish? Just leave the tofu out as this very flavorful noodle and mushroom dish can stand on its own.

tofu-teriyaki-mushroom NOODLES (LOW fat)

prep time: 30 minutes   **start to finish:** 30 minutes   **4 servings**

6 dried Chinese black or shiitake mushrooms (1/2 oz)
8 oz uncooked soba (buckwheat) noodles or whole wheat spaghetti
1 package (14 oz) firm tofu packed in water, drained
1 tablespoon vegetable oil
1 large onion, sliced
1 package (8 oz) sliced fresh mushrooms (3 cups)
8 oz fresh shiitake, crimini or baby portabella mushrooms, sliced
1/3 cup teriyaki sauce
1/4 cup chopped fresh cilantro

1. In small bowl, pour 1 cup hot water over dried mushrooms; let stand about 20 minutes or until soft.

2. Meanwhile, cook and drain noodles as directed on package. Place drained tofu between 2 layers of paper towels; press gently to remove as much water as possible. Cut into 1/4-inch cubes; set aside.

3. Drain water from dried mushrooms; rinse with warm water and drain again. Squeeze out excess moisture from mushrooms. Remove and discard stems; cut caps into 1/2-inch strips.

4. In 12-inch skillet or wok, heat oil over medium-high heat. Add onion; cook and stir 3 minutes. Add all mushrooms and tofu; cook and stir 3 minutes. Stir in teriyaki sauce. Reduce heat; partially cover and simmer about 2 minutes or until vegetables are tender. Stir in noodles, cilantro and, if desired, 1 tablespoon toasted sesame seed.

1 serving: Calories 420 (Calories from Fat 90); Total Fat 10g (Saturated Fat 1.5g; Trans Fat 0g); Cholesterol 0mg; Sodium 1150mg; Total Carbohydrate 58g (Dietary Fiber 7g; Sugars 7g); Protein 24g
% daily value: Vitamin A 2%; Vitamin C 4%; Calcium 20%; Iron 30%   **exchanges:** 3 Starch, 2 Vegetable, 1 1/2 Medium-Fat Meat, 1/2 Fat
carbohydrate choices: 4

Canned beans and tofu stand in for meat, poultry and shellfish, which are widely used in jambalaya recipes. The result—a truly tasty dish that will transport you to the bayou. Take a tip from New Orleans's nickname, and kick back with a "Big Easy" night when you cook this low-key skillet meal.

tofu and sweet potato JAMBALAYA

prep time: 45 minutes   **start to finish:** 55 minutes   4 servings

1 package (14 oz) firm tofu packed in water, drained
1 tablespoon olive or vegetable oil
1 large dark-orange sweet potato, peeled, cut into 1/2-inch cubes (2 cups)
2 cloves garlic, finely chopped
1 can (14 oz) vegetable broth
3/4 cup uncooked regular long-grain rice
2 tablespoons Worcestershire sauce
1/4 teaspoon ground red pepper (cayenne)
1 can (15 oz) black beans, drained, rinsed
12 medium green onions, sliced (3/4 cup)

1. Place tofu between 2 layers of paper towels; press gently to remove as much water as possible. Cut into 3/4-inch cubes.

2. In 12-inch skillet, heat oil over medium heat. Add tofu; cook 6 to 8 minutes, turning frequently, until light golden brown. Remove tofu from skillet; set aside.

3. In same skillet, cook sweet potato and garlic 2 to 3 minutes, stirring occasionally, just until sweet potato begins to brown. Stir in broth, uncooked rice, Worcestershire sauce and red pepper. Heat to boiling. Reduce heat; cover and simmer 10 minutes.

4. Stir in beans. Cover; cook 8 to 10 minutes, stirring occasionally, until rice is tender and liquid is absorbed. Stir in tofu and onions. Cook 1 to 2 minutes or until heated through.

1 serving: Calories 470 (Calories from Fat 90); Total Fat 10g (Saturated Fat 1.5g; Trans Fat 0g); Cholesterol 0mg; Sodium 540mg; Total Carbohydrate 74g (Dietary Fiber 9g; Sugars 13g); Protein 22g
% daily value: Vitamin A 170%; Vitamin C 15%; Calcium 30%; Iron 35%   **exchanges:** 4 Starch, 1 Other Carbohydrate, 1 1/2 Lean Meat, 1/2 Fat   **carbohydrate choices:** 5

Tempeh, pronounced TEHM-pay and also spelled tempe, is a fermented, high-protein soybean cake with a chewy texture and slightly nutty flavor. If you can't find this tasty ingredient in your supermarket, check in a health food store.

TEMPEH STIR-FRY
with yogurt–peanut sauce

prep time: 40 minutes   **start to finish:** 40 minutes   4 servings

1/4 cup creamy peanut butter
1/4 cup vanilla lowfat yogurt
3 tablespoons teriyaki marinade
1 tablespoon honey
2 tablespoons vegetable oil
1 package (8 oz) tempeh, cut into 2 × 1/4 × 1/4-inch strips
1 medium onion, cut into thin wedges
3 medium carrots, cut into 2 × 1/4 × 1/4-inch strips (1 1/2 cups)
8 oz fresh green beans, cut in half crosswise (1 1/2 cups)
1/4 cup water
1 medium red bell pepper, cut into thin bite-size strips
1/4 cup chopped fresh cilantro

1. In small bowl, beat peanut butter, yogurt, teriyaki marinade and honey with wire whisk until smooth; set aside.

2. In 12-inch skillet, heat 1 tablespoon of the oil over medium heat. Add tempeh; cook 5 to 6 minutes, turning frequently, until light golden brown. Remove tempeh from skillet; set aside.

3. To same skillet, add remaining tablespoon oil and the onion; cook 1 minute, stirring occasionally. Stir in carrots, green beans and water. Cover; cook 5 minutes. Stir in bell pepper. Cook 2 to 3 minutes, stirring occasionally, until vegetables are crisp-tender.

4. Stir in tempeh and peanut butter mixture until well mixed. Cook 1 to 2 minutes, stirring occasionally, until heated through. Sprinkle with cilantro.

1 serving: Calories 380 (Calories from Fat 190); Total Fat 22g (Saturated Fat 4g; Trans Fat 0g); Cholesterol 0mg; Sodium 630mg; Total Carbohydrate 29g (Dietary Fiber 7g; Sugars 17g); Protein 18g
% daily value: Vitamin A 210%; Vitamin C 50%; Calcium 15%; Iron 15%   **exchanges:** 1/2 Starch, 1 Other Carbohydrate, 1 Vegetable, 2 Medium-Fat Meat, 2 1/2 Fat   **carbohydrate choices:** 2

TEMPEH STIR-FRY with yogurt–peanut sauce

 the veggie PANTRY

Going vegetarian or meatless? Now is the time to consider what to stock in your pantry, refrigerator and freezer to create great-tasting meals. This list is by no means complete, but it is a good start.

Keep It in the Cupboard

- Baked snack chips
- Canned and jarred sauces: chutney, mustards, pasta sauces, pesto, relishes and salsa
- Canned tomato products: plain and seasoned
- Canned vegetarian soups and broth
- Canned vegetarian baked, chili-style and refried beans
- Canned whole beans: black, butter, cannellini, great northern, kidney, pinto and soy
- Dried fruits: apricots, blueberries, cherries, cranberries, dates, mixed dried fruits and raisins
- Dried legumes: beans, lentils and split peas
- Grains: barley, bulgur, oats, rice, kasha (roasted buckwheat groats), quinoa and wheat berries
- Nuts: almonds, cashews, peanuts, pecans, soy nuts, sunflower nuts and walnuts
- Pasta: wheat pasta or nonwheat pasta like lentil, lupini, mung bean, split pea and rice flour pasta
- Peanut butter and other nut butters
- Prebaked pizza crusts and shells
- Ready-to-eat whole-grain cereals
- Spices and herbs
- Texturized soy protein (TSP) flakes and mixes (chili, sloppy joes, soup)
- Whole-grain crackers
- Whole-grain loaf breads, pita breads and rolls

Keep It in the Fridge

- Bean dip
- Cheese dips and salsa con queso
- Cheeses
- Flour and corn tortillas
- Fresh fruits
- Fresh herbs
- Fresh vegetables
- Fruit and vegetable juices
- Hummus or baba ghanoush
- Milk: dairy and soy milk
- Olives
- Smoothies: purchased ready-to-drink
- Yogurt

Keep It in the Freezer

- Cheese and vegetable pizzas
- Fruit and vegetable juice concentrates
- Frozen fruits
- Meat substitutes (meat analogs): soy-protein burgers, "chicken" patties and nuggets, hot dogs, sausages and vegetable burgers
- Vegetables

vegetarian foods GLOSSARY

With the growing interest in vegetarian foods, more new and unfamiliar ingredients are popping up in the supermarket, in articles about food and on restaurant menus. This glossary highlights some of the most popular ingredients and foods.

AGAR-AGAR is a thickening agent made from dried sea vegetables. It is often used instead of unflavored gelatin, which is made from animal products.

ARROWROOT is a powdery starch that comes from the tropical root of the same name. It's a substitute for cornstarch.

BARLEY MALT SYRUP (MALTED BARLEY SYRUP) is a dark, thick sweetener made from sprouted whole barley. It has a mild caramel flavor and is not as sweet as sugar or honey. It can be used instead of honey or molasses in most baked goods.

BROWN RICE SYRUP is a sweetener made from adding sprouted dried barley or barley enzymes to cooked rice and letting it ferment until it forms sugars. It has a mild flavor that's less sweet than sugar.

EGG REPLACER is cholesterol-free and is made from starches and leavening ingredients that act similarly to fresh eggs. Do not confuse it with cholesterol-free egg substitute products, which are made with egg whites.

KUDZU is a powdery starch that comes from the root of the same name and can be used to thicken soups, sauces and puddings.

MEAT ANALOGS are meat substitutes made from soybeans. They come in many different forms: burgers, sausages, crumbles, hot dogs, ready-made meal mixes (such as chili) and in frozen dinners. For more information, see "All About Soy," pages 258–259.

MISO is a salty, thick, fermented paste made from aged soybeans and sometimes grains such as barley or rice. Ranging in color from yellow to red to brown, this paste is primarily used as a flavoring ingredient instead of chicken or beef granules.

NORI is seaweed that has been dried in paper-thin sheets. Generally, it is used for wrapping sushi and rice balls.

NUTRITIONAL YEAST (BREWER'S YEAST) has no leavening power and is used in making beer. Its flavor is a combination of meaty, cheesy and nutty. It is a good source of vitamin B and is often added to foods in small amounts to boost nutrition.

SEITAN is a versatile meat substitute made by combining whole wheat flour and water. After the dough is mixed, it is repeatedly kneaded and rinsed while immersed in water to remove all of its starch. The resulting dough is then simmered in vegetable stock. You can make your own seitan or buy it in many forms.

SOY PRODUCTS. See "All About Soy," pages 258–259.

TAHINI (SESAME SEED PASTE) is a Middle Eastern classic made from ground raw or toasted sesame seeds and is similar in texture to peanut butter. It's a key ingredient in hummus, a Middle Eastern dip of pureed garbanzo beans.

TAMARI is a soybean product very similar in flavor to soy sauce, but it is more subtle and a little bit thicker.

TOFU. See "All About Soy," pages 258–259.

VEGETARIAN VEGETABLE BOUILLON CUBES are made from vegetables and are used instead of chicken or beef bouillon cubes.

helpful nutrition and cooking information

Nutrition Guidelines

We provide nutrition information for each recipe that includes calories, fat, cholesterol, sodium, carbohydrate, fiber and protein. Individual food choices can be based on this information.

Recommended intake for a daily diet of 2,000 calories as set by the Food and Drug Administration

Total Fat	Less than 65g
Saturated Fat	Less than 20g
Cholesterol	Less than 300mg
Sodium	Less than 2,400mg
Total Carbohydrate	300g
Dietary Fiber	25g

CRITERIA USED FOR CALCULATING NUTRITION INFORMATION

- The first ingredient was used wherever a choice is given (such as 1/3 cup sour cream or plain yogurt).
- The first ingredient amount was used wherever a range is given (such as 3- to 3 1/2–pound cut-up broiler-fryer chicken).
- The first serving number was used wherever a range is given (such as 4 to 6 servings).
- "If desired" ingredients and recipe variations were not included (such as sprinkle with brown sugar, if desired).
- Only the amount of a marinade or frying oil that is estimated to be absorbed by the food during preparation or cooking was calculated.

INGREDIENTS USED IN RECIPE TESTING AND NUTRITION CALCULATIONS

- Ingredients used for testing represent those that the majority of consumers use in their homes: large eggs, 2% milk, 80%-lean ground beef, canned ready-to-use chicken broth and vegetable oil spread containing not less than 65 percent fat.
- Fat-free, low-fat or low-sodium products were not used, unless otherwise indicated.
- Solid vegetable shortening (not butter, margarine, nonstick cooking sprays or vegetable oil spread as they can cause sticking problems) was used to grease pans, unless otherwise indicated.

EQUIPMENT USED IN RECIPE TESTING

We use equipment for testing that the majority of consumers use in their homes. If a specific piece of equipment (such as a wire whisk) is necessary for recipe success, it is listed in the recipe.

- Cookware and bakeware without nonstick coatings were used, unless otherwise indicated.
- No dark-colored, black or insulated bakeware was used.
- When a pan is specified in a recipe, a metal pan was used; a baking dish or pie plate means ovenproof glass was used.
- An electric hand mixer was used for mixing only when mixer speeds are specified in the recipe directions. When a mixer speed is not given, a spoon or fork was used.

COOKING TERMS GLOSSARY

BEAT: Mix ingredients vigorously with spoon, fork, wire whisk, hand beater or electric mixer until smooth and uniform.

BOIL: Heat liquid until bubbles rise continuously and break on the surface and steam is given off. For rolling boil, the bubbles form rapidly.

CHOP: Cut into coarse or fine irregular pieces with a knife, food chopper, blender or food processor.

CUBE: Cut into squares 1/2 inch or larger.

DICE: Cut into squares smaller than 1/2 inch.

GRATE: Cut into tiny particles using small rough holes of grater (citrus peel or chocolate).

GREASE: Rub the inside surface of a pan with shortening, using pastry brush, piece of waxed paper or paper towel, to prevent food from sticking during baking (as for some casseroles).

JULIENNE: Cut into thin, matchlike strips, using knife or food processor (vegetables, fruits, meats).

MIX: Combine ingredients in any way that distributes them evenly.

SAUTÉ: Cook foods in hot oil or margarine over medium-high heat with frequent tossing and turning motion.

SHRED: Cut into long thin pieces by rubbing food across the holes of a shredder, as for cheese, or by using a knife to slice very thinly, as for cabbage.

SIMMER: Cook in liquid just below the boiling point on top of the stove; usually after reducing heat from a boil. Bubbles will rise slowly and break just below the surface.

STIR: Mix ingredients until uniform consistency. Stir once in a while for stirring occasionally, often for stirring frequently and continuously for stirring constantly.

TOSS: Tumble ingredients (such as green salad) lightly with a lifting motion, usually to coat evenly or mix with another food.

metric conversion guide

VOLUME

U.S. Units	Canadian Metric	Australian Metric
1/4 teaspoon	1 mL	1 ml
1/2 teaspoon	2 mL	2 ml
1 teaspoon	5 mL	5 ml
1 tablespoon	15 mL	20 ml
1/4 cup	50 mL	60 ml
1/3 cup	75 mL	80 ml
1/2 cup	125 mL	125 ml
2/3 cup	150 mL	170 ml
3/4 cup	175 mL	190 ml
1 cup	250 mL	250 ml
1 quart	1 liter	1 liter
1 1/2 quarts	1.5 liters	1.5 liters
2 quarts	2 liters	2 liters
2 1/2 quarts	2.5 liters	2.5 liters
3 quarts	3 liters	3 liters
4 quarts	4 liters	4 liters

WEIGHT

U.S. Units	Canadian Metric	Australian Metric
1 ounce	30 grams	30 grams
2 ounces	55 grams	60 grams
3 ounces	85 grams	90 grams
4 ounces (1/4 pound)	115 grams	125 grams
8 ounces (1/2 pound)	225 grams	225 grams
16 ounces (1 pound)	455 grams	500 grams
1 pound	455 grams	1/2 kilogram

MEASUREMENTS

Inches	Centimeters
1	2.5
2	5.0
3	7.5
4	10.0
5	12.5
6	15.0
7	17.5
8	20.5
9	23.0
10	25.5
11	28.0
12	30.5
13	33.0

TEMPERATURES

Fahrenheit	Celsius
32°	0°
212°	100°
250°	120°
275°	140°
300°	150°
325°	160°
350°	180°
375°	190°
400°	200°
425°	220°
450°	230°
475°	240°
500°	260°

NOTE: The recipes in this cookbook have not been developed or tested using metric measures. When converting recipes to metric, some variations in quality may be noted.

index

Complete your cookbook library with these *Betty Crocker* titles

Betty Crocker's Best Bread Machine Cookbook

Betty Crocker's Best Chicken Cookbook

Betty Crocker's Best Christmas Cookbook

Betty Crocker's Best of Baking

Betty Crocker's Best of Healthy and Hearty Cooking

Betty Crocker's Best-Loved Recipes

Betty Crocker's Bisquick® Cookbook

Betty Crocker Bisquick® II Cookbook

Betty Crocker Bisquick® Impossibly Easy Pies

Betty Crocker's Complete Thanksgiving Cookbook

Betty Crocker's Cook Book for Boys and Girls

Betty Crocker's Cook It Quick

Betty Crocker's Cookbook, 9th Edition— *The* **BIG RED** *Cookbook*®

Betty Crocker's Cookbook, Bridal Edition

Betty Crocker's Cookie Book

Betty Crocker's Cooking Basics

Betty Crocker's Cooking for Two

Betty Crocker's Cooky Book, Facsimile Edition

Betty Crocker's Diabetes Cookbook

Betty Crocker Easy Family Dinners with Rotisserie Chicken

Betty Crocker's Easy Slow Cooker Dinners

Betty Crocker's Eat and Lose Weight

Betty Crocker's Entertaining Basics

Betty Crocker's Flavors of Home

Betty Crocker 4-Ingredient Dinners

Betty Crocker's Great Grilling

Betty Crocker's Healthy New Choices

Betty Crocker's Indian Home Cooking

Betty Crocker's Italian Cooking

Betty Crocker's Kids Cook!

Betty Crocker's Kitchen Library

Betty Crocker's Living with Cancer Cookbook

Betty Crocker's Low-Fat Low-Cholesterol Cooking Today

Betty Crocker More Slow Cooker Recipes

Betty Crocker's New Cake Decorating

Betty Crocker's New Chinese Cookbook

Betty Crocker's A Passion for Pasta

Betty Crocker's Pasta Favorites

Betty Crocker's Picture Cook Book, Facsimile Edition

Betty Crocker's Quick & Easy Cookbook

Betty Crocker's Slow Cooker Cookbook

Betty Crocker's Ultimate Cake Mix Cookbook

Betty Crocker's Vegetarian Cooking